The Subject as Action

The Body, in Theory
Histories of Cultural Materialism

Editors
Dalia Judovitz, Emory University, and
James I. Porter, University of Michigan

Editorial Board
Malcolm Bowie
Francis Barker
Norman Bryson
Catherine Gallagher
Alphonso Lingis
A. A. Long
Jean-François Lyotard
Elaine Scarry
Jean Louis Schefer
Susan Stewart

Titles in the series:
*The Subject as Action: Transformation and Totality
in Narrative Aesthetics* by Alan Singer

The Subject as Action

Transformation and Totality in Narrative Aesthetics

Alan Singer

Ann Arbor

THE UNIVERSITY OF MICHIGAN PRESS

Copyright © by the University of Michigan 1993
All rights reserved
Published in the United States of America by
The University of Michigan Press
Manufactured in the United States of America

1996   1995   1994   1993   4   3   2   1

A CIP catalogue record for this book is available from the British Library.

Library of Congress Cataloging-in-Publication Data

Singer, Alan, 1948–
    The subject as action : transformation and totality in narrative
aesthetics / Alan Singer.
        p.   cm. — (The Body in theory)
    Includes bibliographical references and index.
    ISBN 0-472-10471-3
    1. Narration (Rhetoric) 2. Literature—Aesthetics. 3. Fiction.
4. Subject (Philosophy) I. Title. II. Series.
PN212.S56   1993
808.3—dc20   93-34668
                                                    CIP

For my mother and father,
Rhea and Bernard

Reading novels has the result, along with many other mental disorders, of making distraction habitual. It is true that a novel, by sketching (though with some exaggeration) characters really to be found among men, gives thoughts the same *coherence* as in a true history, which must always be reported in a certain *systematic* way. Still, it permits our mind to interpolate digressions while we are reading it (namely, to interpolate other happenings we invent), and the course of our thought becomes *fragmentary,* in such a way that we let ideas of one and the same object play in our mind in a scattered way (*sparsim*) instead of as combined (*conjunctim*) in accordance with the unity of understanding. If the preacher, the professor, or the prosecuting or defense attorney is to demonstrate his mental composure in speaking extemporaneously (without preparation)—or, for that matter, in any report—he must show *three* forms of attention: first, he must look at what he is *now* saying, in order to present it clearly; second, he must look back to what he has *already said;* and third, he must look ahead to what he now *intends* to say. If he neglects to pay attention to any one of these three elements—that is, fails to assemble them in this order—he throws both himself and his audience or readers into a state of distraction, and even an otherwise good mind can then be reproached with being *confused.*

    —Immanuel Kant, *Anthropology from a Pragmatic Point of View*

Acknowledgments

I am indebted to many colleagues and friends, whose skepticism, incisive argument, and intellectual conviction have held this book to a challenging standard.

At Temple University I have benefited from the commentary of Timothy Corrigan, Daniel T. O'Hara, and Susan Wells. Above all, Susan Stewart and Steven Cole have given the arguments in this book the shrewdest and most rewarding scrutiny. The four summers Susan Stewart and I taught the Temple Seminars in Art and Culture in Rome together were an invaluable proving ground for many of the arguments contained in this work.

Many others have contributed scrupulous readings and productive criticism of portions of this work: Charles Altieri, Leo Bersani, Anthony Cascardi, Robert Caserio, Kevin Moore, Patrick O'Donnell, and Amy Shuman. Allen Dunn deserves special mention for the years of conversation about narrative and the aesthetic that echo through these pages.

A study leave from the College of Arts and Sciences at Temple University enabled me to rethink and rework the initial plan of this book.

Nadia Kravchenko of the Temple University Word Processing Center gave the manuscript her efficient and careful attention.

Finally, I want to pay tribute to that most generously transformative totality, my family, Nora and Alexandra.

"The Methods of Form" originally appeared in *SubStance* 41, no. 4 (1983). Copyright © University of Wisconsin Press 1983. Reprinted with permission.

"The Totality of Desire: Toward a Historical Formalism" originally appeared in *Enclitic* 8, nos. 1 and 2 (Spring/Fall 1984).

"The Dis-Position of the Subject: Agency and Form in the Ideology of the Novel" originally appeared in *NOVEL: A Forum on Fiction*, vol. 22, no. 1, Fall 1988. Copyright NOVEL Corp. © 1988. Reprinted with permission.

"The Voice of History/The Subject of the Novel" originally appeared in *NOVEL: A Forum on Fiction*, vol. 21, nos. 2 & 3, Winter/Spring 1988. Copyright NOVEL Corp. © 1988. Reprinted with permission. It also appeared, in an expanded version, in *Intertextuality in Contemporary American Fiction*, edited by Robert Con Davis and Patrick O'Donnell. Copyright © Johns Hopkins University Press 1989. Reprinted with permission.

Every effort has been made to trace the original copyright holders of these articles.

Contents

Introduction: Prospect for a Narrative Aesthetics

Nothing particular is true.
    —Theodor W. Adorno, *Negative Dialectics*

This work takes up three cruxes of contemporary literary theory: the critique of the so-called ideological subject, narrative theory, and the category of the aesthetic. The confluence of these trajectories of knowledge in the speculative field of "narrative aesthetics" depends upon my configuring them in the following ways. I take the critique of the subject to be preeminently a crisis of faith respecting the sources of human agency. I take narrative rationality to be the "scene" of that crisis. And I take the category of the aesthetic to be a profoundly determinative phenomenon whereby the crisis of subjectivity might be *met* without being *resolved* on the dangerous coordinates of conceptual knowledge and purposive action.

Accordingly, I use the term *narrative* here in a way that goes well beyond the motives of storytelling proper. For my purposes narrative denotes above all a reflective capacity of mind comparable to Theodor W. Adorno's influential protocol of "second reflection." According to this protocol the category of the aesthetic is endowed with a specifically cognitive purchase on sense. Because in second reflection it is the temporal vitality of cognitive experience that gives access to the aesthetic, the undertaking of aesthetic practice does not entail the abdication of a world of conscientious actions. For such reasons Adorno will loom a larger and larger figure in this work. Though what follows is not purveyed as an "Adornian" philosophy of narrative art, the ramifications of the stance of second reflection taken in *Aesthetic Theory* (1970) and in *Negative Dialectics* (1966) will help me to construe narrative as both a rationalistic and a normative enterprise. In this capacity narrative can maximize the productivity of rational action as a hedge against its latent instrumentality. These, after all, are the powerful Frankfurt School ideals that have been sustained by post-Enlightenment social criticism and political theory but which, I believe, have been profoundly compromised by recent literary theories purporting to connect the work of art with a world of social imperatives.

Of course, this reading of narrative goes against the stronger, however much contested, tradition of treating narrative as epiphenomenal of objective history. It is upon this basis that we have predicated a dubious distinction between historical and artistic knowledge. In this way we obscure the capacity of narrative art for projecting human acts into a world of experience that is limited by neither the metaphysical transmutations of a judgment of "taste" nor the sequestering walls of bodily immediacy. These have been the traditional boundaries of artistic experience that have elicited from its despairingly "tasteful" captives a remarkable proliferation of increasingly complicated mind-body equations. All purport to square the circle of human desire so that rationality and art might be united in the struggle to emancipate human from natural necessities.

We might see the full historical consequence of the problem most quickly by risking a reductive overview here. Since Aristotle literary formalism has been impelled to build its disciplinary authority on the opposition between aesthetics and history. Modern theorists who have sought to end this dualism have taken the opposite approach of legitimating aesthetic works by attacking formalism. They would subsume the solipsistic course of literary aesthetics under the social telos of history. Poststructuralists, neo-Marxists, and sociologically oriented theorists find in formalism the convenient scapegoat of a literary theory that has, they allege, lost touch with its material-historical conditions and which must be redeemed to the ways of the world by means of a radical methodological conversion.

Nevertheless, I want to resist the currently fashionable rhetoric that—no less dualistically than classical aesthetics—privileges the social determinations of literature over formal or aesthetic elements. To the contrary, my work will proceed on the assumption that form *is* historical inasmuch as history is ideological: artworks are formed by social agents. They are therefore symbolically mediated by the very historical-cultural forces that are reciprocally determined in relation to the symbolic discourse of art. Social life and aesthetic value are thus both bound by the phenomenon of determination, the hitherto unrepresented conditionality of all representation. On this basis we can try to transcend the long-standing conflict between material determination and transcendental signification implicit in the aesthetics-history split.

My argument thus will attempt to obviate any substantive distinction between aesthetic form and history by acknowledging their mutual complicity not only in the concept of ideology but also in the empirical domain of human actions presupposed in that concept by its post-Enlightenment progenitors, Destutt de Tracy and Auguste Comte. On this basis, I will promote the idea that the subsequent methods of ideology-critique worked out by theorists as diverse as Marx, Adorno, Althusser, Habermas, Lyotard, and Giddens offer rich prospects for a literary criticism that seeks to legitimate aesthetic values with respect to historical experience without depersonalizing the formal imperative of either phenomenon. We will see that for the most consequential theorists of ideology what has always been preeminently at stake in the critique of ideology is an ethical theory of the human subject. So this must also become the goal of any literary theory that claims an explanatory power extending beyond the logical limits of the individual or generic text.

Particularly in the novel, the no less crucial concepts of action and agency connect the theory of the subject to the theory of ideology. I believe that the missing "subject" of literary theoretical discourse has been the constitutive agency of the Subject itself. The Subject remains too much a given of classical aesthetic theory, whether it is derived from Aristotelian organicism, Plotinan Intellect, British utilitarianism and virtue ethics (Shaftesbury, Hutcheson, Mandeville), or the intentionless objectivity of the American New Criticism (Wimsatt, Beardsley, Brooks). By contrast, the status of the subject remains both the motivating and the driving question of ideology-critique as it is practiced in post-Enlightenment culture.

So it should be clear that, within the rubric of ideology-critique, I embrace a rather broad tradition of critical thought that seeks to understand the grounds of subjective agency, instead of treating subjective agency as the foregone conclusion of all rationally purposive discourse. Although I do not intend a genre study here, I take the novel to be the literary form that most eloquently exhibits the necessity of this critical grounding. We might say that the novel is, in this capacity, a disciplined self-consciousness about the self-problematizing features of narrative totalizing. Indeed, the genre of the novel has been historically obliged to reconcile the "free" subject and the world of historical determination.

On this basis the novel traditionally has been contrasted with the epic, which presupposes a successful reconciliation of self and world, or with the lyric, which laments its impossibility, however sublime that impossibility may prove to be. Because sublimity is so manifestly incommensurable with the fundamental temporality of the novel, I would say that the novel genre is that much more profitably a context for skeptically examining the epistemological pitfalls of totalizing knowledge.

At this juncture I deploy the terms *totality* and *transformation* in order to specify the epistemological polarity within which I believe the significant formal features of the novel are conceptually articulable. First, I will acknowledge the attempted reconciliation of what Kant would later call theoretical and practical reason in A. G. Baumgarten's momentous formulation of the aesthetic as a *cognitio sensitiva*. Correspondingly, I will observe the way in which Baumgarten's project mirrors the dialectic of theoretical totality and practical transformability that gives the novel genre its structural integrity. I will thus suggest that the novel may be seen as a mode of narrative reason that may prove useful in negotiating the gap between practical and theoretical criteria of value, a gap that Kantian and post-Kantian reflection philosophies have not successfully bridged.

Of course, in attempting the reconciliation between transformation and totality, theory and practice, part and whole, the novel consistently has foundered upon the very internal contradictions that the "form-history split" precipitates. On the one hand, aesthetic formalists typically have treated the subject as an ideal at the expense of the world, promulgating the subjectivist excesses of romance. On the other hand, the antagonists of formalism have treated history as an autonomous deterministic order, at the expense of subjective freedoms, thereby promulgating a reductive realism.

Nevertheless, I will argue that the novel is most fully revealed to be itself precisely as the embodiment of these contradictions. Such contradictions constitute the genre's most compelling conditions of possibility. Thus, attending to the formal imperatives of the genre in light of the corresponding imperatives of ideology-critique, we might reformulate the theory of the novel so that it more sharply elucidates subjective agency. Such elucidation might now be taken as the chief conceptual warrant of the genre itself. In other words, this book will not be a history of the novel but, rather, will be an analysis of the most tenacious conceptual problems out of which the history of the novel has been formulated as a coherent field of speculative inquiry.

I must therefore frame my inquiry with the assumption that, unlike the lyric or the epic, the novel is the preeminent discursive genre of modernity to acknowledge form itself as a dissimulation of the self, or as constituting the self in dissimulation. This is so if only because the novel incorporates multiple points of view that are caught in a paradox made famous as a problematic of modernity by the proto-Hegelian philosopher of human activity J. G. Fichte: disunity cannot be deduced from unity. The principle of opposition (disunity) cannot be deduced from a principle of unity because what opposes the subject, facilitating its self-reflection, also excludes it. Accordingly, the ethical aspiration of the novel to redeem an original unity through disunity determines its dissimulating identity. There is a significant methodological shift implicit in this Fichtean line of thought: the assimilation of unity or totality to transformation, through what Fichte postulates in *Wissenschaftslehre* (*The Science of Knowledge* [1794]) as a concept of "self-activity," or what I will call the subject as action. Above all else, this assimilation of subject to act portends the watershed epistemological split between a dynamic paradigm of totality, out of Hegel and focused on intersubjective desire, and a static or transcendental paradigm of totality, out of Kantian formalism and focused on the universality of reason.

In the attempt to reconcile the aesthetics of the novel with the complexities of subjective action, I will of course follow a neo-Hegelian path. I want to put the question of action here in a more critical relation to the mimetic claims of traditional novel theory and practice. Against the mimetic dictum that predicates its representational authority upon respect for the rule of natural necessity, I follow a rule privileging logical necessity. I want to locate the significance of act in a causality predicated on the willful interventions of subjects in contexts of value rather than in a causality that purports to be abstract from the subjective circumstance of human conflict. Only in this circumstance do the ultimately Hegelian constraints of contextuality and recognition obtain as the minimal conditions of that action. As we shall see, these are likewise the minimal conditions of narrative intelligibility insofar as it can be made to submit to the procedures of normative judgment.

Furthermore, although I do not strictly adopt the methods of analytical philosophy in what follows, I must nevertheless acknowledge a debt to de-ontological theory for the direction indicated in the previous paragraph. The exemplary figure here is Georg Henrik Von Wright (*Causation and Determination* [1971], *Explanation and Understanding* [1974]), who demonstrates that human action must be construed as the predicate, not the effect, of any putative causality (call it a reality principle, historical determinism, ideology) because only this logic submits to a test of showing necessary as well as sufficient cause. Von Wright importantly stipulates that, in interpretive situations, the demonstration of sufficient cause requires only passive observation of the world, while the demonstration of necessary cause requires, as I have already suggested, that we locate the significance of an event in the interventions of an interpreter. In this work I will be presuming upon the understanding that mimetic theories of emplotment are in fact predisposed to privileging sufficient causes over necessary causes. And, because they therefore preempt an actantial analysis, they preclude the intersubjective sphere of value, which remains our most vital refuge from the hazards of the ontological absolutism that otherwise holds sway in the grand thematizing gestures of the novel genre and in the critical communities that essentialize thematic reading. Only by acceding to the terms of intersubjectivity can the integrity of subjective experience purveyed in a narrative aesthetic remain a credible pretext for practical knowledge of the world.

The steps of the argument that I am announcing here proceed neither in the manner of a history of narrative genres nor in the manner of a narrative history of the aesthetic. Rather, because I am chiefly interested in speculating on the potential inherent in narrative texts for finding a stronger theoretical warrant linking narrative art to the realm of act, my approach must be dialectical. Consequently, each speculative move in what follows is theoretically enabled by a close reading of a literary text. And, true to the dynamics of formalism as I extrapolate it from the historical record of the novel genre in particular, each of the "example" texts to be adduced here has its specific motive in the *techne* of significant formal innovation. So, the practical ground of each close reading is correlatively a place of theoretical impasse. It is formal innovation in itself that prompts the dialectical motion of this undertaking.

Furthermore, because the contextual nature of all dialectical thinking will be a crucial underpinning of my argument, it should be no surprise that each successive chapter carries the argument forward by recontextualizing a relatively finite repertoire of terms and conceptual topoi. With this strategy I want to attain a tightening contextual weave that augments the framework for further speculation rather than attempting to enclose, in some more absolute and exclusive way, its field of reference.

Finally, because the procedure I have just outlined assiduously avoids a strict deductive narrative line, it seems appropriate to fill out the scope of my introduction with a linear and schematic view of the contents of each chapter to follow. By presenting the broadest context of my strategy of recontextualization, I may allay a reader's anxieties that my suspicion of deductive narration will ignore the requirement for narrative conclusiveness (however provisional) upon which the success of my own argument undoubtedly depends.

Chapter 1, "The Methods of Form," elaborates the problematic of form in relation to the concept of ideology and the methods of ideology-critique. I begin with one of the polemical touchstones of antiformalist criticism of the novel: the invidious comparison of "pure" art with the writing of social consciousness—i.e., the alleged displacement of social responsibility by hedonistic aestheticism. From this opposition arise the most popular valorizations of "imitative" aesthetics. I challenge these by pointing out the inescapable paradox of supposing that social responsibility and artistic mimesis are adequate reflections of one another, as Sartre seems to suggest in "What Is Literature?" (1948). Rather, they are paradoxically related only by the transcendental characterization of the subject assumed in each. By examining the transcendental terms of subjectivity assumed in each, I want to indicate the potentially tautological structure of both.

Against this stance I pose the project of a materialist aesthetic. I establish the perspective for this view by juxtaposing a basically Foucauldian formulation of the materiality of the subject with the aesthetic credo of Maurice Blanchot, Foucault's own touchstone of materialist aesthetic practice. This juxtaposition is the occasion to show how, contrary to the ethical indictment of aesthetic formalism as abjectly subjective, the conceptualization of the subject is a common stake of both aesthetic formalism and social action. This is most explicitly the case insofar as the subject's transcendental character must be critiqued in both. For these reasons I want to adumbrate a method of literary criticism that takes its lead from ideology-critique: both practices are concerned primarily with the possibility of theorizing a constitutive rather than a transcendental subject.

In chapter 2, "The Totality of Desire: Toward a Historical Formalism," I discuss how recent poststructuralist critiques of the Aristotelian paradigm of self-identity—based as it is on metaphor and resemblance—nevertheless fail to theorize, in its place, an active agency grounded in historical contingency. Presuming in turn upon the metonymic principle of Louis Althusser's "structural causality," I want to elicit an alternative, "materialist" model of selfhood that does not resort to the escapism of those anti-identity logics purveyed in so much postmodernist polemic. I begin this enterprise of salvaging subjective agency from the metaphysics of an abidingly Aristotelian self-identity by evoking a principle of "agency without a telos." I take this terminological leverage as a means to establish a substantive distinction between the transcendental and the constitutive subject intimated in the materialist perspective of the previous chapter.

My argument proceeds by juxtaposing Paul de Man's representative deconstructive reading of Rousseau in *Allegories of Reading* (1979) with the critical dynamics of the Hegelian dialectic. On this basis I charge the necessity to resist the poststructuralist abolition of the subject in the course of the critique of the subject. This will be the first of several contextualizations of Hegelian subjectivity. Above all we must reconsider the Hegelian subject in light of poststructuralism's assault upon the *geist*-ridden historical truths within which modern consciousness appears to be so tragically enclosed. It is also the keynote of my own polemical refrain that poststructuralism must come to terms with its own Hegelian genesis if its often well-motivated critique of Hegelian totality will amount to more than oedipal spite. Accordingly, this chapter concludes with the suggestion that, under the skeptical pressure of ideology-critique, the transcendental cogito might yield more profitably to a theory of mobile subjectivity than to a theory of its liquidation.

In chapter 3, "The Dis-Position of the Subject: Agency and Form in the Ideology of the Novel," the warrant for a mobile or positional (rather than transcendental) subject is considered both as the motive of ideology-critique and as an "unconscious" historical premise of novelistic form. Georg Lukács's contradictory stance (in *Theory of the Novel* [1971]), of equating irony with freedom and so theologizing critical understanding, will here be counterposed with the critique of transcendental subjectivity, undertaken expressly as a theory of the novel, by Julia Kristeva, M. M. Bakhtin, and Leo Bersani.

In unspoken accord with Althusser each of these theorists seeks the constitutive ground of the subject in effects rather than causes. Each of these thinkers appreciates how the mobility of the subject is immanent to the methodological contradictions that, I allege, the novel displays to exemplary effect. Thus, each is involved in an attempt to mobilize the subject against the reifying formalism of a putative nonnarrative or antinarrative history. I intend to show how, by contrast with the mobile subject, the notoriously displaced subject of nonnarrative history would be an unacceptable alternative, the refuge of an increasingly metaphysical utopianism. Only on this basis may we establish credible guidelines for a revisionary "theory of the novel" that does not betray the materialist premise of ideology-critique postulated by our most exacting and productive philosophers of contradiction: Hegel and Marx.

Appropriately, the specific literary context for this discussion is the "early history" of the novel. My example here is the protonovelistic discourse of Thomas Nashe's *The Unfortunate Traveller* (1593). A reading of the salient formal aspects of Nashe's text incorporates the various tenets of materialist philosophy already posed against the Cartesian *cogito*. In this way I attempt to conjure a more vivid sense of the novel's original speculative aptitude for the historical experience that materialism purports to comprehend: action.

Chapter 4, "The Voice of History / The Subject of the Novel," more fully articulates the links between the formal problematic of the novel and the critique of Cartesian subjectivity. I follow the antifoundationalist consensus that the Cartesian or idealist subject is flawed most fatally insofar as it aspires to a unity beyond its own formal enunciations and is thus bound to remystify its origins. Bakhtin—particularly his concept of *degradation* in *Rabelais and His World* (1965)—will be adduced again as a figure who has simultaneously internalized the idealist tradition and critiqued it in his much celebrated, though still too uncritical, concept of "dialogism." It is this dialogism that enables him to diagnose the methodological impasses of Hegelianism, Freudianism, and Russian formalism, which also sought to reclaim the subject from the metaphysical recesses of Cartesian idealism. But at the same time Bakhtin epitomizes the tendency of the contemporary critics of these postidealist "systems" to indulge a subject without agency (what Adorno calls the "subjectless subject"), to concede the subject's irresistible slide into ironic regress. The critique of the subject devolves too precipitously in Bakhtinian theory to the negation of the subject.

In contrast, I propose that Hegelian contradiction, stripped of its

telos, is the implicit but unacknowledged impetus of the antisystematic,
anti-Hegelian critique carried out under the banner of Bakhtinian dialogism. Here I believe the program of the Frankfurt School offers a more
productive reckoning with the failure of recent materialist theories to
rescue the subject from the oblivion to which they consigned it in the
critique of idealism. The preceding analysis will prompt a fuller account
of the mobile or positional subject. We will see how the concept of the
positional subject is already incipient in Adorno's promulgation of the
negative dialectic, derived in turn from the headless Hegelianism posited
above. This discussion will give ground for a forceful defense of my earlier
claim that aesthetics constitutes an indispensable supplement to social
theory and the methodological framework of materialist ideology-critique.

The advantage of taking contradiction as a basis of subjectivity is its
accommodation of a mobility that might reconcile aesthetic totality with
the phenomena of transformation and determination. These are, after all,
the proverbial touchstones of all social/political revolutionary utopianism.
But now the project of resolving contradiction is rejected in favor of a
notion of contradiction as self-development. As we will see more clearly
in later chapters, in this "expressive" frame of reference narrative intimates that desire need not be conceived so crudely as the remedy for lack
but, rather, as its mode of intelligibility. Following Hegel's work model
of subjectivity, I hold this consciousness to be self-transformative.

The remainder of chapter 4 examines how the foregoing theoretical
claims are developed productively by the formal innovations of a
significant postmodern fiction: William Gaddis's *Carpenter's Gothic*
(1985). Precisely because Gaddis is among the most reverenced but also
the most unread of the so-called postmodern novelists, he offers access to
many presuppositions of postmodern narrative theory hitherto unexam-
ined as a consequence of their familiarity. Above all else, however, Gaddis's novel is part of an ambitious aesthetic project that I believe articulates the internal contradictions of the novel genre made apparent in
chapter 3. In the course of analyzing *Carpenter's Gothic,* I show how the
conceptual and formal resources of contradiction, so crucial to the work's
aesthetic unity (and its power to theorize new unities), are derived from
the Hegelian problematic.

It will be important to note, however, that the power of such forms
as Gaddis presents in *Carpenter's Gothic* are too often subverted by the
preemptive construal of contradiction as irony by postmodern critics, who

more and more dogmatically elevate irony to the status of a master trope of the novel. Indeed, if we followed their initiative, we would be turned back toward the very thematic sublimation of form that I originally set out to discredit. Irony, in this critical perspective, would paradoxically serve as both the pretext for and the discrediting of any attempt to ground knowledge in aesthetic terms.

In chapter 5, "The Burden of Thematics: Transformation and Totality in Blanchot's *Récit,*" the need to outthink irony in order to comprehend the formal project of the novel becomes a crux of argument. I lead up to the idea that thematism must be supplanted by historicism with the understanding that aesthetics and history are continuous in the phenomenon of determination. I examine how determination is, after all, the common term of Baumgarten's aesthetics and Fichte's "self-activity." A related argument here proceeds toward the conclusion that any account of human agency, act, or motive must perforce be narrative. The "determinative vitality" of the Fichtean subject is indeed articulable only through contingency and contradiction. Fichte demonstrates this understanding in his claim that the self is "at once the agent and the product of action." Contingency and contradiction entail narrative. Thus, the constitutive subject is necessarily a narrative subject—a subject constituted *as* the dynamic of determination and contingency. This insight proffers to literary theory a new ground for unifying or totalizing experience without reifying the formal totalities of literary canons.

Here I must emphasize the inadequacy of the notion of history conceived as a determinate existential condition knowable independently of narrative contingency. For roughly the same reasons that I take narrative contingency to be analogous to Fichtean activity (Fichte's dialectic of "positing" and "striving"), I take further support for the concept of the subject as action from the increasingly pragmatist purview of recent British social theory. This deeply Wittgensteinian perspective is especially well represented by Anthony Giddens in his account of the "duality of structure." The corollary notion that history is not an intentional project, though it proceeds from agents with intentions, suggests the direction of argument that will take over in the next chapter. As I have anticipated, what is at stake here is a notion of an agency without a reifying telos.

My consideration of Baumgarten and Giddens, on the relations of subject to form and act to structure, sets up a close reading of Maurice Blanchot's speculative criticism in tandem with a "formal analysis" of his less-well-known narrative fiction, *Madness of the Day* (1981). Blanchot, the genius of the French *récit,* is arguably the figure who most explicitly and most rigorously confronts the contradictions of Enlightenment consciousness in a nonthematizing artistic practice. In *Madness of the Day* we see the need to supplant the form-theme opposition (which is inherently ironic) with a form-irony dialectic. My postulate of a form-irony dialectic is in effect a procedure for recognizing contradiction as a structural condition of consciousness rather than as a finite and inherently abstract content of consciousness. This form-irony dialectic restrains the ironic consciousness from leaping prematurely to abstract teleological/theological truths and unities by rendering irony a transformative, instead of a negative, agency. The form-theme opposition is here deemed to be a semantic phenomenon expressed as an ahistorical irony. By contrast, the form-irony dialectic is deemed to be a syntactical phenomenon expressed as temporal act. In Blanchot's *récit* theme must be made assimilable to the dynamics of act vis-à-vis a recursive principle if it is to comprehend and participate in the temporality that is its condition of intelligibility.

On the basis of my reading of Blanchot I propose a nonthematic or expressive aesthetic that once again incorporates a conspicuously Hegelian "work" model of subjectivity. Transformation is thus the modality of knowledge of aesthetic judgment par excellence, a mode of knowledge that I must demonstrate to be ethically reflective but not ethically reductive. I must furthermore show the need to modify Hegelian *arbeit* by bracketing its teleological structure. In the context of my argument work is distinguished as an activity from its product; it is conceived of as an *energeia,* not an *ergon.*

Chapter 6, "The Figuration of Contingency: The Subject beyond Irony," focuses on Henry James (*What Maisie Knew* [1897]), an aesthetic formalist whose preoccupation with narrative modes of knowledge, I suggest, leads to a critical anatomy of irony like that contemplated in the previous chapter. In other words, where irony traditionally has been acknowledged to be the organizing "center" of James's fiction, I will locate instead the pretext for a potent critique of the subject conceived under the impersonally abstract terms of ironic distance. The modernist truism (so mightily buttressed by the Jamesian oeuvre) that irony is the fullest expression of the novel form will be alleged in this context to result from the misapplication of critical categories improperly derived from lyric idealism.

To establish a perspective for such claims we must remember that for Lukács irony entails self-abolition, which leads him fatalistically back to the very idealism from which he originally sought to emancipate alienated consciousness. By contrast, my Fichtean dialectic of form and irony (the ironizing of irony), because it would sustain the project of the self as a positive activity—rather than a blind negation—draws us back from the precipice of metaphysical idealism. Thus, it maintains the phenomenon of determination as the material continuity between aesthetical and historical knowledge.

Inasmuch as James's novelistic practice devolves to shifting interpretive emphasis from a metaphysical or purely negative irony to a form-irony dialectic, he points the way to making ironic knowledge a more self-conscious rather than an ever more unconscious result of the irrepressible contradiction between form and theme. This shift constitutes a new determinative vitality of ironic consciousness by its construal of ironic contingency as a fully cognizable human circumstance. And for this reason I warrant that the conceptual matrix of the shift must serve as the basis for any credible thematization of the formal complexities by which James challenges orthodox notions of thematic meaning that would otherwise expressly bar contingency from the field of aesthetic valuation. James's appropriation of contingency (instead of ironic distance) as a conceptual armature of style intimates an alternative construction of the totalizing project of the novel genre.

Specifically, this contingency appears in James's most challenging fiction as a radical strategy of syntactical overdetermination that puts the adequacy of thematic reading—that is to say, thematic totality—profoundly into question. I believe the full consequence of this stylistic choice depends on our seeing how such overdetermination displays a strong affinity with the psychoanalytic paradigm of the unconscious. That is, it denotes a destabilizing of the relation between individual agency and the constraints of social structure. We are thereby compelled to reconceive the unconscious as instantiating a principle whereby *structure* and *action* are rendered as reciprocal terms. I characterize this principle as a temporal recursiveness wherein recursiveness denotes the self-augmenting productivity of human time-consciousness. The Lacanian accounts of the unconscious and the *objet petit a* help to contextualize these claims.

I furthermore adduce Giddens on the reciprocity of structure and act, Adorno on negation as determination, and Paul Ricoeur on mimesis as act in order to demonstrate the generalizability of this recursiveness in the realm of conscious action as well as "unconscious" motive. This discussion leads us back to a consideration of the mechanics by which such recursiveness in Jamesian prose is inevitably syntactically operated. Syntax, in contrast with semantics, "figures" the temporal gap on which reflection depends and without which reflection itself would become narcissistically tautological rather than productively speculative.

Finally, we must see that the most compelling virtue of a syntax-based theory of recursiveness is that it assimilates the ideality of self to the exigencies of time and change. Syntax is always self-transformative. That is, it entails a mediation that assimilates totality to transformation. It is for this reason, I speculate, that *peripeteia,* the principle of transformation par excellence in narrative emplotment, must be taken in a more complex way than our canonical notions of Aristotelian *poesis* incline us. Whereas *Poetics* seems to stipulate that the order of *anagnorisis* succeeds and thereby supplants or sublates the order of *peripeteia,* I maintain that, by sacrificing reversal to recognition, we lose our cognitive purchase on the transformability of context determined within the dynamism of their relation. This transformation is the most emphatically productive dimension of narrative and intimates the most compelling terms for disclosing the pragmatic bearing of narrative art on practical experience. This discussion points the direction of the concluding two chapters, where the stakes of narrative aesthetics shift from achieving a more lucid grasp of the subjective agency immanent to narrative form, to the possibility of achieving a better fit between the self and the social within the emphatically contextual constraints of ethical life.

In chapter 7, "Determining the Aesthetic: Beauty Beholds the I," I speak directly of the contradictory imperatives of transformation and totality as they imply the problematics of formulating a narrative aesthetics. I examine how the traditional opposition of narrative and aesthetic values is founded upon an unduly heuristic dichotomy between cognitive and sense experience.

By constellating three rather different perspectives that give access to the cognitive bearing of *aesthesis*—Adorno on "second reflection," Nelson Goodman on the concept of "aesthetic repleteness," and Sartre on the "project" of "pre-reflective choice"—I improvise an analytical framework wherein transformation and totality may be seen to complement one another as aspects of subjective agency.

I argue that only such a framework is adequate to the daunting formal complexity presented by John Ashbery's densely syntactical, speculative narrative, *Three Poems* (1978). In turn, Ashbery's path-breaking narrative serves to elaborate the motives for theorizing subjectivity in a way that bears on the cognitive purport of aesthetic practice. Indeed, Ashbery's greatest achievement here may be his reflection that the conditions of narrative experience are ever more richly construed as an inverse proportion of their lack of fit with any of the thematic rubrics of novelistic discourse.

The exposition, both of narrative aesthetics in general and Ashbery's unique poetics of prose, hangs again on the phenomenon of *peripeteia* and in particular on the necessity to demonstrate the inseparability of *peripeteia* from *anagnorisis* if it is to serve as an adequate pretext of pragmatic subjectivity.

In chapter 8, "Thinking *Peripeteia* / Peripetic Thinking," the reconceptualization of the subject through narrative aesthetics is recontextualized with the explicitly ethical goal of a *sensus communis*. *Sensus communis* is, not coincidentally, the bridge between subjectivity and the world that obtains in the Kantian sublime as a corollary of the Kantian aesthetic judgment. The most challenging task of an argument that pursues this goal is to elude the metaphysical drift of the Kantian notion of community without losing the practical warrant for intersubjective knowledge with which Kant so soberingly tantalizes us. Accordingly, the burden of analysis in this concluding phase of argument is to re-pose the question of the alleged incompatibility of the narrative and the aesthetic. This time the question is couched in terms of a communitarian ethic whereby the subject's "aesthetic" emancipation from ideological and narrative totalizing does *not* devolve paradoxically to the solipsism of sheer sensuous intensities from whence all narrative desire first arose. This is, after all, the vicious circle from which aesthetics, since Baumgarten, has promised to emancipate us.

By contrasting the reciprocal deficiencies of Jean-François Lyotard's self-styled postmodern "political aesthetic" and Jürgen Habermas's de-aestheticized politics (by which Habermas alleges the project of modernity may be more constructively continued), I elicit the premise of my conclusion. Both Lyotard and Habermas are perhaps unexpectedly relevant figures in a work on narrative aesthetics and the novel insofar as their first concern is to contend with the contingency of human existence in some way that sustains the project of freedom. The inherent risk of such an undertaking is to contrive a narrative so totalizing in its rationalization of contingent particulars that it effectively preempts the very possibility of freedom it was intended to realize. Indeed, such are the ironies of post-Enlightenment culture that Lyotard and Habermas both conscientiously confront.

My point, however, will be to go beyond the self-inhibiting and mutually excluding differences between the Lyotardian and Habermasian ideas of community, both of which conspicuously depend on the narrative-aesthetics split. The thrust of my analysis of their separate projects is to demonstrate their mutual inability to realize how reversibility and recognition make the narrative imperatives of intersubjective life plausibly ethical in a way that does not deny the aesthetic or rational underpinnings of human ethos. The peripeteic turn of narrative, by enlarging the context of the choice of self-recognition, in turn augments the repertoire of human motives. It reinvigorates the contextuality of living.

Finally, we will see how this analysis permits us to understand that, contrary to much postmodernist cant, contingency need not be confused with the apocalyptic horizon of subjectivity. This work, then, is a challenge to the popular idea that the critique of subjectivity entails an antinarrative discourse. I warrant that there is no "missing part" of historical narrative that a critical antinarrative would be destined to complete, as, for example, utopian Marxism alleges. As Paul Ricoeur—to my mind our most trenchant narrative theorist—maintains: "There are only histories of the possibilities of the present." The acceptance of the constitutive role of contingency in the novel and in novel theory is the revelation that the subject of action in the novel is activity itself: in other words, subjectivity cannot be theorized independent of the contingencies of action. Only in this way does the art of the novel approach a meticulous discipline of self-reflection rather than a merely impressionistic reflection of those other disciplines of knowledge with which it contends, resentfully and tautologically, as form has always contended with content throughout the annals of literary history.

1

The Methods of Form

Unhappy is the path that turns around to look at the man walking on it.

—Maurice Blanchot, *Death Sentence*

There are many ways to transcend formalism but the worst is not to study forms.

—Geoffrey Hartman, *Beyond Formalism*

Writing Social Consciousness

The project of a narrative aesthetics must contend with the historically persistent antagonism between the realms of the narrative and the aesthetic, between time and sensibility, between the world and the self. It is a problematic that is perhaps best signaled in the ameliorative rhetoric of the expression "socially conscious" writing. But the political imperative of this phrase founders upon a constitutive contradiction. Social reality presupposes consciousness, yet the idea of socially conscious writing typically asserts an ontological priority of social form over aesthetic form—and perforce over forms of consciousness—that is not sufficiently reasoned.

Moreover, the implied invidious comparison between politically "engaged" fiction and mere aestheticism has too narrowly determined popular expectations about the novel of social consciousness, pitting realists against aesthetic formalists in a fruitless antagonism. This assimilation of aesthetic practice to social practice has been most eloquently argued in our time by Sartre, whose espousal of "committed," or engaged, writing became the keynote of the existentialist polemic against solipsistic aestheticism: "prose . . . is by nature significative . . . words are not objects but designations. In short it is a matter of knowing what one wants to write about" ("What Is Writing?" 35). In this Sartrean perspective (which is often misconstrued as the pretext for a simplistically brute realism) politically committed literature defers to the forms of a preexisting social reality—even in its purport to change that reality—because

17

the alternative would be to grant the aesthetic dimension a substantive rather than an accidental status in artistic practice.

Adorno presents a useful counterpoint to the presuppositions of Sartrean engagement when he writes in *Aesthetic Theory* that "Social conflicts and class relations leave an imprint on the structure of works of art. By contrast, the political positions art works explicitly take are epiphenomenal. Frequently they work to the disadvantage of elaboration, ultimately undermining even the social truth content. In art little is achieved by political convictions alone" (329–30). Indeed, Adorno gives fair warning that, before we leap too quickly to privilege empirical practice on the basis of respect for empirical law, we might remind ourselves that a lawfulness obtains equally, but differently, in the form of the artwork as well.

Furthermore, it might be useful to observe that the debate between aesthetic formalists and social/existential realists about the relative priority of language and forms of life actually recapitulates an older theoretical debate about the difference between literary work and world. This is the enduring problematic of representation. Particularly since Wittgenstein, language philosophers and literary critics alike have admonished that, if we want to make effective use of the concept of representation, we must shed the moral framework that situates the writer with respect to an essentialist truth and concern ourselves more with the variability of conditions that might be satisfied by our notions of truth. Can we deny that, if we valorize the knowledge derived from narrative fiction without examining the conditions under which this knowledge is possible, literary criticism falls short of the insights powering its adjacent critical disciplines of philosophy, social theory, and linguistics?

By conditions of possibility I obviously do not mean embodied forms of social reality (the basis of a naturalistic mimesis) but, rather, the conceptual ground upon which social forms and hence literary forms both subsist: the category of the subject that makes all objects originally possible, or at least interesting in their possibility. Upon the category of the subject hangs the entire post-Cartesian *episteme:* the state, the forms of social reproduction, etc. In this chapter I will discuss a body of theoretical work (creative and critical) that points our efforts to understand the relation between aesthetic forms and social praxis toward an implicit reassessment of these fundamental categories of experience.

Much contemporary thought suggests that "valid" perception of so-

cial and literary representations is inhibited by the narrative logic facilitating our knowledge of both. For this reason Michel Foucault, in the early
works *The Order of Things* (1966) and *The Archaeology of Knowledge* (1969),
willed away the category of man—that is, the subject—as an interpretive
ground. His claim is predicated on the observation that historical narrativity falsely dresses up the patchwork of human cultural experience in
the elegant robes of a seamlessly uninterrupted, legislative will or intention. Foucault responds to this state of affairs by denying that the
significant events of human history are the actions dutifully recorded by
our historians. These are merely the product of narcissistic and self-
replicating narrative modes. For Foucault the forms of knowledge by
which we explain our actions inherently repress what is incompatible with
our desire to explain them, reducing the manifold of cultural experience
to uniform versions of egocentric subjective consciousness. On the contrary, he asserts that for an "effective history" to emerge the *énoncé*, or
statement of fact, must now be understood as a ratio with *énonciation,* the
invisible laws operating behind the articulation of facts. Otherwise, we
consign ourselves to forms of knowledge that escape critical reflection.[1]

If we are going to see narrative as repressive, however, we might do
well to see it in relation to the phenomenon of ideology. Like the study
of narrative, the study of ideology is an inquiry into the modes of production of social representation. It will be necessary to significantly compli-
cate the concept of ideology over the course of this work. But for the
moment it is enough to observe that the dubious "work" of ideology is
the replication of modes of production. In other words it does not produce
an analysis of them. For this reason contemporary Marxist theorists in
particular contend that the Sartrean view of socially conscious writing, or
artistic commitment, is naively complicit with ideology insofar as it does
not produce a concept of its own perceptions; that is, it does not distance
itself or account for the *necessity* of its own being.

Literary critics might add that aesthetic forms that merely replicate
the modes of human self-representation in a given social reality are not
adequate to the Foucauldian knowledge of history because they also do
not provide any way of inhabiting their conditions of possibility or ac-
counting for their production as objects of knowledge. The term *production*
figures powerfully in the minds of theorists of ideology such as Louis
Althusser, who understand that the subject of discourse (author or reader/
critic) is always produced, or "interpellated," in ideology.[2] An abiding

rationale of social realism—as represented in the "classical realism" of Balzac, Tolstoy, and Stendhal—has been the authorial subject's critique of dominant ideology, specifically the technological determinism of late modernity. But late-twentieth-century theories of ideology have radically changed the framework of this assumption, putting the category of authorial subjectivity itself under critical suspicion. Post-Hegelian thinkers such as Althusser reason that, if socially committed narrative must critically engage the ideology from which it arises, it must dialectically displace the speaking subject interpellated in the very act of speech. The speaking subject must be made to stand outside the position of its own speaking in order to achieve the detachment instrumental to dialectical insight. There can be no historically consequential cultural production in lieu of the dialectic, since the subject otherwise bound within the metaphysical horizon of ideology merely replicates the modes of self-representation.

Concomitantly, we might reason that any narrative form that fails actively to produce the subject, to rethink or to escape the ideological positionality of the subject, represses knowledge of the subject's conditions of possibility that are incompatible with its merely self-reflexive ways of knowing. Such narrative courts a fatally false consciouness of the subject's constitutive functions. Yet literary theory born under the star of post-Cartesian subjectivity exhibits a striking irony with regard to this insight. Narrative artists who have remorselessly dispensed with the autonomous, or so-called ideological, subject as a controlling formal device—in works as disparately "radical" as Joyce's *Finnegans Wake* (1939) and Marguerite Duras's film *India Song*—have typically been denounced as the laboratory technicians of an arid formalist experiment. Formal experimentalism is judged to be socially complacent by the very post-Cartesian theorists who assign the purpose of social change to literature in the first place. In this critical context form is revealed to be the "culprit" of political apathy. Yet the critical partisans of social conscience proffer no alternative agency in place of the formalistic subversions of the self-replicating thematic subject that otherwise authorizes the "unity" of narrative genres.

For this reason I take the position that the concept of form itself must now be analyzed beyond the needs of a banal art-versus-life debate, if it is to be transportable—for the purposes of affecting social life—across the boundaries of art. In what follows I will argue that only a more rigorous formalism than we have yet conceived might fit criteria for socially conscious narrative that would be consistent with the Foucauldian critique of history. The urgency of these criteria will become increasingly evident as we come to see the full degree to which the production of forms itself is the threshold of the intelligibility of the concept of ideology.[3]

Form and Theme

Of course, we need not resort to philosophically exotic theories of ideology to know that ideology is as closely wedded to the theory of narrative as is the genre of the novel. History is the text of ideology, and our desire to find ourselves in the structural order of history is analogous to our reasons for reading novels. Yet our relation to ideology is in one crucial respect different from our relation to novels. Marxist critics typically pick out the distinction as follows: in the political analysis of representational modes contradiction and not unity obtains as the threshold of knowledge. On the contrary, when we read novels the rules of genre frequently compel obedience to the principle of an irresistible closure. This is the elaborately codified discipline of thematics. I will have much more to say about this in chapter 5, "The Burden of Thematics."

Suffice to say for the moment, however, that thematics has always been extraordinarily parasitic on the novel, since this genre characteristically assimilates the density of the particular moment to a generalizable fate. Theme elides the materially *productive* moment of rhetoric. It is in light of this assumption that I want to posit the necessity for a notion of literary form that we can locate at the level of its discursive production, either by making thematic unities provisional or by scrupulously displaying the conditions of their possibility as objects of knowledge. In this way we will establish contradiction as a methodological preserve for the formal density of the text. Contradiction roots us in the processes of discourse by reflecting the contingencies of narrative closure.

By contrast, the critical orthodoxies presiding over the realist novel, in particular, privilege nondiscursive structural elements instead of submitting them to the further contradictory mediation (such as their linguisticality) that under the pressure of teleological closure, they necessarily dissimulate. In this sense classical realism is always *an already produced commodity*,[4] inaccessible to any critical inquiry that is not already bound within the forms of its own dissemination. As Peter Bürger has recently noted, this reifying determinism extends to the fictional representation of human subjects. Of Zola Bürger observes, "according to his scientific concept of the notion of literature individual subjects simply possess a functional role" (*Decline of Modernism,* 111).[5] It would seem that we must find a form of representing subjectivity that moves us beyond such a tacitly ahistorical and mechanical threshold of immediacy. Or, such is the case if narrative discourse in general and the novel in particular are to be exploitable for artists seeking the kind of self-consciousness to which critics of social reality aspire.

Foucault theorizes that the complex discursive formations undergirding the institutional edifice of human history can be interrogated only on the point of their dissolution/contradiction, since the events of which they are composed constitute "a materialism of the incorporeal, free of the burdens of mechanical causality or ideal necessity" (*Archaeology,* 178). For Foucault the historical "event" is not an observable phenomenon. It marks the emergence of culturally buried discursive forces that operate remote from the stage where history is played out. Cut off from events, we enjoy immediate access only to the "arrangements of knowledge," the relational structures of power that dominate the scene we inhabit. Precisely because arrangements of knowledge are not commensurable with the events of history in Foucault's scheme, his goal of an "archaeological knowledge" depends on a systematic excavation of the discursive forces that cultural institutions bury beneath their weighty authorities.

The dualism of rhetorical (formal) and thematic (teleological) levels structuring literary models of narrative coherence suggests a complexity comparable to that which operates in Foucault's historical narrative. Though the literary text emerges at the level of the locutionary, the narrative telos paradoxically supersedes particular determinations of a textual matrix in order to make the work a totality. The relations of part and whole are effectively tautological and, as I will show, have often been rendered so by an unreasonably reductive reading of Aristotelian peripeteia. Accordingly, where telos thematically subsumes formal particularity the relevant verbal event is ambiguous, both seen and not seen in its constituent elements. Since Foucault insists that narrative telos inherently belies those forces that are not compatible with what it permits us to recognize as narrative, literary critics and artists might usefully be bound by the same methodological scruple that constrains political theorists to dispel the false consciousness of ideology by setting the concrete particular in some more authentic relation to the whole of historical/textual experience. We might then observe how critics who write about the socially conscious novel all too often fail to take their thinking to its logical conclusion. They do not acknowledge that it leads inevitably to the problem of language: the proverbial standoff of form and content. This dualism is the virtual fetish of a literary criticism predisposed by its rationalist/humanist lineage to substitute for the locutionary density of the text (treated as a comparatively inessential epiphenomenon of discourse) the more indeterminate category of phenomenal subjective consciousness.

But, if we accept that ideology is a fixed set of representational places for the subject within a discursive/cultural matrix and that the subject reinforces those practices that determine subjective places, we might project a different perspective for artistic production and critical inquiry both. The writer who would put herself in a critical relation to the ideological determinations of the particular moment in history must therefore take up a negative position with respect to the *practices of signification,* not the *codes of signification* manipulated by those practices. Therefore, the subversive artist must deal not in plots of political subversion or their counterparts of tragic knowledge but, rather, in the knowledge of his or her *motivation* to construct such plots in the first place. The prevalent objection among humanist pundits is, of course, that this is an implicitly self-annihilating aesthetic. It presupposes a radical loss of the narrative point of view that makes it possible to objectify a world in the first place. I would prefer to view this prospect in a less apocalyptic light and say that such an aesthetic merely expresses the need for a style or form that resists the preemptive categories of thematic unity itself.

I would, in fact, link the aims of an antithematizing aesthetic with the critique of ideological practice as it bears directly on the register of human action. Just as the Althusserian critique of political action situates analysis at the level of material contradiction, the form of narrative that will interest me in this work has its creative impetus at the level of ruptured locutions or contextual disjunctures—where thematic unities are diversely mediated by a contradictory array of locutionary particulars. This implies the reciprocity of intentions and consequences that is both key to the effectivity of act and is explicitly elided by theme.

In *Act and Quality* (1981) Charles Altieri has given a consummate account of levels of action in the text as they relate to levels of interpretation and performance. He reminds us that, while thematic criticism can deepen our awareness of human situations, it often proffers simplistic conceptual substitutes for verbal/situational complexities that otherwise would make it impossible to take the text as a satisfactorily representative instance of cultural generalizations. Our conventional narrative structures

and conventional structures of thematic knowledge both subsist on underdetermined middles, whereby rhetorical density is dissolved in a solution
of linear causality or strictly instrumental teleology. Our appetite for
encompassing generalizations can lead us to confuse meaning with theme,
encouraging a dogmatic forgetfulness of the text as a self-organizing
particular. As Altieri importantly stipulates, "themes contribute to the
meaning of a text but don't constitute meaning" (234). The narrative
styles I will consider in this work demand a deeper knowledge/reflection
of the constitutive processes of a text, and hence a more exhaustive critique
of thematics, in order to authorize a politically significant self-consciousness.

Sentencing Thematics: Exemplifying Blanchot

My remarks about narrative form here will make more than just polemical
sense as I now begin to situate them within view of an actual literary
practice. I have taken my epigraph from Maurice Blanchot's astonishing
récit Death Sentence (*L'Arrêt de mort* [1948]). This is a work that struggles
in its form with the forms of knowledge that enable its composition.
Because Blanchot's work is not a story and makes minimal demands upon
criticism for summary, I need only adduce some typical rhetorical gestures
to sketch out an aesthetic justification consistent with the kind of narrative stance toward thematics that I have been advocating in these pages.
My purpose here is simply to indicate the conceptual parameters of the
narrative project to be developed in subsequent chapters. Blanchot is an
important touchstone of the larger argument of this book. Chapter 5, in
particular, will offer a broader consideration of the formal "work" undertaken by Blanchot in the inception and practice of the *récit*. But for the
moment I seek only to intimate rather than explicate the full epistemological trajectory of this thinking.

   Geoffrey Hartman, one of the few critics willing to comment on a
formal project that does not lend itself readily to critical apothegm, has
called Blanchot's work anti-Aristotelian (*Beyond Formalism*, 93–110).
Blanchot, Hartman says, is all middles. Paradoxically, the reader's
difficulty with Blanchot arises from the aura of end-determined coherence
provisionally endowing the narrator's authority. In the course of the
narrative, the subjectivity denoted by the convention of the first-person
narrator (unifying events within the structures of an egocentric will)
spectacularly fails to encompass the locutionary heterogeneity of the text,

heightening the tension between plot and language. In the presence of this text we are therefore tempted to assume that the category of the subject ceases to be a relevant pretext for interpretation. But this would be premature. In fact, a similar misconception held sway over the place of the subject in the materialist dialectic when Marx purged "the beginning" and God from the Hegelian system.

Althusser for one has made it a given of his own theoretical project that what is proposed by an elision of the beginning in the narrative of history is not the suppression of the subject but, rather, "a simultaneous reflection on the separation and reciprocal action of two categories, subject and object" (*Lenin and Philosophy,* 202). Althusser says the subject inevitably becomes a problem of contradictory moments. The subject is determined in contradiction. Every act of reflection presupposes between subject and object a disjuncture that our holistic theories of the subject can rationalize only at the price of a more profound self-delusion, since rational thought can never rationally coincide with its authenticating ground. For Althusser contradictory moments that are presumptively reconciled by the devices of teleological closure are the elements of a specifically ideological reification of the subject.

Similarly, Blanchot's most characteristic writing constitutes a powerful inhibition to narrative teleology, de-creating (rather than deconstructing) the very structures of subjective consciousness out of which he presumes to write. Blanchot's fiction presents the subject in conflict with itself through contradictions that it can never assimilate in a relation of self-identity. Appropriately, *Death Sentence* is a *récit* (as distinguished from *roman,* wherein the author enjoys a more peaceful habitation of the text), in which narrative confronts its own motives without displacement into the categories of objective character, setting, plot, which otherwise dissociate authorial action from dramatic mise-en-scène. On the basis of this description we might be tempted too quickly to see Blanchot as implicated in the practices of deconstructionist philosophy (whether those of the French Derrideans or of the Yale demystifiers) in a self-trivializing ironic regress.

On the contrary what distinguishes Blanchot from the host of deconstructionists who also wield the rhetoric of a radical skepticism, and what makes Blanchot more worthy of discussion here, is that he is not a programmatic ironist of the self-conscious metafictionist art that has been in such vogue on the contemporary scene of American and French literary culture.[6] Deconstructionist irony salvages negation as determination in a virtual Hegelian synthesis. For the ironist the moment of *aporia,* or negation, is simultaneously the determination of the subject: the objects of attention become the leverage for self-consciousness reinstating a transcendental subject as a discursive center. This negation becomes, in effect, an inner confirmation. The objections of materialist thinkers to the abiding transcendentalism in Hegel are consonant with Blanchot's stylistic refusal of a structure of ironic reversals that would finally resolve into a generalizable negation (i.e., a positive negation). Unlike the deconstructionist, Blanchot eschews the ebullient reaffirmation of authorial prowess implicit in the ironic excesses of a radically self-conscious artifice.

Hegelian negation (as distinct from deconstruction) does seek a conceptual rapport with historical conditions. But in Hegel conditions are no more than phenomena with respect to the noumenal essential: the negating consciousness. In Blanchot, however, conditions (in this case verbal predications of the text) do not assimilate to a transcendental substrate of negating consciousness. Rather, they coexist in uneven relations of partiality. In Blanchot negation is not immediate determination, as would be the case in irony, because, as we shall see, the contradictions of the text reveal their conditions of existence as already contradicted and irregularly distributed. The unity of the structure is thus to be found in the totality of the structure (uneven contradictions) and not in subordination of phenomenal part to essential whole. If consciousness is not ordered by a beginning point for which the end serves as perfect confirmation, then the conditions or causes of perfectible knowledge are only construable through contradiction, or on the threshold of self-transformation. Only on these thresholds of knowledge can we confront and articulate what is otherwise left out of our hapless idealist purview and thereby integrate a totality without a self-referencing terminus. Our interpretive priorities therefore shift to relations of *transition* rather than relations of closure: consciousness is now significant insofar as it creates the problem that engages it or calls it into being.

The passage from which I have taken my epigraph particularly shows how Blanchot makes knowledge of conditions of possibility a significant threshold of narrative meaning without resorting to discredited idealist abstractions.

> Very close to me was a great unhappiness as silent as a real unhappiness can be, beyond all help unknown and which nothing could cause to appear. And I felt this was like a traveler walking down a road in

the middle of nowhere; the road has summoned him and he walks onward but the road wants to see if the man who is coming is really the one who should be coming: it turns around to see who he is and in one somersault they both tumble into the ravine. Unhappy is the path that turns around to look at the man walking on it: and how much more profound was this unhappiness, how much more enigmatic and silent. (*Death Sentence*, 37).

As I have said, the convention of the first person in this narrative is the ruse of representation to which the author is manifestly betrayed. First-person narration is structured thematically out of the historical context of human intersubjectivity. So, it is not surprising that the readerly predisposition toward thematic extrapolation emerges as Blanchot's nemesis in this passage. The conflict is focused where the thematic meaning of the first person is systematically overdetermined in the progress of his narrative. The attempt to present unhappiness "which nothing could cause to appear" appears as the cause of the parable of the road. But the expository force of the parable of the road is strictly antithetical to the rhetorical purpose of the simile/personification that performs it.

Appropriately enough, enigma is a key term of the passage. And the intelligibility of the passage is relative to its enactment of enigma. But this does not represent a hermeneutic intelligence; it unfolds as an augmenting of relations of interpretation that complicates the original problem or question. As Hartman suggests, Blanchot supplants thematic priorities with the epistemological priorities of a *problematic:* "To study the problematics of art would be to consider each work as standing in a dialectical relation to consciousness and a critical relation to the whole activity of art" (*Beyond Formalism*, 109). The enigma of this passage is a deliberate inversion of contextual priorities; the simile of the traveler ostensibly lending particular concrete qualities to the abstraction of "un-happiness" becomes, through personification of the road, a second-order referent shifting the reader's interest from the level of character analysis to the level of rhetorical complexity. The epigrammatic "unhappy is the path . . . " epitomizes the ambivalence of the narrating voice poised midway between self-certain prediction (the aphoristic conclusiveness of the statement) and the self-negating abstraction of personification. The particular qualities derived from the image of the man on the road, and ostensibly intended to describe unhappiness, become a qualification upon the act of description. The ostensible shift of the burden of psychological exposition to the road makes the original project of description moot. The last clause of the passage confirms the abortive fate of the original intention.

I must repeat, however, that this is not the negation of meaning. Rather, taking up Hartman's view, we may observe how the "divagations" of Blanchot's prose put the narration in a dialectical relation to the consciousness that "speaks" first person. After all, this narrative commences with the sentence "These things happened to me in 1938," offering the prospect that the act of telling may be consummated in the tale. Yet it ends with a curse upon any reader who would purchase an interpretation of the narrative events in exchange for the postulate of an appropriate "ending": one that the narrator confides he is ceaselessly striving after himself. Such a reader "would become the beginning of my own story and he would be my victim" (*Death Sentence,* 81). To begin to tell entails a resistance to the tale. Every positing of an ending sufficient to a beginning is actually a doubling of intentions: "There is no end for a man who wants to end alone" (81).

The *récit* as a putative whole and this episode as an ineluctable particular both offer resistance to the tale by subverting the predicates of thematic knowledge to an act of doubt. It is crucial to repeat that it is specifically not the doubt of negation (i.e., irony) but, rather, the doubt incurred by excessive mediation. If we take the affirmation of any dramatic situation to be a heuristic beginning and the instance of internal contradiction to be the appointed "end," we will see that the quoted passage intimates the structure for a relational whole that is as distinct from the mode of ironic regress as it is from linear causality.

Instead of the beginning point and end point comprising a single complementarity, the two moments are differentially related. Blanchot's *récit* constitutes a decisive break in narrative transitivity, or, as I will argue later, it inaugurates a transitivity that is transitional rather than thematic. This point is elaborated by a structure of episodes in the work that is built upon patterns of repetition that cannily elude assimilation to a controlling theme or identity (character). For example, the narrator or other characters repeatedly appear in strange rooms without knowing where they are or why they are there. In each case our sense of scene emerges through the substitution of different persons in the same situation; since the parameters of significance by which we could know the repetition as such keep shifting, they paradoxically create new conditions of intelligibility with every recognition of the same thing. Whenever knowledge is asserted by resemblance the terms of resemblance undergo significant change. At one point the narrator can recognize old friends only through the interposition of a complete stranger.

Another way of making this point is to say that in *Death Sentence* narrative is approached through the presentation of a consciousness riven with contradictions: the novel is structured out of the exfoliations of these contradictions, positing a diverse range of predicative positions that a subject could inhabit with respect to the language of the text. Hence, the discursive form of the novel does not lead us to conclusions but, rather, posits a relation of the reading subject to the alternatives that conclusive predicates would otherwise preempt. Blanchot makes the most concise commentary on the relation of discursive forms to their conditions when his narrator declares: "A persistent thought is completely beyond the reach of its conditions" (53). Even taken out of context, the narrator's statement conspicuously echoes the Marxist hypothesis that has figured as a significant context for our discussion so far: the ideological mind will be known to itself only as its narrative conditions of being are exposed through the rifts of internal contradiction. But in context the narrator's statement is even more emphatic. It launches a reverie that meticulously performs the sense we have just made of it, thereby linking the narrator's statement to the fate of the author:

A persistent thought is completely beyond the reach of its conditions. What has sometimes impressed me about this thought is a sort of hardness, the infinite distance between its respect for me and my respect for it; but hardness is not a fair word: the hardness arose from me, from my own person. I can even imagine this: that if I had walked by its side more often in these days as I do now, if I had granted it. . . . (53)

We are reminded by the suspensive periodicity of the passage that statements in this narrative can be calculated to be significant as they produce speculation about conditions of their articulation rather than as they denote the scope of preemptive discursive wholes. At this moment in Blanchot's *récit,* the designated subject of the statement, "persistent thought" becomes the object of thought, i.e., "this thought"; the statement about conditions yields to or reveals the conditions of its being thought, distinguishing between the thought thinking and the thought thought.

Specifically, the aphoristic timelessness of the first statement is sub-sumed by the temporally specific moment, i.e., by the personification of the second statement. By contrast, linear narrative would present a "per-sistent thought," incapable of producing a concept of its own emergence because it would reveal a self-perpetuating causality. In Blanchot's non-linear narrative one moment is not causally prior to another—thereby establishing its unique possibility—but, rather, reveals possibilities for its own relation to other, contextually unpredictable (because they are *unpredicated*) moments. The text produces a concept of its own emergence insofar as it comprehends its own limits through transitions to disjunctive contexts. Or, as Hartman says, the text is never unburdened of the "labor of the negative." It is a narrative that, at every moment it determines a position for the subject to inhabit, submits to the contingencies of that determination. Of course, it should be clear that the word *contingency* is not to be taken metaphysically here. It is not an ideal, a priori. It is the marker of an active retextualization: a rearrangement of contextual priori-ties to reveal new combinatory possibilities. It denotes a complex network of real textual determinations.

In a recent elucidation of Marxist aesthetic propositions Pierre Mache-rey and Etienne Balibar suggest what might be a useful analogy between the interpretive difficulties engendered by a materialist aesthetic (as prac-ticed by Blanchot, as theorized by Althusser) and the more sociologically domesticated complexities of Freud's dreamwork. Macherey and Balibar remind us that Freud's dream not only is the object of interpretation but, in its contradictoriness, also serves as the *means* of interpretation (in Mach-ery and Balibar 56). Just so, for Blanchot's reader, the authorial refusal to make the two modes of object (end) and subject (means) mutually exclusive, or even merely complementary, poses the chief obstacle to any thematic naturalization. Nevertheless, this "obstacle" is precisely what makes the fiction a conceptually vital proposition, undeluded by naive totalizations.

Or we might say that the text strives for a Hegelian synthesis wherein the subject produces itself by overcoming its contradictions. But it is precisely in the calculated failure of such a project that Blanchot's text produces its most valuable knowledge. Hartman describes the work as a deliberately abortive courtship of "being." The narrator persists in the conviction that the act of telling can be self-authenticating. But that portentous self is manifestly incapable of representation within the scope of available authorial powers. The labor of the negative, where it is deliberately unsuccessful, implies a unique structural order: it privileges overdetermination as a ground upon which parts and wholes (self and other) are intelligible as they adumbrate a constitutive process of language, and not as they reify a hypostatic object. In Blanchot the Hegelian dialectic, purged of identity (*Geist*) by the perpetration of subject and object as distinct and asymmetrical moments, results in a distinctly anti-Hegelian *episteme*. Blanchot's novel suggests, then, an aesthetic form that is consistent with the forms of knowledge aspired to by materialist critics who reject the transcendent/ideal subject of Hegelian dialectic. Because the moments of negation and determination are not simultaneous, as they would be in the negations of irony, because they are temporally and sequentially articulated, the totality of the text is posited not as an identity but as a heterogeneity, albeit one that, as we shall see in chapter 5, attains some measure of autonomy as an analogue for human activity.[7]

We must recall that heterogeneity is the Marxist term for historical imperatives that belie our interpretive models—based, as they are, on a derived structural totality, synecdochically mirroring wholes in parts. The standard of heterogeneity sanctions a methodological overcoming of the limits of self (the starting point) as a procedural guideline for creative and critical practice. On this point Blanchot's project as a novelist converges with his project as a critical theorist. In his essay "The Narrative Voice" Blanchot calls the active principle of narrative "the neuter," that is, an aspect of language undissimulated by the conventions of self-expression:

> to speak in the neuter is to speak at a distance, preserving that distance without *mediation* or *community* and even experiencing the infinite distancing of distance, its irreciprocity . . . the neuter . . . neither reveals nor conceals. This is not to say that it signifies nothing (by claiming to remove sense in the form of nonsense), it means it does not signify in the way the visible-invisible signifies, but that it opens another power in language. (*Gaze*, 142)

If we can bear with the abstraction of Blanchot's prose, we can draw a relation between the neuter and the Marxist conception of narrative form; both attempt to locate a determinate power of language outside the mediating structures of a reified consciousness. The neuter suspends the "attributive structure of language." Posited as a goal of aesthetic practice, this suspension shifts our preoccupation with meaning from the object of predication to the contingencies of predication. Instead of functioning to situate a subjective consciousness within a network of predications that denote a certain object, hence subject, Blanchot's language expresses the conditions of the predicative constraint itself.

In one sense this is perhaps the most eloquent expression of conditions of existence of the whole (or its totality) since the complex whole can only be known in Marxist terms within the play of its contradictions. Althusser puts it succintly: "each contradiction, each essential articulation of the structure and the general relation of the articulations of the structure in dominance constitutes so many conditions of the existence of their complex whole" (*For Marx*, 205). And because this implies that the thematic structures of our knowing are useful to us as they reveal limits, this notion of formal totality compels our reading to confront language on a threshold of combinatory possibilities. Such was the locutionary level of analysis that we sought to reinstate in our original formulation of appropriate goals for a more rigorous formalism.

I repeat, this is not to eliminate the subject but, rather, to make the category of the subject elucidate a more diverse field of inquiry than the one opened, for example, by classical realism. In this perspective the formal armatures of the genre—plot, character, setting, and especially theme—lend themselves to a standard of narrative coherence as they allow the emergence of new motivational grounds for statements traditionally embodied in them. The linguistic life of the statement will take priority over the life of the "person" to whom we attribute it. The text will thereby deny a fixed locus of signification or representation. In fact, the aim of narrative will be no longer the revelation of a representable knowledge so much as a constructive anxiety about the representability of knowledge. It is an anxiety that nonetheless is not anchored to a Cartesian cogito like that so ironically dramatized by the ironic flights of the deconstructionist critic or the metafictionist novelist.

Blanchot's own account of the narrative cogito more strictly recapitulates the antiphenomenalist critique of consciousness. He assures us that his object is not to dramatize the anxiety of self-conscious knowledge so much as to interrogate the determinations it is heir to:

it could be that telling (writing) is drawing language into a possibility of saying that would say without saying being and still without denying it either—or, more clearly, too clearly, that is establishing the center of gravity of speech elsewhere where the speaking is not a matter of affirming being nor of needing negation in order to suspend the work of being, the work that ordinarily occurs in every form of expression. In this respect, the narrative voice is the most critical one that can communicate unheard. That is why we tend as we listen to it, to confuse it with the oblique voice of unhappiness or the oblique voice of madness. (*Gaze*, 143)

Here any impulse to complain about the abstraction of Blanchot's prose must yield to a belief that the calculated "difficulty" of the prose shares a conceptual burden with the form of his fiction. *Death Sentence* "voices" a narrative intelligence unencumbered by the narrow motives ascribable from its situation. On the basis of the quotation we might elaborate that the presentation of situation is always an "affirmation of being," insofar as situation is an objectification of character. Saying is "saying being" in the sense that it precludes reflection on the categories of knowledge that instantiate it. Just so, thematic structures offer to represent being by enjoining the plot predicates of linear narrative from contradiction. By contrast, Blanchot's own fictional narrative is not bound to traditional categories by which we analyze the actions of physical beings.

Instead, narrative event approaches the status of act in Blanchot, where it reveals its possible pretexts, thereby transforming parameters of contextual inclusiveness that identify it and thus undertaking a rigorous contestation of limits. And in this way the peculiar form of Blanchot's *récit* does suggest a practice fully complementary to the theorizing of "The Narrative Voice." Narrative is linked to social praxis by its capacity to turn value into process. Blanchot's narrative drives further speculation about the political acumen of aesthetic forms along a speculative path that evades the aridity of sensuously immediate or abstract standards of aesthetic value, on the one hand, and the naturalistic overparticulariza-tions of an ideologically naive realism, on the other. *Death Sentence* offers the prospect of a knowledge intimately entwined with the process of its own emergence. Thus, *Death Sentence* takes its widely acknowledged place in the avant-garde movement (that acknowledged asylum for the "voice of madness," the price paid by the path "that turns around") by meticu-lously turning the act of situating particulars within thematic structures back into the problem of the determinations (the particularity) of those structures.

Indeed, one of the most glaring contradictions within the political rhetoric of reformist literary theory is its lack of engagement with avant-garde creative works and its corresponding theoretical complacency vis-à-vis the embodied conventions of classical art forms. From Lukács to Terry Eagleton many of our self-consciously provocateur theorists cleave to a set of formal expectations conditioned out of the subject-centering practices of the nineteenth-century novel. This leads critics into the perverse practice of privileging terms in a literary context that in a historical context they would profess to work their potent demystifying powers on. So, when Eagleton, for example, wants to anatomize the Authorial Ideology of a text, he necessarily begs the question of how an author appears in his or her forms in the first place. Or at best Eagleton articulates a narrow range of possibilities for representing authorial presence in a text:[8] "I mean by 'authorial ideology' the effect of the author's specific mode of biographical insertion into GI [General Ideology], a mode of insertion overdetermined by a series of distinct factors: social class, sex, nationality, religion, geographical region and so on" (*Criticism and Ideology*, 58). Because authorial agency is here deemed to be epiphenomenal of "General Ideology," because Eagleton effectively begins thematically, not formally, in this cardinal formulation, he threatens to preempt the very ground of literary production that he presumes to theorize.

The Marxist critic's dubious goal of making criticism a science—hence, freeing it from ideology—depends on breaking the presuppositional ties that bind us unselfconsciously to our institutional discourses. By contrast with the critical methodology induced by Blanchot's *récit*, however, Marxist critics like Eagleton who approach the novel in narrowly canonical terms often appear to be engaged in the very ideological/thematic mode of inquiry they set out to debunk. I have said that the ideological trap of thematic criticism is its doctrinaire sublimation of the particularity of linguistic utterances (revealed at the level of contradiction) to what Blanchot might call the illusory "being" of historical content. Thematic criticism implements a reifying rather than a dialectical knowledge that, as I will elaborate in chapter 5, is antithetical to the skeptical philosophies on which the social theory of the past hundred years has been founded. If for no other reason, then, Blanchot's work is useful because it helps us to put forth as a commonsensical proposition of speculative inquiry what has hitherto been considered a heretical tenet of feckless aestheticism: that only after we have established a conceptual rapport with radical literary forms—forms that are not self-dissimulating fictions of identity—does it make sense to tout a critical methodology aspiring to revolutionary praxis.

And so we come finally to the necessary conflation of form and method upon which the subsequent chapters of this work presume. In an important essay about form, "Literature and the Right to Death," Blanchot takes his incentive from Flaubert, the most notorious form fetishist of the genre: "form is method" (in *Gaze,* 125). It is probably fair to say that the strangeness of Blanchot's narrative insists, as Flaubert did, upon new conceptualizations of reading. Judging from the formal disposition of Blanchot's work as I have sketched it here, a viable method would, like Foucault's archaeology, facilitate meaningful transitions between incompatible systems of knowledge. Addressing this thought elsewhere in his critical essays, Blanchot himself adduces Wittgenstein's problem as crucial precedent for his own work: "every language has a structure about which one can say nothing in that language" (*Gaze,* 130). Thus, the analytical activity of supplanting one knowledge with another is perhaps the most scrupulous account we can give of ourselves as cognitive agents.

One might object, of course, that this epistemological proposition, by now a commonplace of philosophical inquiry, is a fairly banal point for a novelist to propound. But Blanchot's achievement is to make it a determinate practice of narrative art rather than a predicate of narrative structure. His fiction reasserts the need to preserve the provisionality of the structures within which speech is possible, displaying their conditions of possibility through a calculated, therefore *not* indeterminate, excess of meaning. So, with our ears cocked to the jarring contextual dissonances of Blanchot's mise-en-scène we might now listen more subtly for the harmonious dialectical retort to Flaubert ("form is method") that is everywhere implicit in Blanchot's prose—and method is form.

By invoking aesthetic form as a predicative constraint in this way, we are implicated in the pragmatics of action. Action is inevitably conditioned by constraint. Such an acknowledgment, of course, conjures the very rapprochement between subject and history that is augured in the projects of ideology and ideology-critique, both of which I have adduced here as significant frames of reference for any substantial account of narrative aesthetics. Now we must see that within this frame our inclination to assimilate form to act will compel us to reckon with the dynamics of human desire, without which any such frame of reference would be fundamentally incoherent. Particularly the dynamics of Hegelian desire will impel us to see the *trans-formative* imperative of aesthetic form and hence the ineluctably narrative rationality of the aesthetic.

2

The Totality of Desire: Toward a Historical Formalism

> Each of the parts of philosophy is a philosophical whole, a circle rounded and complete in itself. In each of these parts, however the philosophical Idea is found in a particular specificality or medium. The single circle, because it is a real totality, bursts through the limits imposed by its special medium, and gives rise to a wider circle. The whole of philosophy in this way resembles a circle of circles.
>
> —G. W. F. Hegel, *The Logic*

> Within the epistemological labyrinth of figural structures, the recuperation of selfhood would be accomplished by the rigor with which the discourse deconstructs the very notion of the self.
>
> —Paul de Man, *Allegories of Reading*

Metaphorical Desire

Desire in its most transitive urges is a dream of totalization. Desire dreams the identity of the one with the many, the plenitude of truth, the absence of difference. Literary texts and philosophical systems alike proffer this dream as a corrective to the grim wakefulness of historical experience. Fredric Jameson evokes the pathos of such projects when he says, "History is what hurts, what refuses desire" (*Political Unconscious,* 102). History is a tragedy because it remains an unrationalizable contingency of individual fate. It remains intractably other. If, in its turn, human desire remains intractably (if naively) opposed to the temporal otherness of history, then language, the *techne* of desire, might be said to express its fundamental idealism best in the strivings toward resemblance enacted by Aristotelian metaphor. Metaphor, as the trope of resemblance, has been a refuge from the ruthless dispersions of historical time dating from the earliest classical tropologies to the last formal rhetorics of the eighteenth century.

And the desire for a conceptual rapprochement between human subject and historical continuum remains vital in the trope of metaphor.

But, for recent literary theorists seeking to develop a rhetorical analysis of the processes of human desire, the polarities of the conflict are reversed. Now metaphor is posited as a dispersive ordering of sense; history (deemed synonymous with ideology) is posited as a reified system of resemblances, the fruits of an identity principle overripe for deconstruction. The totalizing desire of the project of selfhood is radically rethought in this reversal.[1]

For deconstructionist critics such as Paul de Man the conflation of desire and language assumed in metaphor is radicalized by the claim that all language is metaphorical. In *Allegories of Reading* de Man avers that selfhood is not a substance but, rather, a figure (170). In this view language would appear to supplant man as the agency of artistic practice insofar as the metaphoric ground of language resists the repressive determinism of meaning (reference) and frees the human spirit from its fatalistic embodiments in the finitude of individual action.

In other words, the deconstructionist postulate of the metaphoricity of all language clearly preempts the very totality, unity, satisfaction of desire, toward which Aristotelian metaphor otherwise hearkens in its struggle for resemblances. The metaphoricity of all language admits no originating center of discourse and hence no movement toward those most fabled expressions of the totalizing impulse of narrative desire: identity and closure. Instead, for the deconstructionist metaphor evokes comparison with the principle of human need organizing the Freudian *Ich* around its relations with unattainable objects of desire—most longingly, the body of the mother.[2] Deconstructionist metaphor thus devolves to the vacuum of irony into which all recognizably determinate reality disappears, stripped of the illusions of being.

By contrast, in semantic readings of Aristotelian metaphor as reconciling unlike things (and in the unreflective consciousness that is the corollary of such a conceit) a founding resemblance belies the contingency of subjectivity by collapsing need into identity. This nullifies all but the most metaphysical possibilities for the subject as a historical agency. Such a pure, untroubled, identity is, as the oedipal child knows most traumatically, the absent center of a linguistic system, which finally expresses only its own incompleteness as a "system" of meaning. So, the deconstructionist critic concludes that Aristotelian metaphor, with its willed escape from the determinate contingencies of history, ossifies into an ideological *ressentiment*. Predicated as it is on such moribund idealism, it remains an unfit category for historical analysis.

Contrary to the appearance that we are consigned to dualistic thinking

here, however, my purpose in this chapter is to forestall any easy supplanting of old with new hypotheses. I want to suggest instead that, if the
implications of deconstructionist metaphor are closely examined, we
might see how it is complicit in the very evasion of the hurts of history
that Aristotelian metaphor, through the deceptive remedies of metaphysics, has promised to cure. I want to suggest that the limits of metaphor
(when it serves as a model for the constitutive desires of self) need to be
reexamined. We must consider the possibility that the identity principle
of Aristotelian trope and the ironic relativism of deconstructionist trope
verge at their extremes on the same intellectual fate: foreclosing the
material particularity of the subject. Perhaps this evasion of history is the
worst hurt of all, since it eliminates the refuge either of faith or of
skepticism.

In order to understand better the limits of metaphor as the trope of
desire, let us put it back into the context of human need, but specifically
within the historical framework that the Aristotelian theory of metaphor
appears to eschew. Let us remember, however, that the significance of
metaphoric trope derives from its historical complicity with narrative
teleology. Aristotle's most influential formulations of metaphor in *Poetics*
and *Rhetoric* make it operationally subordinate to *mythos* or plot structure.
The overarching concern of Aristotelian argument, particularly in *Poetics*,
is for the maintenance of plot unities. Just so in *The Nichomachean Ethics*
the admonition to strive for an ethical mean subsumes the violence of
tragic agency to a metaphysical holism that vitiates the active will.[3] The
epistemological scope of metaphoric figure projected by Aristotle in the
example of proportional metaphor confirms this prejudice (*Poetics*, 43) in
its attentuation of metaphor to the status of "an ornamental word." We
can speak of the object of metaphor at all only by virtue of its subordination to the narrative telos of subjectivity, within which the notions of
resemblance and identity preserve their original warrant.

Teleological thinking in plot performs its reduction of difference to
identity on the model of the reduction of reality by theory. Praxis, as
deconstructionists will tell us with some polemical bravura, inevitably
incurs the contradictions of contingent possibility that the human subject
in history and the history of the Cartesian subject in particular belie. From
this point of view what the structures of metaphoric resemblance and
narrative telos have in common preeminently is that they both disguise
the contingencies of existence. Therefore, if the epistemological entangle-
ments of such disguise can be unraveled, we may improvise a more useful

construal of metaphor, not as an autonomous figure but, rather, as part of a dialectical process more intricately knit into the fabric of historical existence.[4]

Nietzsche probably offers the most succinct refutation of the autonomy or epistemological stability of metaphor in "On Truth and Lies in a Nonmoral Sense" (in *Philosophy and Truth*, 82–83). This essay, so loudly resonant in the jargon of deconstruction—e.g., "différance," "textuality," "supplementation"—explains how the philosopher's wish to know the leaf of the physical tree entails a conceptual reduction of the differences instantiated in every specimen of the reality he designates with the word *leaf*. Its truth, in other words, is owed to a lie about its contingent relations. As the rest of "Truth and Lies" makes plain, what Nietzsche shows us in his exemplum is not simply that the constraints of meaning are phenomenological as well as epistemological (that the act of naming is articulated by limits, not by substances) but also that those limits must be dialectically engaged if the project is not to devolve to the solipsistic dogmatism of Nietzsche's "rational man." Because, conceptually, metaphor preempts contingency (i.e., limits) and participates in the idealism of subjective narrative telos, the task of a more historicized rhetoric might be to restore contingent possibility as a proper mediating force of subjective will.

De Manian Desire and Detotalizing Selfhood

The justice of conflating modes of personality, modes of rhetoric, history and art, as I am proposing here, is aptly summarized for my purposes in Paul de Man's provocative reading of Rousseau's "Pygmalion." This work at once makes the task of metaphor appear to be more than an empty rhetorical gesture and renders the conditions of human action an inescapably rhetorical predicament. Even more important, "Pygmalion" serves as a crucial prop to the de Manian assertion that launched these speculations: that self and figure are interchangeable. After all, Rousseau's "Pygmalion" is a meditation on the nature of artistic will and its object of desire. It attempts to define the terms of human creativity vis-à-vis creator (subject) and creation (rhetoric, or *techne*).

Correspondingly, de Man's notion of agency, and what he understands as access to the realm of the political, remains genealogically tied to the affective origins of language. Rousseau recounts these "origins" in the famous anecdote from "Discourse on the Origins of Language": a man intuits the concept "giant" in the threateningly "other" presence of a stranger, albeit another man. Rousseau goes on to specify that the act of naming the giant, a metaphoric moment of "passion" charged by the fear of an other, is a counter for the will, which is nonetheless immediately devastated in the succeeding recognition of mistaken identity. In this knowledge of contingent error the will is helplessly transmuted to a self-consciousness of human need. For de Man the important point here is that passion is an articulation of self through a suspension of reference: the real man supplanted by the name giant. This meaning is tantamount to the preemption of an other and the denial of contingency. Need, by contrast, makes itself felt by instancing the determination of the referent and thus denotes the inescapable existential contingency of metaphoric meaning.

Similarly, as de Man tells us, in Rousseau's "Pygmalion" the artist's creative will first appears in the totalizing gesture of image making. The artist closes the distance between the inner and outer worlds by reducing the diversity of nature to the identity of self. We are meant to see that the notion of form implicit in this act of forming the image is, in all its narcissistic specularity, tautological or figural. Yet it is inexorably disfiguring and self-shattering in its drift toward an ontologizing mode of consciousness. The object desired by the creative will annihilates as much as it appears to satisfy, since the artist's conflation of self and other obliterates the material particularity that can only be significantly determined in difference. The totalizing gesture becomes detotalizing because it is grossly underdetermined in the tautological relations of part and whole or self collapsed into other. De Man himself points out that Pygmalion's creation acquires real power only because its material form (marble) dissimulates against the artist's self-image. He then asserts that it is the "discrepancy" between the specular self projected by the sculpting hand and the formal materiality of the marble that makes a goddess of Galatea, not the mere act of creation. *Discrepancy* is, significantly, de Man's term for a dialectical movement between self and other by which human being realizes its most effectual nature.

There is more than a hint of Hegelian master-slave in the ceaseless reversals between the creative will and its self-transcending other, as de Man sketches out the plot of "Pygmalion." De Man wants to make the point that the evolution of self, following the model of linguistic trope, issues in an unending semiosis. "There can be no escape from the dialectical movement that produces the text," de Man says, with emphasis on the unstable juxtaposition of fullness and lack that all human will succumbs to in the totalizing gestures of subjectivity. In other words, the totalizing act of self-expression reduces self to the matrices of deconstructionist metaphor. The self attains formal integrity in the perpetually shifting registers of the literal and the figural, so that form devolves to the structures of difference.

Yet, paradoxically, the very concept of difference de Man needs for his critique of the metaphysical claims harbored by Aristotelian metaphor is fated to become ontologized in the manner of the Platonist teleology exampled in Nietzsche's leaf. What de Man wants to celebrate in Rousseau's writing is actually negated by his own exposition of it. That is to say, the concrete dimension of contingent possibility that would make the question of what *is* dialectical is eroded by the implications of de Man's critique of canonical trope/self.

I agree with deconstructionists such as de Man that what is wrong with the totalizing impetus of reifying selfhood is that it precludes knowledge of what constrains its meaning. Hence, it nullifies the possibility of self-transformation upon which every viable notion of self since Hegel depends. Another way of saying this is to point out that telos intrinsically precludes agency. What is wanted in its stead, therefore, is *an agency without a telos*. The specular image of the self makes selfhood intolerable because it nullifies desire, the motor of Hegelian subjectivity. We must remember that the Hegelian subject enters history through the transformation of nature. The emphatically contingent reality of the slave in fact epitomizes for Hegel the greatest potential for self-realization. The form of self we posit in our speculations about the formal possibilities of metaphoric thinking ought therefore to enable us to situate meaning with respect to contingent determinations, in order to avoid a deadly tautology. While de Man shows us how totalization masks need with identity in the forms of Aristotelian metaphor, de Man's own conception of metaphor as unstoppable difference renders particular need just as irrelevant and unknowable as the totalizing will he and Rousseau want to discredit.

The flaw of this thinking links de Man's/Rousseau's self with the problematic of the Kantian sublime. de Man himself accepts this complicity when he explains how the self, caught up in the processes of its own production, succumbs to conceptual paralysis: "the sublime dimension is production of a self awed by the knowledge that he is the agent of his own production as radically other" (*Allegories,* 179). This is Pygmalion's predicament exactly. Yet it cannot escape our notice that the very exclusion of an agency or intentionality, which formerly rendered Aristotelian metaphor an unsuitable model of self-production (collapsing need into identity), is valorized here, and in the doubly unreasonable name of sublimity, as a basis for undeluded self-consciousness.

After all, the problem with the Kantian sublime, for the practical purposes intimated by de Man's analysis, is that sublimity is posited as a term that has no concrete determinations to authorize the purport of its own determinate situation. As Kant says, "the sublime is not contrived in natural things but in our consciousness" (*Critique of Judgment*, 121). For Kant the failure of the imagination to produce an image in accord with the understanding—unity of the manifold—is an index of human nobility, because in the intuition of this impossibility the mind surpasses itself. This ennobled mind, however, exhibits no qualities and hence is the agency of no actions, presuming as I am that agency ought to make specifiable the qualities (i.e., the conditions) of every action. Similarly, the freedom of the self that de Man posits in deconstructionist metaphor offers no ground for the free exercise of the faculties it endows.

Paul de Man and the deconstructionists are right that the naive totalizing gesture of Aristotelian metaphor fails because it belies the contingencies of the totalizing self, but I would suggest that this failure might more profitably lead us toward a reconceptualization of part-whole relations that meticulously articulates the terms of contingency (of self) rather than toward the endless drift of differences, or self-annihilation. In other words, the worst failure of the deconstructionist project is that it does not provide a way to situate the social subject historically. It furthermore inhibits the possibility of action because difference is not specifiable as a contingent reality. Difference becomes effectively a nonrelational term. To the contrary, I believe the relationality of difference is crucial to any project that seeks to escape the tautologies that both idealism and radical skepticism are heir to.

As I will show in more detail later, difference, in a simple Hegelian negation, reveals the ground of its determination but cannot examine the more recondite determinations of that ground. Thus, it instances a subject rendered static in the grip of illusory will or ideological reflection. When difference is not a relational term it is only an index of unending diversity or transcendence. Because, like the Kantian sublime, it lacks specifiable qualities, nonrelational difference reveals itself to be an inapt mode of analysis for thinkers committed to the critique of a historically idealized subject, or self.

Contrastingly, I want to suggest that the model of form that would be most adequate to this critique would have to be capable of *producing fresh contingencies,* preserving, as de Man himself says, the discrepancy between specular and formal self as a basis of expression without ontologizing or nullifying the agency of expression. I am making agency equivalent to contingency in this discussion, and, by stressing agency so, I mean to preserve the semi-autonomy of contingent need as a constitutive element of meaning. Later in this chapter we shall see how the separation of the question of agency from the question of intentionality will facilitate such thinking.

For the moment, however, we must consider that any critique of the idealizing momentum of Hegelian dialectic hinges on a reversal of determinations in the direction of particularity, that is, the situation of the subject constituted in its determinations. I have said that, paradoxically, de Man's argument dovetails with the naive teleology he rejects in virtue of his effective reduction of material differences. Such is the price of unrelieved skepticism. Since the conceptual authority on which the opposing viewpoint subsists is metaphor, my call for a more historical formalism—conceiving form in terms of a production of contingencies rather than a disguising of contingencies—prevails upon a complementary trope for its elucidation: Jakobsonian metonymy.[5]

The difference between Aristotelian metaphor and Jakobsonian metonymy is that the latter is a trope predicated on difference rather than on resemblance. While metaphor, because it reifies the intending subject, appears to offer a tempting model for determining the satisfactions of human need, we have seen from de Man's analysis how the framework of intentional subjectivity supplied by metaphor threatens its own ground of determinations. Despite the fact that the totalizing gestures of Aristotelian metaphor fail, however, de Man's account of this failure fails, in turn, to inform the ground of any alternative reckoning with human need. Rather, need is reinstated in de Man's dynamic of self-production because it remains absolutely remote from its potential satisfaction. It therefore remains tragically unsituated in any particular existential context.

Metonymy, on the contrary, is articulated by contiguity, not semantic proximity. In Jakobsonian metonymy meanings are determined by combination or contiguity in the message, independent of contiguities in the linguistic code (semantic proximity). Jakobson coined the term *contexture* for the process by which "any linguistic unit at one and the same time serves as a context for simpler unity and/or finds its own context in a more complex linguistic unit" (60). Hence, the subjective positions metonymy describes are a function of the contingent relations it articulates rather than any semantic identity that might be presupposed in it. Because contexture is a variable of direction within a discursive code, it expresses need as a situation to be inhabited rather than as an "Other" to be overcome.

Thus, we might say that metonymy offers an alternative to the agency-erasing telos of metaphor. It sets forth conditions as determinate, rather than denying them in the name of autonomous subjective will or unstoppable difference. To know conditions is more historical than a mere assertion of the conditionality of meaning, since this involves the preservation of the integrity of subjective agency. Furthermore, such a particularized knowledge presupposes a mediation that is differentially relational rather than dualistically hierarchical in the manner of Aristotelian metaphor.

It is important to observe here that, for Jakobson, differential relations are determined in the possibility of contingent error, arguably a corollary of de Man's notion of discrepancy. This is the case insofar as the rule of contexture inscribed in verbal relations external to meaning is nonetheless accessible to meaning through the reconstructive possibilities of contradiction. Contexture renders the discursive subject "erroneous" with respect to the multiplicity of contextual imperatives that it cannot assimilate to universal discourse. In other words, because relational difference is predicated in contexture on the shifting positionality of the subject, it is discoverable only through the determinate contradictions of discourse—contradictions otherwise veiled by the forms of ideological closure. The possibility of contingent error, which is therefore the recognition of overlapping and competing contextual patterns within a seemingly closed discursive field, preserves access to the conditions of meaning by denying to language a transcendent principle. And, since contingency is only discoverable through contradiction, the self presupposed by this knowledge is constituted *in* determinate need rather than in either the satisfaction of need or in the enigma of indeterminacy.

This version of self might now be plausibly described as an agency without a telos. It is historically articulate insofar as history is a condition to be endured, not escaped. We shall see shortly how ideology is its escapist antagonist in the dramas of historical change.

Frailties of Desire: Structural Causality and Dialogism

Like de Man, I am interested in a notion of form and a concept of
subjectivity that might be wrested from the preemptive totalizations of
ideological narrative will. And, like de Man, I see that such a notion
must be predicated upon a kind of intransitive desire such as seems to be
proposed in the deconstruction of Aristotelian metaphor. But, unlike de
Man, I still want to preserve need, or agency, as a predicate of the notion
of totality, because I want to equate form with subjective positionality in
determinate discourse. In other words, I want to preserve the attributes
of intentionality without telos in order to preserve the particularity of
need. Not coincidentally, I have been arguing that the unspecificable
contingency of need, synonymous with deconstructionalist critique, fur-
tively reinstates the telos of naive desire structures as an *inner necessity*
(Aristotle) or as an always immanent causality. Thus, deconstruction
sabotages its own best intentions, despite the ironically self-preserving
ironies that sustain the skeptical powers of deconstructionist rhetoric.

My concerns here are given particularly rich exposition by three
thinkers whose speculations on desire and the problematic of totalization
bear directly on the political implications of reconceptualizing the subject—hence, on the question of ideology. It is noteworthy that the critical
enterprises of Louis Althusser, Fredric Jameson and M. M. Bakhtin hold
a common stake in a metonymic rhetoric or causality such as I have already
discussed. All are concerned with elucidating the totalizing imperatives
behind artworks and social forms alike. But, unlike their idealist or
deconstructionist counterparts, they are respectors of difference as the
crucial mediator of this knowledge rather than as an index of infinite
diversity or pure contingency. These theorists do not think the detotalizing effects of metonymic form apart from the causality of totalization.

Jameson invokes metonymy in the guise of differential relations that
determine meaning as a specifically "structural causality."[6] Structural
causality, a fundamental Althusserian concept, has been appropriated for
Jameson's analysis of narrative as a "socially symbolic act" because it
theorizes, in the manner of Jakobson, a mediation of parts and wholes
that transcends the worn-out dualistic hierarchies of Hegelian Marxism.
Following Althusser, Jameson indicts the intrinsically metaphoric form
of Hegelian mediation whereby one set of values is transcoded to another:
base into superstructure, epiphenomenal particular into noumenal whole,
etc. (*Political Unconscious*, 39–41). Althusser finds the specific authority

for this identity-based mediation in the causal or totalizing principle of Hegelian dialectic: an expressive causality. The Hegelian subject of *The Phenomenology of Spirit* brings itself into existence by overcoming internal contradictions through the displacements of a negating consciousness. Jameson and Althusser both observe what Marxists have always observed in turning Hegel on his proverbial head—that the subject's being, insofar as Hegel's philosophy can capture it, inheres in the negative principle itself. Therefore, the material differences that constitute the subject in social relations are said to possess only a spiritual unity in the principle of Hegelian negation. The actual contradictions inherent in material existence are conveniently sublated.

These material differences thus never have any existence for themselves and only manifest the unity of the internal principle alienated in them. Althusserians conclude that there are no situations to be grasped by the *Geist*-driven Hegelian dialectic. What is more, there is no possibility of a Hegelian politics in which a determinate subject acts within determinate conditions of existence. Writing on the materialist dialectic, Althusser puts the point succinctly:

> This is because natural or historical conditions of existence are never *more than contingency* for Hegel, because in no respect do they determine the spiritual totality of society. For Hegel the absence of conditions (in the non-empirical, non-contingent sense) is a necessary counterpart to the absence of any real structure in the whole. (*For Marx,* 208–9; emphasis added)

Althusser's structural causality, by contrast, treats the contradictions of social reality as the condition of the existence of its totality. The totality is not constituted, as in Hegelianism, through the overcoming of contradiction. Neither is it constituted in the unity of a subject whose identity coincides with the presupposition of a centered social reality, whether theocentric, ethnocentric, or phallocentric. In the framework of structural causality the conditions of the contradiction constituting any subjective moment are, in Althusser's own words: "no more than the complex whole (of the social totality) in a determinant situation" (*For Marx,* 204). This notion of ideology, Althusserians will claim, accounts for the place of the subject in a social totality that does not belie its own mode of production in contradiction: it does not hide its historicity.

On this basis the Althusserians distinguish themselves from "vulgar"

Hegelian Marxists: by founding theoretic praxis on a historical subject rather than on an abstract ideality. For Althusser material contradiction is the most significant basis for construing the subject relative to the social whole, precisely because all positive forms of representation serve merely to replicate their conditions of existence—at least insofar as their contingency with respect to conditions of existence is unselfconscious. Alternatively, structural causality posits the reflection of the conditions of existence within itself. This is tantamount to a reciprocal conditioning of cause and effect. Althusser proclaims structural causality, on this basis, to be the most profound insight of the Marxist dialectic.

This need for a more complex causal explanation of subjectivity likewise impels Bakhtin's formulation—though in a different historical and intellectual milieu—of the concept of the dialogic word as a predicate of discursive analysis. As Michael Holquist has explained, for Bakhtin "all transcription (transcoding) systems are inadequate to the multiplicity of meaning they seek to convey."[7] Just as Jameson/Althusser attack the structures of Hegelian mediation, in which one code mirrors itself in another, sacrificing its constitutive autonomy to the expression of a homologous relation (Jameson, *Political Unconscious*, 39), so Bakhtin insists that the transcriptive system of thematics, the unity of literary language, blinds us to the fact that it is posited within the constraints of a determinate social dialogue. He eschews the premise of a nondiscursive given, blind to the contingencies of its predication. If criticism is to unfetter itself of this handicap, we need to posit a formal principle that accounts more meticulously for the conditions under which it is socially produced.

Bakhtin's consciousness of the need for such a formalism takes the ironic form of an attack on Russian formalist method. Bakhtin attests that the Russian formalists are complicit in the very sin of unreflective thematism that they programmatically denounce: positing meaning as a nonrelational phenomenon (*Formal Method*, 73-82). The Russian formalists want to privilege the aesthetic device, making it a source of original determination by construing its determinacy only as the negation of "material." Material is everything that has immediate ideological significance in discourse. This amounts, in Bakhtin's words, to a simple negative determinism, reminiscent of the critique of Hegelianism already discussed. Bakhtin observes that while the formalist describes the relation between material and device as causal (108)—V. B. Shklovskii says the material is a "motive" of the device—the intelligibility of the device is ultimately indistinguishable from a discursive form of the material. This is, in effect, a tautological proposition about the determinacy of form itself.

The Russian formalists' claim for the integrity of the aesthetic device is based on the term *perceptibility*. The form of poetic language is rendered "perceptible" where it interrupts the unreflective transitivity of ordinary discourse. But Bakhtin then must ask what exactly this makes perceptible. His answer reveals the emptiness of the question:

> The construction (the device) itself must be what is perceptible. But we know that it is the purpose of the construction to create its perceptibility. Thus we arrive at a paradoxical conclusion: we arrive at a perceptible device, the sole meaning of which is to create perceptibility! This absurd conclusion is completely unavoidable! (*Formal Method*, 111)

As long as Jameson and Bakhtin both want to preempt the spiritualization of part-whole relations, thus to preserve the semi-autonomy of relational elements that constitute any discursive whole, both thinkers may be deemed advocates of a materialist *episteme*. As it has been described by Rosalind Coward and John Ellis in *Language and Materialism* (1977), the materialist stance toward the theory of the subject complements my own preference for conceiving form as the fundamentally metonymic ordering of subjective positions in discourse: "[the] social formation is constituted by unequal elements that are in contradiction with each other: movement and change are provided by the struggle between [these] elements" (63). Rather than further elaborate the predicates of this description, however, I want to specify how the metonymic corrective to metaphoric indeterminacy evokes, with some vivacity, the idea of the more historical formalism toward which I gestured at the beginning of this chapter.

Precisely because historical formalism seeks to preserve the semi-autonomy of need by positing a materialist subject in contradiction, it will privilege contingency distinct from idealist/formalist intentionality, as a site of agency. Thus, it licenses the critic/artist to retain the discursive leverage of determinate meaning, positioning the subject within a concrete discursive situation. It furthermore evades the idealist reductions of teleological structure that would otherwise attenuate the subject to a virtually nondiscursive positionality. Historical formalism in this way posits a narrative authority predicated on the contingency of relations rather than the transcendence of relations. I now wish to suggest that such a formal principle would make possible a significant critique of ideology from within literature—which, by no coincidence, both Jameson and Bakhtin conceive to be the real historical burden of literary theory and practice.

In fact, Althusser's definition of ideology anticipates precisely this notion of a form that is determinate but not simplistically deterministic: ideology is "the representation of the subject's imaginary relations to his real conditions of existence" (*Lenin and Philosophy*, 162). Althusser hastens to explain that, while circumstantially the subject is constituted *of* and *in* contradiction, society requires that there be an uncontradicted subject in order that any predication or communication may occur. So, the imaginary identity of the subject produced by ideology closes off the *movement* of contradiction, thereby endowing the subject's consistency. Such consistency is, of course, inevitably belied by the irrepressible contradictions of social reality that are disguised in it. Althusser exploits the Freudian nomenclature of "overdetermination" to express this inevitability and the new idea of subjectivity, in relation to social totality, that is implied by it. For the term *overdetermination* denotes the inherently multiple determinations of all representations, a multiplicity that may be grasped only by positing the simultaneity of incompatible levels of discursive analysis.

Such a solution to the antinomy of overdetermination demands a mobility of the subject that is otherwise narrowly restricted by egocentric models of subjectivity. Ideology and the forms of subjectivity it fosters are therefore inevitably contradicted by the conditions of existence, which they cannot reflect to themselves and which therefore cannot be meaningfully represented within the repertoire of conventional literary forms. It is perhaps upon the basis of such insights that the Marxist literary critic might now meaningfully forecast a revolution of the subject predicated on aesthetic form and thereby make more dialectical the orthodox Marxist determinisms of Lukács, Goldmann, and Williams, which all tend to grant a simple ontological priority of forms of life over forms of representation in art.

In Jameson/Althusser's structural causality, and in Bakhtin's dialogic (or *heteroglot*) discourse, materialism is a response to empty formalism, to ideal totalizations that constitute intrinsically ideological versions of the subject insofar as they do not reflect their conditions of existence. It may therefore clarify this point to redefine materialism, following Jameson's lead, as fundamentally a "limit philosophy" ("Imaginary and Symbolic," 57–61). We should see form, he says, like the referent of a text, as something constituted not in the act of totalization but, rather, in the limits of totality. By contrast, any materialism, hence any formalism, based on substance must be judged complicit with idealist intentionality. It is corrupted by the narcissistic desire structure that deconstruction has already demonstrated to be inherently self-annihilating. Such idealism simply nullifies the historical contingency of the subject.

On the contrary, along with Jameson, Althusser, and Bakhtin I wish to reinstate the determinacy of the subject, at least as a specifiable site of conflict. This materialism accords with my original wish to establish a threshold for the study of forms by postulating an agency without a telos, thus facilitating a separation of agency from intentionality as the new ground of formal totality: a totality without a totalization.

The naïveté of intentionalist formalisms may be historicized, in other words, by making the irrepressible discontinuity between parts and wholes—instead of the homology of part and whole—the basis of inter-pretation and textual production. Agency in this case denotes the purely extensional relation of parts, which, as we will confirm in our reading of Baumgarten, can only lend themselves to a metonymic standard of intelli-gibility or causality like that intimated by Jakobsonian rhetoric. Since intentionality, by contrast, denotes an intensional (and transcendental) relation of parts to whole, it preempts knowledge of contradictory forces that would only otherwise be expressed as the semi-autonomy of need.

Philosophers such as Donald Davidson have argued the need to find a model of agency divorced from intentionality and from intensional relations. This makes possible an understanding of the contingency of actions—and in this case I am treating the formal transformations of text as actions—upon descriptions rather than making descriptions dependent upon actions (57–61). Davidson argues that too often we confuse features of an act with the description of the act when we try to determine what is happening all around us. The materialist subject insists upon the dis-tinction between the two, and this is materialism's causal principle. When they advocate the reconceptualization of form as a critique of ideology materialist thinkers such as Jameson and Bakhtin are suggesting a way to account for the kind of contingency acknowledged in Davidson's analysis, albeit for ultimately incommensurate purposes. For Jameson and Bakhtin what is at stake is an account of the social forces embodied in literary forms, an account that is usually preempted by the self-productive illusions of humanist subjectivity. Ideology is, after all, the self-replicating authority of egocentric desire that reduces historical experience to a finite repertoire of cultural plots, precisely because it posits the coincidence of an egocentric subject with a centered and therefore reifying social reality.

Jameson's recognition that "history is what hurts, what refuses desire," is thus an eloquent credo of materialism in its recognition—shared by Bakhtin—that the totalizing epistemology prompting older formalisms must escape the traps of its own specularity. For my purposes this escape is proffered through the predications of an agency without a telos. For both Bakhtin and Jameson the escape from specular idealism is tied to a reconceptualization of the totality, whether it is the aesthetic whole or the social whole. Since both Jameson and Bakhtin valorize the site of contradiction as the ground of a new totality without a telos, we might conclude that all forms of representation not founded on contradiction and relational difference are thereby doomed to replicate their conditions of existence. This would be so at least insofar as their genesis from such conditions remains unselfconscious and therefore unchanged. And, as I have already said, material contradiction critiques the conditions of existence of contradiction by reflecting them within itself (Althusser, *For Marx,* 207). Therefore, I would suggest that the form of reflection advocated by both Jameson and Althusser is a form of agency, because it marks a uniquely mobile positionality of the subject; it offers escape from the replication of the subject's conditions of existence without denying them. As long as the mobility of the subject is a function of its overdetermination, the subject's genesis in contradiction, it denotes an agency distinct from intentionality.

The materialist elucidation of mutually conditioned terms—self and aesthetic form—tends to confirm both the deconstructionist mistrust of metaphoric identity and my own suspicions of a veritably self-less deconstruction: the materialist philosophy looks toward a reconciliation of self and historical moment in a metonymic causality that neither belies difference nor concedes the indeterminacy of differential relations. It produces what I will want to characterize in subsequent chapters as a *subject in process.* This is not a subject set adrift on the ever swifter currents of the slipping signifier so heroically navigated by deconstructionist wit but, instead, one more humbly resituating itself within the textual constraints of its own incompleteness. The subject's incompleteness, insofar as it is reflected to itself, articulates the theory of its incompleteness and hence endows the agency of its transformation.

This idea of subjectivity has obvious affinities with the work of Julia Kristeva and Michel Foucault,[8] for whom the totalizing will, whether its animus is the Freudian ego or the strategies of institutional power, is necessarily *ex-centric*. But because, as I have emphasized here, the ex-centricity of this self is always the determinate condition of its existence (and the knowledge it bestows), it permits an account of its transformations that is neither mechanically external to its relational structure nor altogether commensurable with such structures.

We can therefore see that the recent theories of the subject do not so much herald the painful destruction of subjectivity (an all too common misconception) as its pleasurable embodiment in the masochistic desire for an ever more hurtful history. The masochistic subject is broken on the body of its own desires, where its limit term, *contradiction,* becomes the threshold of its reconstitution, hence the resumption of its polymorphous perversities. Now we might imagine that the morphology of these relations will designate the proper scope of the study forms. And the pain will always be perversely indistinguishable from pleasure where desire is its own necessity, where subject and object are bound by the cruel asymmetry of their articulations.

Finally, I do not frivolously dress out these concluding remarks in the provocative garb of psychoanalytic allusion. *Masochism,* as we shall see in the next chapter, is pointedly a relational, not an oppositional, term, when Freud elucidates its dynamic with sadism in "The Economic Problem in Masochism." To deploy the term as a metaphor for the subject's relation to history is therefore to stress that the conflictual nature of subjectivity may now be viewed as precisely what *enables* a coherent account of transformations in human discourse, rather than rendering that discourse merely the most burdensome pathos of human tragedy.

Now the subjective mobility aspired to in these speculations must be recontextualized within the discourse of ideological-critique proper. Only in this way can we persuasively indicate the degree to which its stipulated relationality may be judged to be something more than a free-floating phenomenon. On the contrary, we will see that this relationality offers a cognitive grasp of particular human acts and of human motivation in general. For it is inscribable within the narrative dynamic that plays between intentionality and the unintended consequences that invariably constrain the rationality of intentional acts. We shall see that it is this constitutive disjuncture of all meaningful or interpretable acts that occasions both the consciousness of ideology and the narrative self-consciousness of its critical trajectory through the whole history of human affairs.

3

The Dis-Position of the Subject: Agency and Form in the Ideology of the Novel

The interpretation of given reality and its abolition are connected to each other, not, of course, in the sense that reality is negated in the concept, but that out of the construction of a configuration of reality the demand for its [reality's] real change always follows promptly. The change-causing gesture of the riddle process—not its mere resolution as such—provides the image of resolutions to which materialist praxis alone has access.
—Theodor W. Adorno, "The Actuality of Philosophy"

Ideology and Subjective Holism

The concept of ideology in the discourse of culture critique is an unmistakable child of Cartesian trauma. The Enlightenment dualism of *res cogitans* and *res extensa* reverberates loudly in the split between ideas and actions that the savant Destutt de Tracy took as the enabling condition of ideological practice. Stuart Hall has noted that the study of ideology, from the time of its first formulation as a positive scientific enterprise in de Tracy's *Elements d'Ideology* (1801–15), has held out the promise of a critique of idealism (141).[1] Ideology-critique has always presupposed that ideas are potentially disjunctive with the actions that purport to express them and so tragically belie their effectivity. The ineluctable certainty of this split is reiterated with radically incommensurable motives, by thinkers from Napoleon to Marx who have all nonetheless appropriated the concept of ideology as a rhetorical vantage point from which to attack the inadequacy of words to deeds or the emptiness of ideas rendered abstract from the exigencies of human praxis. Practically, the critique of ideology puts into question the unity of human experience it aspires to comprehend by asserting that the forms of experience intrinsically dissimulate human nature.

Burdened as it is with the dualist prejudices of Kantian formalism, the question of form in literary study bears a distinct family resemblance

55

to the critique of ideology. Like ideology critique, literary formalism
proceeds through a Cartesian doubt about the possibility of reconciling
phenomena and noumena, words and worlds, truths and actions. The
concept of literary form powerfully sustains its appeal by envisioning the
reconciliation of the split it so eloquently describes. Because the study of
ideology and the study of literary forms prompt roughly the same agenda
of questions, the literary speculation of theorists such as Lukács, Benjamin, Adorno, and Marcuse, has intimated the usefulness of treating the
question of form in literature in tandem with the study of the ideological
structures of social life. Particularly as we follow the lead of the more
contemporary Althusserian school in assuming that the study of ideology
is principally concerned with positioning and repositioning human subjects vis-à-vis the discourse world, we may see how our understanding of
the phenomenon of ideology can offer a perspective within which literary
texts, by their own ideological complicity, more convincingly open onto
a world of action. By attending more closely to the agency of the subject
than to the identity of the subject, we may arrive on the threshold of a
political aesthetic that is neither a mechanically reductive realism nor a
metaphysical fancy.

Before we pursue the rationality of juxtaposing methods of literary
formalism and ideological critique in more detail we should however
observe a difference: we must begin by noting that the critique of ideology
is programmatically critical of the forms it discovers, while its literary
counterpart valorizes the forms that legitimate its activity. Organicism
(certainly the most potent formalism propelling literary tradition since
neo-Platonism), like the study of ideology, established the positionality
of subjects with respect to a world of objects as a ground of representation.
But its unity is predicated upon a principle of formal closure whereby the
objectification of reality is too simply rendered a function of temporal
stasis. The positionality of the subject is reified in this formalism by a
narrative teleology that makes all incidents of plot meaningful as they are
reconcilable with the moment of dénouement. This Aristotelian principle
prevails both in narrative plots and in criticism of the novel. So, despite
the fact that the positionality of the subject, whether a narrator or a
character, is a constitutive element of literary form and hence a premise
of formalist aesthetics, that subject is denied the very mobility upon
which ideology-critique presumes in order to theorize the transformations
of discourse.

Particularly in the New Criticism, a veritable apotheosis of organicist aesthetics, subjective positionality is reduced to a counter of synchronous relations isolated within the borders of the text by the Aristotelian constraints of closure—dénouement and peripeteia—even as these devices become the vehicles of ironic consciousness. In other words, the plot form that sustains this organicism presents an analogy to a naive or untroubled ideology: a set of ideas that objectify experience as a peaceful totality. In this regard literary organicism effectively renders subjectivity a predicate of form as if the constitutive properties of any form of reality were prior to the subjective agency they reflect. By contrast, such idealizations are taken as the target of ideological critique precisely insofar as its aim is the transformation of discursive positions that confer social identity.

I. A. Richards is a literary formalist whose acceptance of the notion of agency or subjectivity as a predicate of form indicates the epistemological dilemmas to which such thinking succumbs. For Richards science, the authentic realm of agency, "can never answer any question of the form: what is so and so." "It can only tell us how such and such behaves" (84). Science can totalize but cannot yield totalities. Thus, for Richards it cannot serve to heal the "dissociated sensibility" of high modern culture. By attempting to make form intelligible apart from agency, and thereby to abstract it from the contingencies of time, Richards denies it any effectivity. As many critics have pointed out, he denies it the very sociological ontology that might have resolved the split between art and science, form and agency, that fundamentally troubles all of his critical speculation.[2]

While Richards's definition of "pseudo-statement"—"a form of words which is justified entirely by its effect in releasing or organizing our impulses and attitudes" (91)—superficially reconciles form with agency, agency is nonetheless rendered only a reflection of the virtually oracular intuition embodied a priori in formal tradition. That is to say, a functionalism obtains between form and subjective agent that is the effective elision of agency as a constitutive moment. As I have already suggested, such thinking is perceived within the critique of ideology, from Marx to the Frankfurt School to Althusser and contemporary social theorists such as Anthony Giddens, as crucially flawed insofar as the eliding of agency nullifies the possibility of formal transformation or simply renders transformation an ontological instead of an epistemological proposition. By contrast, in ideological critique, in which the possibility of changing the discursive position of the subject within a discursive matrix is the prerequisite of changing the discursive order, we accept the necessity of revising priorities, such that form is rendered a predicate of subjective agency. In other words, form is produced in subjective mobility. It should be clear, then, that I will follow the methodological lead of ideology-critique when I propose to adopt a notion of form in literary practice that is predicated on subjectivity. In this way I wish to counter the reifications of objective form in literary theory that cut aesthetic discourse off from the ethos of transformation. We might remember that the Aristotelian rationale for art is originally founded on the principle that mimesis is the imitation of an action, a making in time, a transformation.[3] It is specifically in the challenge to elucidate this principle of transformation that the argument for comparing ideological critique and aesthetic form seems to me to find its greatest urgency.

Of course, the idea that literary formalism must seek predications other than form itself is not new. It was promulgated by George Lukács in *Theory of the Novel* (1920) and *History and Class Consciousness* (1923) as the first premise of a nascent materialist aesthetic. His own neo-Kantianism notwithstanding, Lukács posited his materialism in order to lift the veil of Kantian transcendentalism obscuring the historical determinations of social practice. Lukács sought to reconstitute formal identity as an agency instead of an objectified reality. In *History and Class Consciousness* Lukács asserted that the human subject is the producer of forms and that the activity of this production is not separable from the comprehension of all such historical forms taken up in the life of the human subject. Accordingly, I would like to suggest that the predication of form on subjectivity or agency opens a perspective of knowledge about the relation of subject and object that is narrowly inhibited by the apolitical and ahistorical formalism of a literary aesthetics that cannot accommodate the Lukácsian insight. Furthermore, I will assert that the genre of the novel, which Lukács points out has always made the question of form its central problem, uniquely grasps the implications of the new formalist perspective. It thereby prefigures a significant revision of our own expectations about the relation of formal innovations in literature in particular to cultural change in general. The desire to make literary form a predicate of subjectivity rather than to make subjectivity a predicate of form thus impels a seeking after new strategies for mobilizing the human subject against the epistemological rigidities of humanist self-knowledge.

The concept of form has nevertheless long been synonymous with the resolution of conflict or difference and thus with an essentializing inertia of the humanist subject. Though the theoretical demystifiers of humanist ethics indict the idealization of subjectivity as the greatest inhibitor of critical self-awareness in the human sciences, the idealist subject nonetheless preserves a methodological privilege in social theory and in literary theory alike. For the German sociologist Georg Simmel, whose study of form marked a propitious convergence of critical disciplines in the 1920s and 1930s, form specifically emerges to shape the content of experience when undifferentiated immediacy is ruptured. Yet Simmel's analysis of form as a social practice, while suggesting a reconciliation of form and agency in its almost Deweyan emphasis on practical experience, nonetheless insists that the burden of form is primarily to preserve the integrity of subjective mind: "We become cultivated only when all of them (knowledge and skills) serve a psychic unity" (42). Literary critics similarly compensated themselves for the loss of subjective immediacy in modernist culture, with the category of aesthetic wholeness. As we saw with Richards, the New Criticism (coming of age in the 1930s and 1940s) complements Simmel's conflation of form with the redemption of a whole subjective immediacy. The infamous New Critical sequestering of the text from history and society only makes explicit the implicit ascendancy of form over agency in the subjectivity endowed by the modes of lyric sincerity and negative irony.[4]

We must recall, however, that in Simmel's *Conflict in Human Culture* optimistic holism reverted to a painful realization: far from conferring mastery of objective experience, form inevitably reveals the incommensurability of subjective will with objective spirit. In the knowledge of the irreducibility of temporal subjective experience to the forms of subjectivity Simmel resigns himself to an insurmountable tragedy of human culture. Precisely because literary criticism is implicated in the same holistic premise, we must see how it is implicated in the same tragic knowledge. This is especially apparent when we realize how doggedly New Critical literary formalism seeks its truth through the concept of a unified self. For the organicist totalization of self is undermined by the very Freudian model of consciousness without which the theme of selfhood in literature and literary criticism is virtually mute.

Mobile Subjectivity

Freud's analysis of the function of artistic forms is pervaded by a sad recognition of its largely compensatory nature insofar as subjectivity in art remains predicated on form: "Art," Freud says in *The Future of an*

Illusion, "offers substitute satisfactions for the oldest and most deeply felt
cultural renunciations" (in *Standard Edition,* 14). In this account art articulates a specifically remedial consciousness, healing the gaps of a nature
that is inherently disjunctive with itself. This is not equivalent to saying
that art is delusional. But, in Freud's prospectus, art is clearly assimilable
through the mechanism of sublimation, to the modality of conscious
development he calls the secondary process. Distinguished from primary
process by object cathexis, secondary process paves the developmental road
to mature personality. In secondary process the evolution of subjectivity
proceeds through sublimation of uncathected, or polymorphous, desire
into static objectifications of human need. By contrast, the formless mobility of primary process inhibits development. Freud's extensive mapping
of the development from primary to secondary process led to the hyposta-
sis of the subject in Anglo-American analysis. But the relatively recent
French revision of Freud has insisted that the progress of mature personality through sublimation perversely ignores the ascendancy of primary
process, which is theorized in Freud's most mature treatises. Because this
is an analysis of the subject as intrinsically conflictual, I want briefly to
chart the course of this revisionary process with two literary critics,
Samuel Weber and Leo Bersani, for whom all the French signs point to
serious consequences for aesthetic formalism.

    Weber, in his book, *The Legend of Freud* (1982), implicitly links the
fates of aesthetic formalism and secondary process when he shows how the
elaboration of secondary process depends upon "the expectation of an
intelligible whole." From this point of view secondary process and the
structure of personality in general are the expressions of an intrinsic
narcissistic drive that predicates identity on exclusion of difference or
partiality. This is a version of identity that is cognate with systematic
philosophy and literary formalism in its emphasis on closure. Yet Weber
and Bersani, who develop their respective positions from a Lacanian perspective, have both pointed out that what appears in early Freud to be a
program for resolving conflict in mental development turns in Freud's
later considerations toward a recognition of the inescapability of
conflictual desire. Weber summarizes:

    The pursuit of meaning; the activity of construction, synthesis,
    unification; the incapacity to admit anything ireducibly alien, to leave
    any residue unexplained—this indicates the struggle of the ego to
    establish and to maintain an identity that is all the more precarious

and vulnerable to the extent that it depends on what it must exclude.
(13–14)

For Freud this conflictual self-recognition entails a return to the
theory of primary process for the fullest account of mental life. It is argued
that this is specifically the case insofar as Freud's attempt at a reconciliation between the ego as aim determined (narrowly teleological) and the
ego as agency became an increasingly difficult enterprise, an unresolvable
contradiction at the heart of metapsychology. Weber points out that
Freud's antagonism with Adlerian psychoanalysis flows from his adamant
assertion that the ego is not original but, rather, is produced by conflict,
in which case conflict is not an other to be cathected but, instead, is
constitutive of self. In other words the constitutive conflicts of self are
resolvable only as strategies of deflection from an ultimately unresolvable
problematic: the schism between conscious and unconscious mind. From
the viewpoint of the *Ecole Freudienne* it is Freud who makes our proposed
revision of the causality that plays between form and subjectivity necessary
insofar as his "energetic" metapsychology privileges psychic movement
over psychic inertia. Form is always a contingency of subjective dynamism, of primary process.

If our formal description of Freudian consciousness is thus to be
revised (in light of a reintegration of primary process into analytical
discourse), we can follow through on our original purpose of linking the
question of form in ideology and literature. We can begin by speculating
how the primary process might be rhetorically related to the project of
mobilizing the conscious subject against the discursive rigidities of its
social places and aesthetic forms. For Bersani, in particular, there is
already a guide for such speculating in the dynamic of masochism and
sadism, the exposition of which is roughly contemporaneous with the
ascendancy of primary process in Freud's thinking.[5] This aspect of Freudian metapsychology compels our attention because it contains a narrative
component that implicates it in the study of literary forms without the
necessity to construct an extensive and perhaps unwieldy analogy between
the disciplines of psychology and literature. It furthermore encourages us
to resist any temptation to essentialize desire. As I implied in my earlier
discussion of Hegelianism, we must understand instead that desire can
be formulated more strategically in relational terms.

According to Bersani, Freud establishes a threshold of narcissistic
will in a nonsexual stage of sadism that always precipitates what he

designates as a "turning around" of the object relations. "Fixed" states are thus rendered as a dynamism of mobile positionality. While the hetero-aggression that triggers the sadomasochistic dynamic is initially a nonsexual urge, the resultant suffering of the victim sends a "thrill" of recognition through the torturer, which accords pleasure proportionately as it represents to the torturer a shattering of the constitutive limits of physical subjectivity. I take this shattering to be a decisive threshold of mobility. Representation creates desire by instantiating a lack (difference) in the observing consciousness.[6] In other words desire entails an irreducible interchange between primary and secondary processes. Because Freud seems to predicate sexual pleasure and the eroticizing of sadism on the representation of sexual excitement (in this case, as Bersani points out, sexual excitement must be represented *before* it can be felt), he privileges the mobility of subjective desire over its particular embodiments.

In a second stage of sadism the quest for domination of the other that began in the mind is reborn in the body of the tormentor as a fantasy of identification with the victim and in a third stage as a quest for a new object (subject of aggression); the subject or agent comes to self-realization through movement. In the dynamic of sadism and masochism Bersani, like Weber, sees the return of the repressed "other Freud," the Freud of primary process. By contrasting the mobile subjectivity inherent in sadomasochism with the subject produced by the narrative sublimations of Anglo-American analysis and literary formalism, he specifies the consequences of that repression. In his incisive essay "The Other Freud" (1978) Bersani contends that, through its valorization of the Freud of the secondary process (genetic development through sublimation), humanist aesthetics has had the effect of privileging a narrative violence, which he treats as a version of sadism. Violence is here understood as a formal strategy whereby time is nullified in the privileging of a cathartic moment over the undifferentiated flow that distinguishes it. Narrative catharsis produces a comparable structural violence or stillness in its conflating of the proairetic events of narrative with the expressive function of a timeless holism. This all too heuristic whole in turn nullifies the particularity of the events that constitute it.

In order to develop the argument beyond the terms of the psychoanalytic model Bersani shifts its ground from the Freudian dynamic of sadism and masochism to the Sadean text of *120 Days of Sodom*. Sade reveals the affinity between the Freud of secondary process and the dominant conventions of narrative closure. Bersani sees in the structure of the Sadean spectacle, in which sadomasochism is reified as a "stilling" of otherness, the essence of narrative. With its "rigidly hierarchical organization of people and events into major and minor roles . . . the calculated progress of a Sadean narrative is toward a violent act which, in a sense puts an end to all calculation [i.e., movement]" ("Other Freud," 42–43). It is appropriate that an ideal climax in sadism is murder, since this helps us to understand calculation in terms of an entropic discursive mobility. Death is the ultimate immobility, "an end to all calculation." Bersani asserts that, just as the Sadean master brings the other into relationship with his own will as victim—by removing him first from the world and then removing a part of the body from its respective whole—narrative produces its meaning, achieves a comparable immobility, by gradually conflating the discrepancies that differentiate the part from the whole.

In rhetorical terms more instrumental to literary analysis we might say that narrative dénouement, or what we will have to designate more specifically as peripeteia in subsequent chapters, seems to be predicated on a synecdochic causality. That is to say, it produces an identity between parts and wholes that elides time into space, mobility into stasis. Narrative plot reduces each incremental episode of action to a proleptic type of the cathartic reversal. Thus, the multiplicity of subjective positions that constitute plotted, narrative discourse are effectively sublated into a singular position. My idea that dominant organic models of literary formalism mistakenly make subjectivity a predicate of formal determination dovetails, I believe, with Bersani's critical assessment of narrative mastery. Organic formalism subsists on the paradox that the process of subjectivity remains a contingency of its own formal reification or idealization.

The expansive subtleties of Bersani's argument need not be detailed here. It will suffice to say that what is sacrificed in organic formalism is the idea of transformation as the modus vivendi of subjectivity. Significantly, the synecdochic and hence reifying causality that I take to be the basis of organicist models of narrative form has a counterpart in the prevailing Western paradigm of interpretation: wherein meaning is articulated by an allegorical (not to say Sadean) master text. For Fredric Jameson this paradigm serves as the specific impetus of ideological critique and a methodological access to the political unconscious. As Jameson says, ideological critique is always essential where we understand that, "if indeed one construes interpretation as a rewriting operation, then all of the various critical methods or positions may be grasped as positing, either explicitly or implicitly, some ultimate privileged interpretive *code* in terms of which the cultural object is allegorically rewritten" ("Marxism and Historicism," 41). Such codes, we might conclude, warrant critique because they preempt the mobility of the subject. The mobile subject belies the privilege of allegorizing consciousness.

For Jameson the critical discourse most aptly suited to working out this insight is, as we have already seen, Marxism. Jameson compares Marxism favorably with competing methodologies on the basis of its powerful critique of expressive causality.[7] If we can say that the problem Jameson identifies is the problematic inertia of the subject presupposed in organicist models of formal totality and that this formalism belies the principle of mobility implicit in Freudian epistemology and ideological critique, then we can at least cautiously begin to speculate upon the possibility of a notion of formal totality that permits a more positional subject. Since Jameson points out that the trope of the expressive, or nonpositional, subject is allegory (where transformation and totality are mutually exclusive), we must look for a tropological expression enabling new part-whole relations such that transformation and totalization, or agency and totality, might be assimilable to one another. I have been suggesting that such a form is incipient in the genre of the novel. Correspondingly, the form of the novel historically expresses the conflict between agency and totality, between the Freudian/Marxist revisionary subject and the organicist subject, as its condition of possibility.

I will have to specify my understanding of the novel here. I take Bakhtin's notion of *heteroglossia* to be a perspicuous grounding of the distinction between novel and lyric, epic, and dramatic modes.[8] I believe the concept of heteroglossia permits us to speak more responsibly of an ideology of the novel that might be continuous with the forms and methods of ideological-critique. For Bakhtin's analysis suggests that the subject in the novel is not instantiated as an essential discursive position. The subject is more lucidly understood (as exampled in the vicissitudes of sadomasochism) as a discursive disposition: a putting in place that is already a displacement in relation to the other places of discourse. We shall see that the agency of this displacement is indistinguishable from the discursive relationality it articulates.

Dialogic Mobility

Like Freudianism and the concept of ideology, our understanding of the concept of the novel has been revised in the late twentieth century by a

self-reflexive epistemology. This strategy of making the threshold of totalizing agency reflexive is largely an attempt to preserve the contingency
of human relations that cultural ideologies so commonly transcendentalize
in their representation of culture. This was precisely Bakhtin's motive
when he pointed out that the mistake of formalist critics of the novel was
to assume that language was a fixed code, independent of the discursive
situation and thus unresponsive to the transformational exigencies of social immediacy. Bakhtin's supplanting of the centrality of the concept of
language with the concept of "utterance" stipulates that the threshold of
intelligibility in discourse is its dramatistic contingency. This is almost
Kenneth Burke's sense of a grammar of motives, but with the further
qualification that the coordinates of dramatistic meaning are seen as vari-
ables of social practice, always in flux. Specifically, the poles of subject
and object are taken to be reversible.

Julia Kristeva, one of the first poststructuralists to give a productive
reading of Bakhtin, has also been the first to speculate upon the innovation in novelistic form that is entailed by Bakhtin's regrounding of the
novel in the concept of dialogism: a mandate for the reversibility of subject
and object. Kristeva designates this innovative prospect as the "subversive" novel, a text that formally presents itself as a dialogue between the
subject of narration and an addressee (the reading subject). The dialogue
obtains as a splitting of the writer into the subject of enunciation and the
subject of utterance (*Desire*, 75). The subject of enunciation, the authorial
self, is present as a signifier for the reader. But, Kristeva asserts, the reader
becomes a signifier for the authorial subject by virtue of the fictional
character (subject of utterance) who represents the subject of enunciation
for the reader.

This complex mediation between author and addressee by the subject
of utterance (Bakhtin calls the trajectory of this communication "exotopy," that is, finding one's self outside)[9] recapitulates the heterology
of language in general, whereby the utterance, always already spoken by
its very conventionality, functions as an interpretant between the one who
utters and the one who understands. As Kristeva says, the novelistic word
thus marks the possibility of permutation from the position of the author
to the position of the addressee. This possibility of permutation would
accord well with a formalism grounded in the principle of transformation.
Because of the unusual mediational status the novelistic word possesses,
it does not merely represent; it is also always the object of representation.
Its discursive coordinates are produced out of the discrepancies between

subject and object compounded within the history of the word's usage. With the understanding that language is always already inserted into a social discourse and that the terms of meaning are variants of position within the dramatic scene, we might conclude that heteroglossia denotes the priority of subjectivity over form in the novel simply by virtue of the mobility it entails. Bakhtin explicitly approaches the conclusion that subjectivity is fundamentally an axis of change, when he characterizes the novel text as "a transformation of another text." Here transformation supplants telos as the burden of novelistic excursus.

It is well known that "carnival" is the social text out of which Bakhtin reads his theory of the novel. In carnival the individual is both subject and object. The most controversial rhetorical ramification of the carnivalesque is its apparent nullification of intentionality, which thus seems to preclude agency as a term of analysis in any social/interpretive situation. Bakhtin's notion of the dialogic appears to obviate intentionality as the basis of narrative logic precisely because it makes the possible transformation of the subject's position in discourse, rather than the identity of that position, the vital axis of meaning. So, while the modality of carnival instantiates a social place for the human subject, it simultaneously appears to vitiate the claim to meaning that alone can animate the subject in that place.

The specific value of Kristeva's remarks on Bakhtin is her clear disputation of this appearance and thereby her ability to see beyond it to new strategies for recuperating human subjectivity as a meaningful category. Kristeva, associating the subversive novel with the textual embodiments of the carnivalesque, indicates that intentionality and agency are differentiated in the phenomenon of dialogism. Accordingly, intention is understood to be a term of teleological or monologic discourse, and agency is understood to be a term of dialogic discourse, a totality that is in process, not a totalization. The concept of the dialogic is thus revealed to be an implied critique of intentionality as a totalizing term, but *not* an elision of the subjective agency marked in intentionality.

Rather, we must assume a radical reconceptualizing of that subject here. Kristeva prefers that the philosophical order entailed by the concept of intentionality be situated in language rather than be confused with the situation of language itself: "Dialogism situates philosophical problems within language" (*Desire*, 89). In other words it seems Kristeva would replace the pair intention-telos with the pair agency-totality as the ground of formal utterances. The terms [substance-causality] of intentionalist-teleological discourse are in her view supplanted by dialogism, which "absorb[s] them within the concept of relation": "It [dialogism] does not strive towards transcendence but rather toward harmony, all the while implying an idea of rupture (of opposition and analogy) as a modality of transformation" (88–89). We will remember that the modality of transformation is precisely the formal axis upon which the discourses of psychoanalysis and ideological critique have been seen to converge in their demands for a subjectivity that expresses agency without telos. Implicitly linking her project to those other two, Kristeva's ideal of the heteroglot subject promises a literature that "will perhaps arrive at a form of thought similar to painting: the transmission of essence through form, and the configuration of (literary) space as revealing (literary) thought without 'realist' pretensions" (88–89). Because the elucidation of such a "form of thought" and the subject it would denote must be reconciled with an economy of transformation that does not transcend its own discursive situation, we must look for its unity only in the subjective mobility it occasions. This constrains us to the rhetorical situation anticipated in the preceding pages, in which history may be confronted with all the discursive specificity that ideology specifically occludes.

We will not, of course, forget that carnival, or dialogue, is a place of ideology inasmuch as it is a ground of representation. But, because the Bakhtinian dialogue makes representation a self-consciously relational practice, the ideology of carnival and the novel can now be understood as a logical process that is inherently recursive. In this way does it follow the epistemological trajectory of ideological critique. This recursiveness (contrasted with the monological practice of ideology)[10] appears most explicitly in the novel's radically foregrounded performative aspect. We know from Lukács that authorial performance in the novel always subsists as a ratio of immanence to mimesis in which the authorial consciousness projects the appearance of a world and thus expresses a contradiction at the heart of all mimetic desire. This is the ineluctable contradiction between form and form-giving consciousness. For novelistic mimesis makes a claim to immanence that form necessarily belies. As we saw earlier, Lukács proposes that the novel expresses the transformative capacity of human identity by virtue of its ironic structure: since the novel reveals that the producer of apparently immanent forms is not separable from the comprehension of those forms, the novelistic act of mimesis always redounds to the facts of authorial contingency, which in turn modifies the conditions of mimetic desire.[11] As we shall see later, Lukács's abortive effort to resolve this performative contradiction in *History and Class Consciousness* results in a sobering cautionary for the literary theorist to inhabit more scrupulously the place of contradiction rather than to seek its transcendence.

The Example of Thomas Nashe

It is now appropriate to point out that the history of the English novel, which begins conspicuously in the performative contradictions of classical rhetoric, reveals a striking continuity with the Lukácsian premise for a materialist reading of the novel genre. In *Unredeemed Rhetoric* (1983), a recent and well-reasoned study of the protonovelist Thomas Nashe, Jonathan Crewe has implicitly showed how classical rhetoric is traversed by the very problematic confronting Lukács in his analysis of the novel. Crewe has situated the study of classical rhetoric (and Renaissance fiction) within the conceptual framework of human idealization. Here value is predicated on the tension between immanence and act. As is the case in Lukács's account of the irony of form, the strict and highly elaborated decorum of Renaissance prose demands an adequacy of word to occasion that literature (contingent on political, market, editorial imponderables) can best express only as an invidious comparison between the authentic act (the ideal decorum) and the dissimulating performance (the textual enactment of decorum). It becomes remorselessly clear to the Renaissance author that a perfect execution of language would in fact vitiate the ideal. Or, as Crewe argues, the perfect execution "must fall short, since such an order is ultimately unthinkable without transcendental foundation" (25). All language, then, if it is to enact the values of an ideal decorum, is already a self-admitted likeness. Therefore, it paradoxically attains perfection only as it becomes a more perfect likeness of likeness. In other words the claim of immanence, to which language aspires in rhetoric, gains veracity only in the self-conscious forms of failure, which reify the ideal by distancing it.

So, however much it may have seemed a digression, it should now be clear how my point that performance expresses contingency may serve to link a discussion of textual formal totalities based on ideal decorum with our original notion of establishing subjective mobility as a formal principle. Because contingency, treated as an intrinsic rhetorical feature of narrative prose, emphatically makes the concept of form accommodate the transformation that contingency entails (i.e., temporality), it suggests a notion of formal totality governed by a transformative principle.

In light of the preceding remarks it should come as no surprise that I choose Crewe's subject in *Unredeemed Rhetoric* as the perfect exemplar for linking the historical identity of the novel with the theoretical problematic of ideology. It is precisely because Nashe's fiction seems inadequate to the task of mastering a rhetorical decorum that his critics, from Gabriel Harvey to Rosemund Tuve, have judged him harshly to be an author without a style. My own purpose in showing how this apparent lack of style is generative for a concept of form in the novel is nowhere better served than in a reading of Nashe's prose narrative *The Unfortunate Traveller* (1593). Nevertheless, what I propose is not an exhaustive explication of the text. Instead, I offer a sampling of its characteristic rhetorical moves as they answer the questions raised along the way of my own speculative travel toward a revisionary formalism. Nashe offers only the first of several literary exemplifications of this developing theoretical stance. Though it is perhaps the most schematic, it is like all the others intended to indicate the degree to which the theory I am advancing is no less emphatically a practice of reading. Reading, considered as a praxis, will be increasingly important as a premise for seeing how the aesthetic dimension of subjectivity may ultimately serve social ends.

Accordingly, Nashe's text declares its intention to recount the life of Jack Wilton, narrator, with a stipulation to the reader: "if you come in company with any man which shall dispraise it [the account] or speak against it, you may straight cry 'Sic respondeo,' and give him the stockado. It stands not with your honours, I assure ye, to have a gentleman and a *page* abused in his absence" (253; emphasis added). The statements of the text prove, before they are uttered, to be a contingency of the reader's sense of decorum, which is quite self-consciously an artifact of the textual. Crewe points out that Nashe is credited with the first use of *page* to refer to the technology of print, acknowledging therein a further dimension of verbal contingency, since the page defended here entails pages of reading to which the reader must submit as a condition of his contract. Thus, the page is permitted to rise above his social station. What we have here is, in effect, an eloquent dialogism, which I would argue might be the most compelling ground of the claim that Nashe is a seminal English novelist. Nevertheless, I need not make a case for his primacy in the canon, but only for the power of this text to exemplify the formal/

transformational principle that I am arguing links the understanding of the form of the novel to our grasp of the problematics of ideology. It is on this threshold of knowledge that the novel genre becomes a rich reflection on human action to which ideology, after all, always consequentially devolves.

As the quoted passage illustrates, Nashe's rhetorical performance engages the problematic of ideology in its ability to express the desire for expression as an already conflictual order (conflictual with respect to reader and decorum). As we have seen, ideology, a seminal post-Enlightenment concept intended to express the necessity for a critique of prejudice and tradition, has ever since and on that basis made the conflictual order a condition of knowledge. Therefore, ideology has always presumed upon a transformative moment as its threshold of expression. This transformation denotes either the fatal reification of ideological positions within a discursive matrix (the dissociation of appearance and reality) or the Marx-inspired dream of the end of ideology (the conciliation of appearance and reality).

In either case, as recent critics of ideology such as John Thompson and Anthony Giddens have suggested, the term *ideology* demands to be understood as a relation to power and domination. This is particularly compelling insofar as Giddens defines *power* rather restrictively as "transformative capacity" (88). Within the bounds of this definition power is arguably indiscernible from the fundamentals of the concept of action, a claim that will be borne out with close argument in subsequent chapters. For the moment it suffices to know that Giddens argues, along with Habermas (*Towards a Rational Society*, 99), that ideology is "coeval with the critique of ideology." After all, to identify knowledge as ideological is to assume the existence of another language with competing validity claims. In turn, this is to acknowledge contingency again as a kind of generative principle. The discursive positions produced by ideology and the methodological rigors of ideological critique must be seen to subsist on one another.

In Nashe's narrative, as in the power relations that structure ideological knowledge/experience, the subjectivity of the narration reveals its constitutive ground to be precisely the contingency of other places of discursive leverage or power. These are expressed as proliferating motives in the rhetorical displacements of voice into different performative registers. Kristeva's phrase "the subject-in-process" takes on considerable concreteness in the rhetorical complexities of Jack Wilton's narrative. As we shall see, the mimetic function of the text reflects a totality wherein the reciprocity between subject and form appears to be generative rather than reiterative. The totality is integrated in an expanding economy of discursive places of exchange (complementary to the Freudian dynamic of sadomasochism), in which any sense of structure or totality must be assimilated to the concept of transformation.

The famous climactic scene of *The Unfortunate Traveller*, the confession and death of Cutwolfe, gives us our best example. Here, in order to know who is speaking, a reader must understand how one voice is both the pretext and the outcome of other voices. The scene is a public execution—the public square is the primal scene of Bakhtinian dialogue—where social practice has deposited a thick sediment of public discourses. Accordingly, Nashe's narrative excavates a remarkable depth of contextual strata. First, the law places Cutwolfe on display for the moral reproof of the assembled public. In turn, this occasion provides the borrowed premise of Jack Wilton's own narration. Cutwolfe speaks in a conspicuous quotational space obtruding Jack's presence but at the same time echoing his own past. For Cutwolfe's present speech echoes a previous oration, delivered as prelude to murder while holding his victim, Esdras of Granado, at sword point. It is for this murder that Cutwolfe is to be punished. Esdras, the murderer of Cutwolfe's brother, in turn performs his repentance within the quotational space of Cutwolfe's oration. As a ploy to stay *his* executioner's hand, Esdras projects this personal guilt onto Cutwolfe. This is a rhetorical reversal whereby he narrates the record of sin and guilt that will be bequeathed to Cutwolfe should the latter accede to his murderous impulse and become no better than his victim. Cutwolfe responds to this hypocritical moral parry by enthusiastically embracing damnation as his only state of grace. Thus, he performs on the verbal level the very reversal of roles that Esdras offers to undertake in person by promising to stand in for Cutwolfe as the perpetrator of future damnable acts. These, he says, will accrue to the spiritual depravity of the surrogate, leaving Cutwolfe free to delight in the contemplation of crimes without endangering his soul in the commission of deeds.

The bargain is proffered by Esdras as the best of two worlds. But, because the worlds of word and deed are effectively indistinguishable in this presentation, the bargain is a veritable nullification of choice and hierarchy, except as exigencies of transformation and reciprocal agency. In other words the structure of this narrative, complementary to the rhetorical exigencies of its author, entails an agency that is inseparable from the process of dialogue in Bakhtin's sense. We could say that Jack

Wilton's narrative is the performance of performance, insofar as its intelligibility is linked to the recursiveness of its reference. Every rhetorical gesture is rendered as a transformation of its constitutive agency. The subjectivity of Nashe's narrative, speaking out of deeply recessed quotational space, appears as a succession of performative stances that are unified not by the unfolding intention of a transcendent or intentional subject but, rather, by the contextual discrepancies multiplied within it.

Certainly, the subjective mobility exhibited here can be extrapolated on a thematic level as a flight from the self-deluding traps of univocal subjectivity. Just so, Nashe's rhetoric is described by Jonathan Crewe as a flight from the self-erasure of rhetorical ideality. It would be a fair hypothesis that Jack Wilton, like the author (epigone to his rhetorical model), seeks to evade the moral lesson proffered by his own account of Cutwolfe's execution, understanding, as he does, the inherent hypocrisy of baiting morality with the violence of the reader's voyeurism. But such thematic reading simply translates instead of productively engaging the unique discursive situation of the text.

On the contrary, the rhetorical strategy of subjective mobility is understood more crucially with respect to the central questions raised in this chapter when it is analogized to the conflictual ground of ideology. Ideology in its epistemological instability entails a self-subverting agency of knowledge. In this light Nashe's rhetoric shows how subjectivity, embodied as a transformational principle rather than a topos of identity, renders all questions of formal totality subordinate to its own reconstitution. By situating the novel so decisively in performance, Nashe reflects the genre's aptitude for a critique of the formal imperative contained within it. We must appreciate that such a critique would be inhibited by any alternative rhetoric that made form the predicate of a hypostatic, unconflicted subjectivity.

The fullest discursive ramifications of Nashe's project are made explicit in the conclusion of the dramatic action. Having gulled his victim into trading his life for a black oath against God, Cutwolfe's final deed is to punctuate the string of Esdras's self-damning blasphemies with a musket ball in the mouth. It is a doubly traitorous act confirming Esdras's betrayal of God's trust with a betrayal of Esdras' trust in Cutwolfe. This act is consecrated by Cutwolfe in the name of revenge: "the glory of arms and the highest performance of our valours; revenge is whatsoever we call law or justice. The further we wade in revenge, the nearer come we to the throne of the Almighty. . . . All true Italians imitate me in revenging constantly and dying valiantly" (Nashe 369). The previous words of Esdras are mirrored in the present rhetorical performance of his judge and tormentor, Cutwolfe, as he recounts his own guilt in the public arena. But when Cutwolfe's admission of guilt is finally revealed to be a calculated incitement to mimesis, a renunciation of guilt, Cutwolfe's words are in turn redeemed to high moral ground by the author/narrator, who claims them as the catalyst of his own professed moral reformation. Such a reformation, of course, serves to rationalize the mimetic veracity of the entire narrative episode, which Jack Wilton carefully completes with the account of Cutwolfe's own torture and death. This is an execution that the reader cannot mistake as anything but a reenactment of Esdras's demise. That is to say, it is simultaneously an authorial revenge upon Cutwolfe's crime and an elaboration of the very lascivious rhetoric of sadistic spectacle that revenge moralizes upon.

So, if we ask who has acted in this context, we must consider that the description of such action entails a subordination of characterological motivation to more diverse motivational grounds marked in the transformations of performative agency. In all of this we are reminded that revenge, the mimetic act par excellence, is the perfect metaphor for the practice of Nashe's rhetoric. Like revenge, every performative act of the text betokens another *actantiel* grid, which is its reconstitution on adjacent grounds. Like revenge, every act in the text is intelligible as the motive displaced. The motive of Jack's performance is both borrowed from and constitutive of Cutwolfe's, as Cutwolfe's is both borrowed from and constitutive of Esdras's. Like revenge, the reversibility of positions in the dramatic context is more important than any specific action represented in it. Finally, Jack Wilton cannot be sorted out of the mobility of the subjective agency that unifies this episode, except in the most banal thematic of moral teaching, which the novel conspicuously ridicules by making it the ex post facto motive of the narration. In sum, one must speak of the narrative subject apart from the narrative persona if one wants to respect the complex rhetorical relations of such a text.

Unlike Jonathan Crewe, however, I am reluctant to characterize Nashe's rhetoric too simply as "narrative 'blockage,' a frenzied stasis of pure performance" (Crewe 91) or as a prescient deconstructionist acknowledgment of the "seemingly inexhaustible (malign, hidden) implications of rhetorical performance" (90). Crewe's valuable reading of Nashe is, I believe, too simply invested in the tenets of deconstructionist wit, which he celebrates here. Crewe himself admits that there is a "more philosophical possibility" in all this that remains unexploited by Nashe and his contemporaries. I would like to identify this possibility with the prospect offered by Leo Bersani's critique of subjective immobility: the ideal of a subjectivity that resists the teleological pull of its own formal disposition while preserving the constitutive properties of conflicted will as its epistemological animus.

My point, after all, is not that Nashe gives us a blueprint for the novel as conceived by contemporary theory. Rather, the rhetorical predicament that gives rise to the early novel in general and that informs Nashe's aesthetic in particular expresses a notion of human subjectivity that is methodologically congruent with the situation of human agents circumscribed by ideological practice. It is this affinity of the novel for the conceptual tasks of ideology-critique that, for Lukács and implicitly for Bakhtin, give the genre its historical importance. It is through this affinity, we are encouraged to believe, that the novel can be linked to the freeing of historical subjects from the stasis of self-deluded history.

But it is not my purpose here to indulge Lukácsian utopianism about the fate of culture vis-à-vis the novel. Rather, I would like to conclude by simply suggesting what is to be gained provisionally by pursuing the relation of the form of the novel to the methods of ideology-critique. The scope of a single chapter is not adequate to the demands of my initial hypothesis that, by linking the methodology of the novel with ideological critique, we may begin to contemplate a political aesthetic that is not preemptively thematic. Nevertheless, we have taken steps in that direction. For the notion of the positional subject, which posits form as a predicate of subjective agency, effectively binds form and subject dialectically, making it impossible to conceive one too reductively as a function of the other. This reaffirms the methodological priority of taking the conflictual order as constitutive of meaning rather than as a premise of or an obstacle to meaning.

Such is the ground that critics of ideology such as Anthony Giddens want to cultivate for evaluating social action. They are reacting against what Giddens himself calls "functionalist" models of subjectivity and what I have been referring to as intentional, or Cartesian, models of subjectivity (best exemplified by the New Critics). For theorists such as Giddens the limit of this paradigm of subjectivity is that it is always simplistically deductive from a static idea of structure or form. It is thus inarticulate with respect to the imperative of human action.

Giddens has voiced his specific objection to this functionalist model of subjectivity in order to overcome a methodological impasse in the study of social action. The tradition of treating agency and structure as separate or ideal moments has resulted in the eliding of temporality as a variable of social determination. In Giddens's judgment such a representation of temporality fails to account for "the fundamentally recursive character of social life" (*Central Problems*, 69). By attacking this notion Giddens has emerged as an antagonist of structuralist theory. Alternatively, his approach has been to presuppose what he calls a "double structure." The double structure, or "structuration," posits a reciprocity between agency and structure reminiscent of Kristeva's/Bakhtin's supplanting of the pair intention-telos (monologue) with the pair agency-totality (dialogue). The double structure expresses the mutual "dependence" of structure and agency (Giddens 53), which, if rationalized in any other way, we must conclude would consign analysis to the familiar wearisome dualisms of failed idealism.

In the context of our present discussion the conceptual premise of the double structure gives us a strong intimation of what literary form must entail in order to accommodate the positionality (temporality) of the subject that is inherent in the rhetorical structure of the novel, at least insofar as it is described by Bakhtin and exampled by Nashe. Just as important, the subject put in process by Giddens bears directly on the long-standing ethical warrant of literary study: the attainment of a self-knowledge adequate to the historical exigencies of a self-transforming culture.

In this chapter I have been arguing that what has been missing in literary formalism is precisely a serious engagement with that transformative ethos. It is true that Lukács tried to undertake this engagement by privileging praxis over subjective identity, or Nature, as the crux of human knowledge. His shift from a static taxonomy of subjective positions in the *Theory of the Novel* to a dialectical model of subjective relations with the objective world in *History and Class Consciousness* warrants comparison with Giddens's desire to accommodate time to form, or, as Lukács himself would say, to chart a path home for the human subject. But there are insurmountable problems with Lukács's argument. These are ironically traceable to the fact that in *History and Class Consciousness* he abandons the novel as a site for analyzing the conflict of subject and object, positing instead a premature reconciliation of subject and object in the proletariat class. According to Lukács, the proletariat renders the subject truly historical in the knowledge that the forms of social life are the products of its proletarian labor, hence the access to a consciousness of self as a universal object.[12]

It is at precisely this point that *History and Class Consciousness* lapses into a regressive holism, because the resolution of subject and object envisioned in the proletariat is revealed to be an unapproachable ideal. It was quite clear to Lukács himself that members of the proletariat did not actually possess the consciousness that made them their own object, even if that consciousness was implicit in their historical condition. If the consciousness that would warrant our understanding of the proletariat as an objectification of subjective will must be imputed (as Lukács said, borrowing Weber's term, "objective possibility"),[13] while the complementary object world needs no such conspicuous rationalization, then the subject of Lukácsian praxis redounds to a functionalist predication upon form. This functionalism is strikingly reminiscent of the subject figured in the organicist ideal of literary form. As we saw earlier, the New Critical valorization of organic form effectively preempts the subjective mobility marked in the contingency of forms. It resigns us to a formalism that is incapable of expressing transformation as a principle of self-knowledge whereby all things, as Martin Jay puts it, "would dissolve into processes" and "Being would be understood as Becoming" (*Marxism and Totality,* 111). By contrast, because form in the Bakhtinian or Kristevan novel, like Giddens's double structure, does not permit the conflation of subjective consciousness with narrative form or subject with object, it necessitates treating the subject as always interacting with a pre-given object, thus preserving subjective agency as a more effectively historical moment.

If the idea of the novel adumbrated in the confluence of Giddens, Bakhtin, and Kristeva constrains us to this understanding, perhaps we will move in a direction that Lukács's prefatory arguments in *Theory of the Novel* (not coincidentally intended to be a preface for a larger work) pointed but could not follow. Perhaps by apprehending the position of the novelistic subject as its *dis*position with respect to the transformations of discourse, we will finally see in that genre the continuity of art and life that Lukács abandoned the novel to discover. To dispossess the subject of its essence is to pose it as a relation with itself that is mediated by time, to make its positionality constitutive of its meaning. It is to conceive along with Bakhtin, in *Problems of Dostoevsky's Poetics* (1963), the fullest implications of the concept of *exotopy,* that barrier of otherness crossed by the dialogic word. We have seen how easy it is to mistake Bakhtin's understanding of the exotopy of dialogue as merely another allegory of indeterminacy. But Bakhtin himself emphatically reminds us that the dialogic word is not a concession to the infinite semiosis portended on the social threshold of dialogue. The author does not disappear in the text amid the din of voices that echo in his utterance:

> Our point of view in no way assumes a passivity on the part of the author, who would then merely assemble others' points of view, other's truths, completely denying his own point of view, his own truth. This is not the case at all; the case is rather a completely new and special interrelationship between the author's and the other's truth. The author is profoundly *active,* but his activity is of a special dialogic sort. (Bakhtin, *Problems,* 285)

Nowhere in the acknowledged major texts does Bakhtin himself fully explicate the agency imputed here. But I believe that, if we follow the implications of the other theories convergent in the present chapter, we can build Bakhtin's imputation into a more positive assertion. We would say that novelistic agency is irrepressible in the alterity of contingent relations. But the novel produces its meaning at the place where the virtually unconscious overdeterminations of sheer alterity are returned to consciousness as the burden of change.

In the next chapter the discharge of this burden in history and historical consciousness will become the basis for a more critical perspective on Bakhtinian dialogue. We will see the necessity to acknowledge a countercurrent in Bakhtinian theory that induces a veritably subjectless drift of dialogue. That subjectless drift leads Bakhtin into complicity with the very metaphysical totalities against which the dialogic novel seemed to stand as a repudiation. In a broader consideration of Bakhtin's argument we will see the need for the novel to come to terms with the historicity aspired to in dialogue, by changing the terms of its historical comprehension. Specifically, we will need terms that surpass the capacity of dialogism to articulate the problematic of authorial activity and, by inference, the acts of all historical agents.

4

The Voice of History / The Subject of the Novel

> The higher a genre develops and the more complex its form, the better and more fully it remembers its past.
> —M. M. Bakhtin, *Problems of Dostoevsky's Poetics*

> The history of forms is one where subjectivity, the progenitor of forms, ends up being absorbed by them.
> —Theodor W. Adorno, *Aesthetic Theory*

Novelistic History

The novel is our most prescient invocation of the past, of history. In *The Sense of an Ending* Frank Kermode reminds us of the truism that "novelty of itself implies the existence of what is not novel, a past" (117). Perhaps it follows that the novel is so inextricable from our experience of the past because, like history itself, the novel is formally a disjunctive moment expressed as a desire for conjunction. More conspicuously than other genres, the novel seeks its unity through heterogeneity. For it speaks obliquely, and nowhere more obliquely than in the convention of voice itself. Voice, the dominant metaphor for the totalizing power of novelistic form, is the genre's locus of subjectivity. But, as such, it is uniquely problematic, since novelistic voice is inherently and notoriously multiple: no *one* speaks in the novel. In its ineluctable multiplicity novelistic voice subverts the unitary imperative of the very metaphor of human speech that otherwise endows its rhetorical aptitude. Novelistic voice is the annunciation of an intertextuality that shatters the subject who speaks of it.

In this regard recent theorists of the novel who want to assert its perspicuous historicity nonetheless see the problematic of voice as precisely the touchstone of the genre's conceptual richness. Contemporary narrative theorists invidiously distinguish the novel from other literary genres according to the extremity of the problematic of voice.[1] For in novelistic voice, they argue, the human subject has manifestly experienced the vicissitudes of a crisis of self-knowledge, which the genres of epic and lyric escape by their vicarious ahistoricality. By invidious comparison with the novel epic and lyric are deemed to be mouthpieces for a monologic subject, whether authorial or characterological, which is disguised to itself by the single-mindedness (single-voicedness) of its representations.

According to this account, the paradox of voice in the novel is precisely what has made the genre a more rigorously philosophical enterprise than lyric or epic. I have alleged that the longest philosophical shadow cast on literary aesthetics in the twentieth century is that of Cartesian idealism. The idealist tradition has designated the subjective cogito, as a voice tragically divided from the world it speaks about, to be the insurmountable obstacle to its own historical self-realization. For post-Lukácsian theory this is the fate of the self, which the novel has been bound to narrate by its formal complicity with such historical fatalism.[2]

The argument of the previous chapter attempted to clarify the degree to which the recent currency of the theoretical writings of M. M. Bakhtin has given a special urgency to the idea of the novel as a vital confluence of history and subjectivity.[3] The force of Bakhtin's argument is carried in his assertion that the concept of voice is indistinguishable from the concept of dialogue. For Bakhtin dialogical meaning in the novel is always articulated across the barrier of an intractable otherness: author versus character, character point of view versus character point of view. Speech gains intelligibility neither from the systematic integrity of the language nor from the rhetorical fulcrum of authorial intention. Rather, this intelligibility is emergent from the ratio of perspectives that instantiates any social speech situation. In other words novelistic dialogue conspicuously recapitulates the conflict internal to the idealist cogito by virtue of its ineluctable temporality. For time separates identity into otherness. Because novelistic voice mediates our knowledge through differential relations rather than through tropes of identity, Bakhtin maintains that the novel expresses the struggle of historical existence in human subjects with a lucidity unavailable to traditional paradigms of subjectivity. The intertextual imperative of the Bakhtinian novel thus comprehends the temporality of the subject without idealizing its historicity.

For this reason I believe Bakhtin has been so enthusiastically appropriated by poststructuralist literary theory, which has sought to make history a new codex of literary value in order to subvert the hegemonic logocentrism of thematic and formalist criticism. Especially for those critics who identify themselves with "materialist" philosophy,[4] literary formalism, conducted under the sanction of the univocal or monologic subject, inhibits knowledge of how literature relates to the transformations of cultural life it is bound to reflect. This life it can only otherwise articulate in the unconscious gaps of its dogmatically ahistorical discourse. Thus, for thinkers as diverse as Foucault, Derrida, de Man, Jameson, and Althusser the category of history is posed against the "traditional" values of the literary text: formal totality, self, ego, truth. History becomes the methodological pretext for dismantling the authority of the Cartesian cogito, for heralding an end to an anthropocentric *episteme*, for confronting our freedom by stripping off the hokey theatrical vestments of enshrined cultural identity.

In this chapter I want to examine the use of the concept of history as a strategy for regrounding literary value in the uniquely "critical" structures of subjectivity endowed by the novel. In this way I might specify the genre's general usefulness as a tool of speculative inquiry into the nature of human subjectivity. Nevertheless, while I will agree with Bakhtin that the category of history must be invoked to fend off the twin threats of formalist monism, on the one hand, and subjective relativism, on the other, it will be necessary to specify the terms of dialogic history beyond the threshold of sheer otherness, where Bakhtin leaves it. It will become clear, as I argue the benefits of situating his work in the context of Adorno's negative dialectic, that Bakhtin's history, articulated as unmediated difference, must be supplemented with a theory of contradiction and determinate negation if it is not to obscure the very process it is meant to reveal. Only in this way will history and subjectivity be brought into a conceptually productive relation to each other. Only a theory of contradiction—such as that intimated in my discussions of Hegelianism in chapter 2—will constrain us from departicularizing history in the guise of an autonomous transcendental subject or from rendering the subject a threshold of relativity across which history is dispersed into infinite particulars. Only a reconciliation of contradiction and negation that is not a synthesis will salvage an intertextuality that does not nullify its own historical determinations.

Furthermore, because Bakhtin's claim for the novel's unique powers to historicize converges upon the deontologizing postmodern scrutiny of organic form, I now want to engage Bakhtin on the ground of the postmodern American novel. My exemplar will be William Gaddis, in whose work novelistic historicity is made decisively intelligible by the trope of parody. Gaddis's most recent novel, *Carpenter's Gothic* (1985), compels us to see how history can be elucidated through the concept of parody if we remember how parody belies the unity of experience it articulates by proliferating differences on a premise of identity. For this reason I will argue in turn that parody is the exemplary case of Bakhtinian dialogue. I want to test the validity of Bakhtin's attempt to reground formal study of the novel in dialogue and history. But, more important, I want to show how in Bakhtin any notion of history as a corollary of formal totality must entail a model of the subject that is assimilable to the concepts of transformation and transition. Through these concepts we elucidate the experience of contradiction without mitigating its disjunctive and therefore vital temporality. Such, I believe, is the burden dialogue gives to parody in the dialogic imagination.

With this proviso I want to insist that the dialectical path of the Bakhtinian novel in general and Gaddis's novel in particular does not lead us to a reckless dismantling of subjectivity but, rather, to a redefining of subjectivity under the valid materialist constraint that refuses to allow interpretation to rest outside the tumult of historical changes it gives voice to. By refusing interpretation any extralocality in relation to historical change, the materialist subject is the irrepressible parodist of idealist notions of history. It is for this reason that Bakhtin himself specifically elides parody with history as a textual substrate of dialogue. Dialogic voice renders the individual voice indistinguishable from many voices insofar as it is specifically a function of social exchange, once again a counter of temporality. So history, within the expressive scope of the Bakhtinian novel, is a kind of parodic ventriloquism that speaks through the temporal contradictions it engenders. It speaks through the intertextuality of the subject.

The Subject of Dialogue

Of course, if we are to hear the dialogic voice of history in all its subtly audible multiples of self, Bakhtin admonishes us to listen for it under the deceptively peaceful murmurings of the dominant ideology. By vivid contrast, with dialogue ideological discourse enchants us into a stupor of uncritical reflection. Because it seduces us to the delusive harmonies of identity-based (rather than differentially based) language systems, Bakhtin judges ideological discourse to be too one-sided for the historical scope aspired to in dialogue. In this respect ideology is specifically not amenable to the transformative exigencies of time. Therefore, in the Bakhtinian novel the pious patriarchs of history must first be the skeptical children of ideology.

With this proposition we can begin to appreciate the usefulness of the Bakhtinian aesthetic as a fulcrum of ideological critique. Nevertheless, we must realize that, if Bakhtin's dialogue is (on the basis of its powerful historicity) to benefit by invidious comparison with ideological discourse, it must further enable us to conceptualize the subject of history as an agent of historical change better than ideology. Above all, it must be able to specify the mediational terms of subjectivity precisely as ideological discourse does, but without reifying them in the modes of ideological production. In other words, if dialogue is to reveal its unique grasp of change better than ideological discourse, then the concept of dialogue must be reconciled with the perennial paradox of subject-object relations upon which every social or aesthetic totality produced within ideology rests. Yet it must do so, we will see, by proposing a subjective agency comparable to what Kristeva has called a subject-in-process. This requires an agency that is not subsumed within the deductive imperatives of its own telos.

Indeed, Kristeva's portentous opening of the intertextual scene in contemporary criticism conspicuously defers to Bakhtinian dialogue as an imperative of change upon which subjectivity must converge in any self-understanding that does not preemptively reduce itself to a metaphysical reflection. Just as Kristeva says of intertextuality in general, that "it requires a new articulation of the thetic" (*Desire*, 59–60), so it may be said of dialogue specifically that its telos is continually assimilated to the agency that articulates it.

It follows that parody is arguably Bakhtin's most representative case of dialogue precisely because it so strongly intimates a subject-in-process as "a new articulation of the thetic." Parody is technically the appropriation of the voice of another twisted to new motives.[5] But Bakhtin's exposition prevents our construing an overly facile Nietzschean "will to power" by this gesture. On the contrary, because dialogic voice is so exclusively constituted on the threshold of otherness, whether it is the voice of self or other, parody in Bakhtin's special context eschews the teleological traps of intentionality and univocal meaning. Significantly, Bakhtin chooses the term *utterance* instead of *word* to designate the generative locus of meaning in parody. *Utterance* invokes the nonverbal imperatives of speech acts (intonation, scene, time, etc.).[6] The manifest overdetermination of the speech act designated in the term *utterance* requires a more dialectical notion of subjective agency than I believe any intentional-teleological model of interpretation has yet offered. In any case, utterance, as Bakhtin defines it, is mediated too diversely to sustain the unity of the transcendental subject that might be otherwise presupposed in it.

The dialectical charge of utterance impels us all the more strongly toward embracing the concept of a subject-in-process when we consider the dynamics of the social scene out of which dialogue and parody arise, according to Bakhtin. Though dialogue has its textual roots in the rhetorical forms of Menippean satire, Socratic irony, diatribe and the seriocomic, its life spark is the social situation, the public agora wherein one's (authorial) meaning is necessarily mediated by the intentions of others. Bakhtin locates the originary scene of such mediations in the ritual armature of medieval carnival: the ceremonies of crowning and decrowning. The crowning and decrowning of a king is the essential carnivalistic act of Saturnalia, European carnival. The emphasis on movement, transformation, transition, which is so vital to the ritual of crowning and decrowning, celebrates, as Bakhtin says, "the shift itself, the very process of replaceability" (*Problems,* 125). In this regard, Bakhtin points out that the crowning/decrowning rituals in medieval carnival are analogous to the key tropes of Menippean and Socratic irony: *anacrisis* and *syncrisis* (the rhetorical triggers of classical parody), which progress by disjuncture. These tropes, by proposing communication across a brazen contradiction of styles, require a unique agency of transition in order to mediate differences without nullifying the differential play, the parodic spirit that animates them.

Furthermore, it is important to observe that the threshold of otherness crossed by the cultural texts of carnival, parody, and dialogue (all roughly homologous in this perspective) is sharply distinguished by Bakhtin from what he considers to be the insufficiently dialectical mediations of merely "stylized" discourses. In the genre of stylized discourse, arising from a contradictory opposition of forms, meaning is expressed too simply in terms of a resolution of difference. Thus, transition is vitiated as an aspect of meaning, and the mobility of the subject presupposed in transition is rendered discursively inert. Bakhtin's insistence on the distinction between stylized and dialogical discourse compels our attention because it bears out his pragmatic stake in the mobility of the subject. Most significantly, it mandates transition as a mode of intelligibility whereby dialogism must be anchored in determinate moments but not confined to them in its way of articulating them.

With this preliminary understanding we are obliged to see that the warrant for Bakhtin's privileging of dialogue and parody requires him to demonstrate how, in these genres, otherness articulates difference over time without losing its historical specificity. Otherness itself must be reconciled with subjective agency. As if to meet this demand head-on, Bakhtin, from his earliest "Architectonics of Answerability" (1924), elides dialogic/parodic meaning with the concept of action.[7] Action definitively entails a change of state, a transitional moment. Dialogic discourse is deemed, above all else, to be an "activity" by virtue of its transitional recursiveness; in other words, because the meaning of a word in dialogue is determined in the interpretation of "an other," the further dialectical entailment of intersubjective conflict is necessarily part of that interpretation. Michael Holquist summarizes this fundamental principle of dialogue: "Discourse does not reflect a situation; it is a situation" (*Mikhail Bakhtin,* 204). The transitional movement valorized in the crowning and decrowning ritual is thus reflected under this principle with the implicit proviso that the resolution of "situations" in dialogue may never be abstracted from the conditions of their utterance.

Unfortunately, when Bakhtin attempts to elaborate the terms of otherness that would elucidate the analogy of parody/dialogue to action, and thus to render it a plausible site for historical specificity, his exposition attenuates to a set of surprisingly undialogical abstractions. Dialogue is profoundly mystified in the universalizing trajectory of phrases such as "joyful relativity" or "carnival sense of the world." Such characterizations imply that the only relevant "situation" of dialogue is the universality of difference or sheer alterity itself. Within the conceptual miasma of such abstraction it would appear as if the historical "other" were indistinguishable from an ontological "other*ness.*" That is to say, Bakhtin appears to open a methodologically unbridgeable gap between dialogism and dialogue.

Furthermore, Bakhtin's attempts to clarify the meaning of dialogic "activity" by stipulating the relation of self to other, such that one is not lost or subsumed in the other, only result in an apparently irrational juxtaposition of contradictory motives: on the one hand, the threshold of otherness is deemed to be intentional so as to preserve its historical specificity; on the other hand, the threshold of otherness is deemed to be universal so as to transcend the teleological boundaries of intentionality and the subject-object dichotomy that imposes them. After all, the tropological roots of dialogue, anacrisis and syncrisis, which I have already mentioned go so deeply into the Menippean bedrock of dialogue, already adumbrate the contradictory crux of this thought. Syncrisis, "the juxtaposition of various points of view on an object," presumes upon a threshold of unmotivated difference; anacrisis, "a means for eliciting and provoking one's interlocutor," denotes a threshold of intentional difference (*Problems*, 110). Precisely because both tropes are sedimented at the same level in Bakhtin's archaeology of dialogue, he fails to articulate the contradiction between them as a meaningful exigency of the literary praxis he wants to valorize.

To make matters worse, Bakhtin's most sympathetic commentators conspicuously founder on the contradictory coordinates of his theory by ignoring them. For example, in his enthusiastic preface to *Problems of Dostoevsky's Poetics*, Wayne Booth is driven to conflate intentional with differential imperatives in dialogue in order to transcend the necessity of a logical transition between them. The result is that Booth confuses the dialogic moment with temporal immediacy. From that rhetorical springboard Booth is obliged to make the dangerous leap into an airy (because conceptually empty) sublime, asserting that dialogue is unspecifiable except in terms of what Longinus called "a sublimity of freed perspectives" (xx). Quite to the contrary, Bakhtin himself is adamant that sublimity, the definitive measure of the mind's inability to particularize its experience, hence its inability to historicize, is effectively a monologizing negation of nature. More important, the abstraction that obtains in sublimity, through its negation of historical immediacy, eschews the very subjective mobility that gives an ethical burden to carnival in the first place. This degree of abstraction vitiates any concept of authorial will or formal totality by which we would be able to designate some texts as dialogic and others as not.

Finally, Bakhtin thwarts all such logical purifications of his thought, by unequivocally asserting that dialogic carnival is not "naked, absolute negation and destruction (absolute negation, like absolute affirmation, is unknown to carnival)":

> Moreover, precisely in this ritual of decrowning does there emerge, with special clarity, the carnival pathos of shifts and renewals, the image of constructive death . . . we repeat, crowning and decrowning

are inseparable, they are dualistic and pass one into the other; in any absolute dissociation they would completely lose their carnivalistic sense. (*Problems*, 125)

Clearly, Bakhtin wants to sustain subjective mobility as reciprocally a condition of and an end of dialogic intelligibility. For this enterprise he must be able to specify the historical particulars of the dialogic situation dialectically, but without precipitously resolving the dialectic in that gesture. This, I believe, is the methodological demand that dialogism makes upon itself, which it simultaneously denies itself the conceptual resources to answer.

Dialogue as Contradiction

We have arrived at an apparent impasse in Bakhtin's theory. We can see that the concept of dialogue is precisely what makes Bakhtin's theory of language transpersonal and therefore conducive to the critique of idealism pervading contemporary literary theory. But now we must acknowledge that his novel concept also manifestly fails to account for the specific agency of its own unique mediation of difference through transition. It thus fails to elude the solipsistic nominalism of intentionalist (Cartesian) subjectivity on the one hand and to resist the pull of sheer relativity or difference on the other.

For these reasons I want to propose that the most constructive way to follow Bakhtin's arguments to their desired conclusion—that dialogue is a basis of aesthetic form in the novel (intentional) *and* a threshold of sociolinguistics that transcends literary form (relative)—might be to construe Bakhtin's otherness as contradiction per se. In order to transcend the contradiction between intentionalist and relativist imperatives at the heart of Bakhtin's theory of dialogue, parody and the novel, we must construe contradiction itself as the methodological lever of dialogic enterprise. Only by this means can we ascribe agency to the historical experience that Bakhtin is obliged to elucidate. Whereas in Bakhtin's lexicon dialogue is sometimes definable as a variable of intention and sometimes as a variable of free relativity, contradiction reciprocally expresses both the universality of difference and the specificity or determinateness of temporality and plot. After all, contradiction requires a structure of resemblance that is temporally prior to its articulations.

It is true that in *Problems of Dostoevsky's Poetics* there is a curious attempt by Bakhtin to distinguish dialogue and dialectic as if otherness could be divorced from time.[8] But in the Bakhtinian texts that give the fullest scope to dialogism, "Discourse in the Novel" and *Marxism and the Philosophy of Language,* the author seems to realize, as have all powerful theorists of mediation, that, because contradiction depends on resemblance, as well as difference, it preeminently marks the onset of time. Time, in other words, is the difference between contradiction and difference. My claim that Bakhtinian otherness entails contradiction rather than mere difference is buttressed in the fact that temporality is itself fundamentally articulated as contradiction in the speculative tradition that Bakhtin essays to continue.

Contradictions are, after all, the propulsive moments of the Hegelian dialectic. Bakhtin seems to aspire to a Hegelian order of historical determinations in his much touted pledge to restore the time of social reality to artistic language. But Bakhtin is plausibly even more radical than Hegel and therefore even more congenial to recent materialist thinkers precisely because his dialogue does not ultimately render the threshold of contradiction timeless (through *geist*). Rather, dialogue effectively proliferates historically determinate moments by insisting upon the general irreducibility of their contradictions. Or, at least, Bakhtin points this epistemological path by foregrounding the intrinsic recursiveness of the social exchange upon which dialogue is premised. If the dialogic voice can only be intelligible in terms of the response it gets, we might justifiably surmise that the meaning of the whole utterance can only be clarified as a calculable proliferation of contextual contingencies upon which interpretation will thereafter subsist.

The importance of this point is best observed when we recall that a popular straw man in Bakhtinian argument is Ferdinand de Saussure, who privileged the systematic (synchronic) and thus timeless aspect of language over the temporally bounded performance (diachrony) of individual speakers. Saussure's aim was precisely to escape the "unscientific" contingencies of parole. Bakhtin evokes a striking contrast with the Saussurean stance in V. N. Volosinov's *Marxism and the Philosophy of Language* (1929), in which he observes that dialogic utterance is fundamentally a "value judgment" generated out of the contradiction between two aspects of the word: theme, which designates the historical instant of utterance, and meaning, which designates the parts of utterance that are repeatable, the self-identical components of systematic language. The relationship between theme and meaning is necessarily expressed as contradiction, but

it becomes quite clear that contradiction here may be said to be constitutive of utterance precisely insofar as utterance (meaning) is recursive for
theme. Bakhtin specifically elaborates this point:

> there is nothing in the structure of signification that could be said to
> transcend the generative process, to be independent of the dialectical
> expansion of social purview. Society in process of generation expands
> its perception of the generative process of existence. There is nothing
> in this that could be said to be absolutely fixed. And this is how it
> happens that meaning—an abstract self-identical element—is sub-
> sumed under theme and *torn apart by theme's living contradictions* so as
> to return in the shape of a new meaning with a fixity and self-identity
> only for the while, just as it had before. (in Volosinov 106; emphasis
> added)

Because theme is articulated in the instant of speech and is thus, by
definition, unreproducible, the contradictions it embodies are not expressible except as theme is differentially related to the contingencies of its
expression. In other words, theme may only be said to be "torn apart by
living contradictions," as Bakhtin claims, if we acknowledge that such
contradictions constitute a "return" of meaning, that is, the transformation of the relations between theme and meaning, self and other. Bakhtin
generalizes that value, issuing from this threshold of contradiction, always
depends on an "evaluative orientation" with the proviso that "a change
in meaning is essentially always a re-evaluation: the transposition of some
particular word from one evaluative context to another." We must appreciate how Bakhtin's notion of "evaluative orientation" here explicitly
recalls and reemphasizes the transitional moment of ritual crowning and
decrowning in carnival so key to the conceptual efficacy of dialogue. We
will recall that such a moment always redounds to a transformation of the
terms that articulate it. Its intelligibility, then, is intrinsic to its recursiveness, and its recursiveness is a proliferation of its contingencies.

There is a conspicuous and therefore elucidating corollary to the
dynamic of dialogic discourse, as I have just schematized it, in the resurgence of expressive theories of language that occurred in European
thought after the first objectifying delineations of eighteenth-century empirical science. Charles Taylor gives us a positive account of this resurgence by arguing sympathetically with Herder (against Condillac's *Essai
sur Connaissance*) that expressive theories of language are not of necessity

naively subjectivist.[9] The indictment of subjectivism under which Romantic poetry, for example, has been prosecuted by modernist critics, ignores, according to Taylor, the possibility that expression is not simply the product of cognitive activity but also its continuation. No doubt, at the beginning of the eighteenth century expressive theory was vulnerable to empiricist skepticism because it could not satisfy criteria for scientific proof; it apparently gave no access to the objective order of nature that was not self-ironizing. But the designative theories that supplanted expressive theories in the course of the Enlightenment proffered no alternative to alienated subjectivity in their own impersonal and abstract formalizations of language. In fact, designative theories induced a comparably sterile absolutism at the opposite pole of the subject-object dichotomy.

In Bakhtin's attempt to theorize dialogue we witness a similar predicament: here is a critic who desires to escape from the monologic subject in order to enter social reality free of the ahistorical illusions of idealism. Yet this newfound "objectivity," conceived as it is in terms of the sheer alterity of dialogue, utterly vitiates the ground of subjectivity by bowing to the specter of a subjectless relativism. As if to solve this problem, Taylor points out (in his discussion of Herder) that the critique of expressive theory is most deeply flawed where it ignores the self-transformative aspect of all articulations of the speech system formalized in language. For Herder language expresses not the objects it names but, rather, the possibility of expressing a purposive relation to such objects. Thus, what distinguishes us from nonlinguistic species is not our ability to name an object but, instead, our ability to recognize objects as classifiable according to a system of names. In other words language, in expressing its reflective capacity, transforms its reflective capacity. We might find a way of solving Bakhtin's difficulty in formulating the concept of dialogue without courting self-contradiction, if we likewise point out that the expressive agenda Bakhtin attacks in monologue does not necessitate the abandonment of expression altogether (dialogue conceived as a "joyful relativity"). It only necessitates changing his notion of what is to be expressed such that the self-transformative aspect of expressive language is accommodated. This relatively simple proposition will have far-reaching consequences in my subsequent discussions of the relation between Baumgarten's aesthetic and Fichtean self-activity.

As Taylor points out, the critics of expressive theory mistakenly assumed that the expressive capacity is prior to language. If, following Taylor, we adopt the opposite view, that the expressive capacity is constituted in language, we might extrapolate to the case of Bakhtinian dialogue and suggest that it is precisely the contingencies of expression that dialogue preeminently expresses, rather than the mere fact of its own intrinsic otherness. Thus, *dialogism* would no longer float free as a term designating the radical otherness of joyful relativity. It would be more meaningfully anchored in the determinations that change it; transition would be assimilable to formal/social totality. If, in dialogue, contingencies are proliferated through contradiction, we could say that contradiction is *revealed* rather than *resolved* through a mode of representation that, as a result, entails the temporality of reflection. This mode of representation follows the original epistemological path of dialogue, which was intended to move language toward the status of act. Following this deduction, I believe we can more confidently conceptualize dialogue, along with Bakhtin, as a mediation that preserves its own historical particularity but nonetheless transcends the idealism of intentional consciousness through which we first objectified it.

Negative Dialogue: Bakhtin and Adorno

Even Bakhtin's most enthusiastic recent commentators have ignored the line of argument I am pursuing here, in part I believe because it is not congenial enough with the more radical poststructuralist purge of subjectivity. For example, Paul de Man, in his professedly appreciative overview of Bakhtin's achievement (in *The Resistance to Theory* [1986]), observes a metaphysical *impensé* in Bakhtin's exposition of dialogue. This, de Man argues, mitigates its lucidity with respect to the exigencies of textual interpretation. De Man's diagnostic finger points to "Discourse in the Novel" as Bakhtin's most symptomatic text. Here, says de Man, Bakhtin posits the absolute discontinuity between intentionalist discourse (de Man calls it tropological) and dialogic discourse, while ignoring the contradiction that binary opposition is itself tropological, which is to say (intentional) nondialogical. In this analysis de Man rightly sees what we have also noted: that Bakhtin needs to assimilate the notion of agency to otherness in order to realize the fullest conceptual potential of the dialogic principle. But, de Man is quick to observe, Bakhtin cannot specify terms for such a conceptualization that do not devolve to a devastating self-contradiction: "The ideologies of otherness and of hermeneutic understanding are not compatible, and therefore their relationship is not a dialogical but simply a contradictory one. It is not a foregone conclusion whether Bakhtin's discourse is itself dialogical or simply contradictory" (*Resistance*, 112).

I would suggest that de Man does not see how the move from dialogism to dialogue can take place in Bakhtinian theory precisely because he does not see contradiction as intrinsic to dialogic discourse. In his essay on Bakhtin, de Man, like many poststructuralists, will not conceive of otherness except as radical otherness, sheer alterity. Therefore, he cannot construe otherness as a nonatomistic aspect of temporality or as a motor of transition. By contrast, Bakhtin is emphatic in the very text that de Man cites, that the historical reality disclosed in dialogue renders otherness indistinguishable from the process of historical change: "Historical reality is an arena for the disclosure and unfolding of human characters— nothing more" (*Dialogic Imagination*, 114). The significant assertion here is that the determinateness of history is now predicated on a concept of totality, the disclosure of which is its transformation and the consequence of which is its narrative momentum.

So, despite his professed enthusiasm for Bakhtin, de Man might make us doubt the much touted affinity between dialogism and the timeless, subjectless, relativistic drift of the poststructuralist *episteme*. On the contrary, if there is a continuity between Bakhtin and contemporary theory, I would argue that we should look for it in the belated and therefore even more profoundly historical influence of the Frankfurt School. In particular, we should look to the work of Adorno, for whom contradiction as a mediating term that grounds historicizing consciousness, suggests precisely the possibility (contra de Man) that otherness (nonidentity) and hermeneutic understanding can be compatible.

The success of Adorno's effort to salvage Hegelian negation for a historical hermeneutic rests on the term *nonidentity*. *Nonidentity* stipulates an otherness that does not pass away within the negating consciousness. It becomes, instead, a constitutive contingency of the agency expressed or represented in it. Adorno vehemently distinguishes this agency from the Hegelian "negation of the negation." Specifically, it is not subsumed by a Hegelian *geist*. It is true that both Hegel's and Adorno's paradigms of mediation seem to present an equally striking complement to Bakhtinian dialogue. They are even more specifically grounded in contradiction than Bakhtin's, whether it is the contradiction between *begriff* and *sache* (Hegel) or between mental and manual labor (Adorno). Furthermore, the constitutive moment of the subject in both Hegel and Adorno is marked on a threshold of otherness whereupon the subject must adapt to the contours of its object in accord with the constraints of Bakhtinian dialogue. But, as I have already hinted, Adorno radically departs from the Hegelian course. He calls Bakhtin more favorably to mind at precisely that point where he faults Hegel for subsuming the tension between subject and object within the negative moment, rather than redeploying that tension as the generative structure of its own reflection.

Adorno's attack on the Hegelians is sharpest in the charge that "they hope to conceal mediations instead of reflecting them" (*Negative Dialectics,* 70). Here the echoes of Bakhtin's insistence on the ineluctably generative process of dialogue (hence its relation to historical reality) suggest that Adorno and Bakhtin share a commitment to the materiality of the moment, to the realm of temporality that reveals no inner essences. The Hegelian negation in Adorno's view abandons the proper task of philosophy, which is to recover to thought (reflection) the content that subsuming judgment has eliminated, thus preserving in the nonidentity of the reflective moment the dialectical movement of history—what he calls "determinate negation." Bakhtin's dialogic novel satisfies the dialectical requirements of Adorno's determinate negation by similarly resisting any easy conflation of self and other, author and character, part and whole. More important, however, Adorno's negative dialectic suggests how the otherness of dialogue might be specifically conducive to hermeneutic enterprise insofar as it (otherness) entails a "return" to the differences that instantiated it. For the negated (or, in Bakhtin's terms, the dialogized) other necessarily makes the negating subject different from itself. Dialogue temporalizes subjectivity or "interprets" it, rather than making it abstract. For Adorno the moment negated emphatically preserves its historicity when it is interpreted according to the first nature that passed away within it (*Origins,* 50). Once again Adorno contrasts his thinking with Hegel: "In forgetting . . . at each new dialectical stage the right of the preceding one, Hegel produces the very image of what he takes abstract negation to task for: abstract positivity dependent on subjective arbitrariness for its confirmation" (*Negative Dialectics,* 162).

Insofar as Adorno persuades us that the fruits of negation are inextricable from the interpretive (critical) activity that produces them, from the hermeneutic task, I believe that we have grounds to discount Bakhtin's loose phenomenalizing of dialogue as "pure relativity" or "becoming," which likewise eludes any hermeneutic determination.[10] On this basis we have a greater warrant to emphasize, instead, those theoretical moments in Bakhtin that are committed to making history *livable* as dialogue. For in this regard Bakhtin's conceptual ends share more with Adorno than his methodological means might seem to distinguish him from Adorno.

Indeed, at this crossroads of argument Adorno's usefulness for clarifying the mediational imperatives of dialogic discourse becomes even more compelling where Adorno's thinking is worked out in relief against the philosophy of his influential mentor and friend Walter Benjamin. In Benjamin Adorno observes a self-contradictory desire to negate the world while eschewing any ground of determination beyond the negation itself. If we mark the resemblance between Benjaminian negation and Bakhtin's desire to historicize without a methodology whereby he can distinguish historical moments, we will see how Adorno's critique of Benjamin can be brought productively to bear on Bakhtin. We will see more starkly Bakhtin's need for a concept of mediation that might be more dialectical (despite Bakhtin's repudiation of dialectic in *Problems*) than he is inclined toward in his most influential discoursings upon the dialogic imagination.[11] In his critique of Benjamin's essay "The Work of Art in Its Age of Mechanical Reproduction" (in *Illuminations* [1955]) Adorno finds his most decisive occasion for speculating in the direction of more dialectical mediations. His argument is all the more pertinent to the issues raised by Bakhtin because it is specifically an argument in defense of the formal autonomy of the work of art. Thus, it is especially congenial to Bakhtin's project of elaborating a theory of history through the form of the novel.

Benjamin had repudiated the autonomous work of art on purportedly materialist grounds in *The Origin of the German Tragic Theater* (1971). He had long held that historical meaning could be derived from the mediations of consciousness only through a "discontinuous finitude" exemplified by the trope of allegory. Allegory guaranteed a "discontinuous" finitude in its obtrusion of an insuperable otherness (presented by the signifying figure itself).[12] In fact, Benjamin's rich notion of allegory as a work that expresses the nonidentical relation of mind to nature followed suit with Adorno's own conviction that the mediation of subject and object was substantial and so historically anchored only insofar as it was a mediation by the social totality in all its concreteness. For Adorno the detotalizing overdeterminations of the social totality opened upon the process of historical change. Adorno's initial enthusiasm for Benjamin's work on allegory led him (in *Die Idee der Naturgeschicte* [1932]) to declare that the "theme of the allegorical is decisively history" (qtd. in Buck-Morss 358). Allegory facilitated the demolition of the false appearance of totality given by unreflective images of history. Indeed, the myth of history as a structured totality (which is the rhetorical complement of Bakhtin's monologic discourse) was critiqued by both Adorno and Benjamin precisely for its appearance of self-sufficiency.

Nevertheless, when Benjamin went further to analogize mythic history to the aura of self-sufficiency presented by the formal/aesthetic rules of the artwork, he inexplicably ignored what Adorno took to be the most compelling aspect of the artwork: its mediation of the artist and his or her material exclusively according to the technical laws of its own construction/tradition. Adorno accused Benjamin of disregarding an elementary experience embodied by the work of art: "that precisely the utmost consistency in the pursuit of the technical laws of autonomous art *changes* this art, and instead of rendering it into a taboo or fetish, approximates it to the state of freedom, as something that can be produced and made consciously" (*Aesthetic Theory*, 13; emphasis added). Adorno argued that art did not present an impenetrable totalization in its claim to formal integrity. Instead, Adorno postulated art's transformative power, hence its historicality, as brought about by the dialectical relation between the artist and the historically developed techniques of the artwork. Such a relation, which he felt, was already epitomized in Benjamin's allegory.

The negative moment of the artwork is never empty of historical particulars for Adorno because the irreducible facticity of technical laws, relative to praxis, entails the automatic recursiveness of the concept expressed in the work's technique. The artwork exemplifies what Adorno called "the riddle character" of interpretation, which necessitates a transformation of the artistic image. This transformation is catalyzed by the discrepancy between praxis and technical laws that always obtains as the condition of its instantiation. Just as every negation of a primary nature entails not simply a secondary nature but, rather, its "interpretation," so the artistic image, in the necessity it occasions for interpreting technical rules—by executing them—changes those rules determinately. By comparison, Adorno saw that Benjamin's blind negation of aesthetic rules themselves was historically irresponsible. This was especially true where Benjamin postulated the negative potency of the artwork as an inverse proportion of the alienating technologies of modern art production. Within this perspective Adorno realized that the work of art could never get beyond the negative moment itself. The negation of the work of art, unreflected in the rules of aesthetic form, would result only in an irrational fragmentation of mental experience, verging on a politically retrograde mysticism. We can hardly forget that the same charge is hurled against Bakhtin, when, conjuring the aura of a joyful relativity, he loses his methodological grasp of the particular concrete historical determinants of dialogic otherness.

In Bakhtin's *Formal Method,* however, there is a notable complement to Adorno's criticism of Benjamin that will bring us back to the issue of contradiction, where we left off our consideration of literary form proper. It will at the same time reassert the value of juxtaposing Bakhtin with a more methodologically rigorous thinker such as Adorno, in order to unlock the richest methodological potential of dialogue. Adorno's investment in aesthetic form is especially pertinent for the purposes of any literary critic who wants to exploit Bakhtinian theory for literary study, since Bakhtin posits the aesthetic form of the novel as prior to the possibility of any meaningful sociolinguistics. In *The Formal Method* Bakhtin attacks Russian formalism for privileging the literary device over thematic material exclusively. He marshals his attack in terms of its negation of thematic material, rather than, to borrow Adorno's term, the further "interpretation" of the negation. Bakhtin conceives the possibility of salvaging the concepts of motive and device, so integral to traditional descriptions of artistic form (and which he believes the formalists have rendered abstract beyond usefulness), only by attending to a specific quality of the artwork that he deems preliminary to any meaningful judgment of artistic validity:

> We are only provided with a real criterion for a decision when there is an obvious *contradiction* between the artistic plan and its fulfillment, i.e., when the work is immanently unsuccessful. Only such a work contains elements which are superfluous to the construction and only function to introduce others. Other than this, only caprice and crude subjectivism are able to make a differentiation between motivation and device a part of the interpretation of the poetic structure. (*Formal Method,* 116)

Bakhtin's point is that form may be productively engaged by the critic insofar as it is discerned in the self-transformative capacity of its own articulations. Here I believe we can listen for an anticipation of Adorno. Adorno would say that the contradiction between artistic plan and its fulfillment is immanent to the plan. This is the link between the "immanently unsuccessful" work and the principle of transformation that animates the riddle character of interpretation. According to the analysis Bakhtin performs here, we can imagine that his ideal dialogic text would now acquire the historical density of a more determinate Adornian mediation. This is owing chiefly to the new emphasis Bakhtin places on contradiction. For contradiction in the quoted passage would seem to be indistinguishable from a proliferation of contextual contingencies marked in "elements which are superfluous . . . and only function to introduce others." In other words, it is contradiction that, for Bakhtin as for Adorno, would make an immanent critique uniquely possible without relapse into crude subjectivism on the one hand or into mysticism on the other.

The Dialogic Novel as an Agency of Reflection: The Example of William Gaddis

I have already suggested that a useful way of construing parody, as the exemplary dialogic discourse, is to understand it as a proliferation of contingencies within an apparent structure of resemblance. In this way it neither reifies nor absorbs the otherness by which it articulates its meaning. So, standing once again on the threshold of contradiction and now able to see how contradiction can be the motor of a dialectic that does not erase historical particulars, we may return to the parodic impetus of the novel proper. We are now prepared to discuss the novel's aptness as a model of human subjectivity that can, as Bakhtin intimates, redeem historical subjects to a more productive relation with their social totality.

My particular argument that parody is the best representative case of dialogue/novel depends, as we have seen, on a modification of Bakhtinian dialogue, so as to reconcile radical otherness with the temporal constraints of transition and determinate negation. As Bakhtin chose Dostoevsky to be the famous exemplar of novelistic dialogue, I have chosen William Gaddis to be an exemplar for the modifications I am working on Bakhtinian theory. By looking at the enabling conditions of Gaddis's rhetoric in *Carpenter's Gothic,* I hope to give further warrant for the need to take Bakhtin into serious account, thus inversely to make Bakhtin's formulation yield a more serious account of temporality as a determining aspect of literary form.

Gaddis is most conspicuously a novelist of dialogue not merely because his novels are written pervasively in dialogue but, even more significantly, because his dialogue is wrought with such syntactical otherness as to epitomize the distinction between the Bakhtinian parlance and the conventional referent of the concept of dialogue. In Gaddis's dialogue, rendered as it is without secure pronomial markers or linear punctuation, voice crosses the syntactical boundaries of person and theme. The conventional totalizing power of voice is denied by a syntactical fluidity that precludes a punctual thematization. Thus, the distinction between the critique of the subject and its most naive embodiments, so potent in Bakhtin's sense of dialogue, emphatically becomes the crux of narrative development in this fiction.

Bakhtin said of Dostoevsky that, above all, his dialogic novels do what the parodist has done from classical times: call unified language into question. Gaddis's polyphonic prose gives an eloquent gloss on this characterization of the premier dialogist but without indulging the attendant banalities of leaving the "question" open-ended in a relativistic drift of meaning. By denying himself a fixed place in relation to his language, by making voice a shifting horizon of perspective, Gaddis confers on his prose the character of a mediation that specifically mitigates the inside/outside distinction that makes thematic abstraction so seductive. I believe it is this distinction, insofar as it serves as the basis of the form-theme dichotomy, that Bakhtin himself sought to discredit in his most generalized definition of the novel, as any expression within a linguistic system that acknowledges its own limits.[13] We shall see that, despite its seemingly unbounded voices, Gaddis's writing is not reducible even to a thematic of sheer otherness precisely because it inhibits thematic knowledge per se by articulating it at the limit of its intelligibility.

This argument is already under way in the self-mocking reflexivity of Gaddis's title. *Carpenter's Gothic* denotes a Hudson River style of architecture that mimes the stonework of European Gothic architecture in wood. The exterior appearance of large graciously proportioned rooms is belied by an interior without a plan. The artisans worked from design books of European facades, not from the sculptural exigencies of stone and wrought iron. Because the builders were interested only in outward appearance, the interiors were, of necessity, an irrational patchwork. By definition theme is incompatible with form in the hallmarks of this style. The thematic depth inferred from the bold facade returns the gaze abruptly to the material surface. One confronts the self-contradiction of this style like walking into a mirror. By its facelessness the inside renders the outside more conspicuously a facade, but one that cannot be detached to be revealed.

Mr. McCandless, the character in *Carpenter's Gothic* who reflects on these facts most self-consciously, is prompted to see in this architectural trompe l'oeil, a reflection of the inside of his own head. Aptly, McCandless's mind is proffered as a cerebral core of the book, a thematic recess, the "voice" of the book's truth. But, precisely because McCandless's mind is so inextricable from the epistemic problems of the architectural model it reflects, his voice comes under a scrutiny that it cannot bear without revealing its insubstantiality to be its only infrastructure. More specifically, it will become clear that the formal elements of Gaddis's novel mediate the thematic content of voice so as to make thematic meaning, as Bakhtin suggested in *Marxism and the Philosophy of Language*, a contingency of historical development rather than to make history a contingency of theme.

I am proposing that in order to appreciate the formal innovation of Gaddis's novel, we must read it as a critique of the form of the genre conceived under the metaphor of voice. I believe this was Bakhtin's chief impetus in showing how voice is inherently double and so irrecuperable to any thematic gloss that is not itself subject to the temporal exigencies of form (once again mitigating the distinction between inside and outside). Above all, we must understand that, despite its omnipresence in a novel of dialogue, voice in Gaddis's fiction is meant only to be an ever more provisional category of intelligibility.

Parody is a particularly apt tool in this undertaking because, as I have defined it in Bakhtinian terms, it productively entails the time that thematic closure typically sacrifices to the timeless unity of voice. In Aristotelian narrative plot closure confers the identity of voice by eliminating temporality as an ungovernable contingency. In the subordination of voice to plot the reader of conventional linear narrative enjoys a spectacular oversimplification of time whereby the contemplative activity of reading is spatialized in the visual contours of scene. We recognize time to be Gaddis's parodic object in *Carpenter's Gothic* precisely because here time is deliberately complicated (rather than simplified) by voice, producing a ruthless derealization of scenic spectacle. In *Carpenter's Gothic* the proliferation of voices without clear syntactic or pronominal distinctions makes temporality irreducible to voice. By deploying voice to subvert the temporality of conventional plot, Gaddis exposes the secret complicity of voice with plot and theme in all the monologistic modes of conventional fiction. By contrast, the urgency of Gaddis's dialogism relates to our incipient freedom from the thematic constraints of voice and thus to the disclosure of that parodic potential of all plot, which is time itself. Time, the knowledge of which monologic plot eclipses behind the fatalistic tropes of closure, is here found mugging in the mirror of plot's most sobering mimesis.

We can capture the best reflection of time's parodic countenance in Gaddis's prose by juxtaposing the syntactic rigors of a representative passage with the unifying imperative of this novel's would-be theme: the mock-epic "return" of all of the characters in *Carpenter's Gothic* to the primal Gregory Rift in Africa, where human time began. The return to the rift portends the ultimate thematization of historicodramatic plot. It is the ultimate dream of historical self-fulfillment. For in the origin of time is its proverbial negation. All of Gaddis's characters who are seeking to resolve the contradictions of a history that has cheated them of identity are drawn toward the rift, as toward a threshold of self-redemption. Yet the consummation of the thematic "return" to the rift is most spectacularly abortive in *Carpenter's Gothic* insofar as the theme of the rift itself punningly echoes the rhetorical mediations of Gaddis's prose that preempt (at least for the reader) any such interpretive return to monologistic bliss: such is the syntactical rift between voice and person that makes the *contingencies of self-presentation* the sole constraint of thematization in *Carpenter's Gothic.*

Nevertheless, I want to insist that the perspectival drift in the rifted syntax ought not to be read thematically as loss of meaning, or as the nostalgia for an Edenic permanence, even an Eden proffered in the guise of an archaeological site that can be, albeit laboriously, dug up. Neither can the rifted syntax be generalized as the tragedy of human history. History made into a metaphor for loss would be too perversely departicularized in the very access to time. After all, time is otherwise nothing but particular in its mediations of human fate. Rather, I would say that this novel is preoccupied with the *impossibility of loss,* where there is no object to recover from the shifting rifts of perspective. Gaddis is concerned with the mediation of the experience of loss, not the experience of loss itself. As is the case in Adorno's precept that negation entails interpretation for its most decisive knowledge, I believe the apparent loss of syntactical perspectives by which Gaddis's novel progresses presents an interpretive structure conspicuously marked by its own temporal determinations. In other words the rift of perspective itself becomes a reflective ground in Gaddis's prose, which, as long as it obtrudes its own particulars, resists thematic generalization without surrendering thematic rationality.

The complex mediation valorized here insofar as it preserves the particulars of its agency in its transformation has its most dialogic exemplification in a passage in which Liz Booth, Gaddis's Dickensian heroine, is caught up in the doubly duplicitous act of composing/plagiarizing a line of fiction. Appropriately, by mirroring the project of Gaddis's multiply voiced novel, the passage makes the parody of authorship its most eloquent expression of authorial agency:

> Knees drawn up she pulled the towel round her bared shoulders and a shiver sent breath through her, staring at that page till she seized the pencil to draw it heavily through his still, sinewed hands, irregular features, the cool disinterested calm of his eyes and a bare moment's pause bearing down with the pencil on his hands, disjointed, rust spotted, his crumbled features dulled and worn as the bill collector he might have been mistaken for, the desolate loss in his eyes belying, belying. . . . The towel went to the floor in a heap and she was up naked, legs planted wide broached by scissors wielded murderously on the screen where she dug past it for the rag of a book its cover gone, the first twenty odd pages gone in fact, so that it opened full on the line she sought coming down with the pencil on belying, a sense that he was still a part of all that he could have been. (95)

The rifted syntax, inaugurating the paragraph with an unpunctuated dependency, epitomizes the problem presented by Gaddis's prose in its apparent dismemberment of what it seeks to unify. At the same time such syntax portends a deft resolution of this problem. For the run-on of the dangling or dismembered part, "knees drawn up," with the full predication of "she pulled the towel . . . " explicitly entails contradiction as a threshold of its formal reconstitution. Its reconstitution as a scenic/grammatical whole, wherein the knees can be integrated with the rest of Liz's body and the dependency can be integrated with a complete predicate, is an inescapable imperative of its composition here. Simply because the dangling clause is so emphatically a part before it is a whole, temporality conspicuously obtrudes in its representation. Such is the case with the rest of the paragraph, in which all our attempts at assembling parts devolve to a transitional movement between apparently mutually exclusive scenic gestalts.

For example, the knees and the hands of the author are jumbled with those of her character. The diction of the text "belying" authorial presence is transposed with the diction of omniscient narrative, which calls attention to itself belying "authentic inspiration." Furthermore, the "natural" subsumption of verbal particulars to thematic wholes is frustrated by the increasing abstraction of the verbal parts themselves. As the verbal parts are more and more atomized by rifted syntax, and as it is increasingly difficult to parse the integrative functions of words and phrases in this paragraph, we realize how their functions (because they are so insistently mediated by contradiction) may be reciprocal for contradictory contexts: Liz's hands bearing down on the pencil "bear" the hands "disjointed, rust spotted" of the character in her manuscript without bridging the contexts between them.

As we have discussed already, contradiction, founded on resemblance, represents the temporal shift that sheer difference, by its deferral of the representational moment, confines to metaphysical intuitions. Thus, we may generalize that, in this paragraph, the more atomistic the parts, the more their differentials come to be reflected in them as a structure through which they change, effectively rendering the parts recursive for the whole. For example, the "bare shoulders" "bearing down" are only construable "parts" of a totalizing metaphoric intuition when they "belie" their metonymic succession. But the succession itself is contrived so that it articulates itself more fully through the metaphoric structure superinduced upon it.

This reciprocal determination of parts is even more conclusive in the deliberate shuffling of scenic frames that propels the narrative exposition in this passage. An implicit prepositional ambiguity hovers over the entire passage as the agency of transposition: there are the hands represented on/in the manuscript page of Liz's novel, the scissors wielded in/against the "legs planted wide," and the rag of a book located in/beyond the TV screen, where the reaching hands are illuminated by it. The apparent superimposition of scenic coordinates occasioned in this prepositional ambiguity is a result of the elided transitions between discontinuous contextual frames. Paradoxically, this goes to make transition (contingently in space but necessarily in time) the most pervasive aspect of the text, since every contextual frame would seem to open spontaneously onto another contextual frame without an inclusive revelation of its contents.

Finally, the fact that the paragraph culminates in a highly theatricalized plagiarism (where by definition contextual frames are indistinguishable from what they frame) tempts us to abstract the diverse formal parts to the integrative thematic whole, which this prose has resisted so powerfully from the start. In fact, the juxtaposition of the concept of plagiarism with the scenic ambiguities of the prose taunts a facile thematization in terms of the metafictional regress of rational perspectives: wherein fact is revealed to be indeterminately relative to fiction. This, after all, is the epistemological taunt of plagiarism. I believe that, above all else, however, the distinction of Gaddis's fiction is that here the act of plagiarism remains profoundly "a part of all [it] could have been" in such a way that form and theme decisively do not coincide. Gaddis refuses the invidious choice of plagiarism versus authenticity, fact versus fiction. In doing so, he insists that the relative values of each scenic particular of the paragraph can only be said to claim significance in relation to the whole as they elaborate the problem of scenic construal rather than solving it. Thus, the "he" in the last line may now be said to be "interpreted" (in Adorno's sense), rather than thematized, by the conflation of past tense with the conditional future perfect, which articulates his presence.

In fact, the inherently contradictory reference of the pronoun (*he*) to an antecedent that is already temporalized in two directions (*was / could have been*) is an eloquent summary of the conditions of reading Gaddis, wherein every statement must be reconsidered in terms of the conditions of its utterance, changing those conditions determinately. All that is "belied" in the *he* of this passage is inextricably "a part of what he has become"; it lies indisputably revealed in the proliferation of contingencies that animates our reading. In this effect we might appreciate how eloquently Gaddis's prose recalls the promise of Bakhtinian dialogue: to give us access to a discursive reality that is temporalized without being thematized, where transition becomes a mode of recognition, where the novel is interpreted under the sign of parody as a rethinking through contradiction. The novel is history making with the proviso that history remains an activity of mind that can be reflected only through the juxtaposition of irreconcilably distinct moments. This is the experience of time par excellence.

In *Carpenter's Gothic* the contradictoriness of a syntax that unifies by proliferating the contingencies of consciousness fatefully redounds to a displacement of the person (e.g., Liz) from the activity of reflective mind, which otherwise personifies human agency. This consciousness of time, reconceived as the condition of consciousness, obtrudes most momentously in *Carpenter's Gothic* at the profoundly ambiguous moment of Liz's demise, when time proverbially ceases to be a relevant object of representation.

Significantly, the displacement of character that we saw "figured" in

Liz's act of plagiarism, is, at the moment of her death, both echoed and complemented by the abrupt displacement of the reader from all gestures of readerly competence. Gaddis orchestrates a drama of misreading that coincides cathartically with the dénouement of dramatic episode. Here what purports to be the climactic action of the novel, an apparent murder, turns out not to be an action at all but, instead, a cerebral stroke, an involuntary seizure, the revealed absence of a presumable subject (perpetrator) of the deed of murder, which vitiates the deed as act. Having set up the action by placing Liz in a room so melodramatically charged with notice that "the front door had not closed," Gaddis lets a spectral intruder interpose "himself" in an ambiguously objectifying syntactical perspective, which slips from the reader's grasp just as she establishes herself within it:

> The front door hadn't closed, and through its glass panels the bare shadows of branches in the streetlight rose and fell on the black road out there in a wind scarce as the gentle rise and fall of breathing in exhausted sleep. For a moment longer she [Liz] held tight to the newel as though secured against the faint dappled movement of the light coming right into the room here and then suddenly she turned back for the kitchen where she rushed into the darkness as though she'd forgotten something, a hand out for the corner of the table caught in a *glance* at her temple as she went down. (253; emphasis added)

The "hand out for the corner of the table" reaches from a profoundly ambiguous space, an ambiguity deepened by our inability to tell the agency of the action. Does Liz glance at what she had forgotten (the open door, the intruder's presence caught in time to rescue the autonomy of her subjective gaze), or is *she* caught in the glance of another's consciousness, which portends her victimization? The trajectories of the other conspicuously agitated verbal constructions in this passage ("coming right into the room . . . she turned back . . . she rushed into the darkness") are similarly elusive. Misreading is compelled by such ambiguity in inverse proportion to the manifest intransitivity of action. Specifically, the ironic juxtaposition of the overdetermined moment of misreading (prompted by the illusion of an intruding subject) with the moment of Liz's death (the quintessential identity out of time) offers the clearest elucidation of

Gaddis's purpose as a narrative artist who is concerned with the causes and effects of history.

For here the time of interpretation conspicuously becomes the variable of scenic projection, the very success of which in orthodox thematic narrative would contrastingly devolve upon the cathartic death of readerly time—wherein the perspectives of reader and writer fatally coincide. The syntactic ambiguity of the word *glance* in this passage is aptly the pivot of this understanding, just as pronomial mobility was in the earlier passage. Here the glance is made to serve as a counter for both the autonomy of the subject's position as putative agent and of the contingent positionality of the temporalized subject, bound as that subject is to locate itself only outside of itself. The abrupt disappearance of the subject (as a specific agent) behind the readerly glance (at the table) coincides with the materiality of the glance (the blow to the head) that must "strike" the readerly consciousness first in the shock of rereading. In other words subject and object in this scene coalesce in a verbal density as concussive/concatenating for the reader, as the corner of the table is for Liz's consciousness at the moment when it is extinguished: at that moment consciousness proceeds along a trajectory that "returns" to the circumstances of its own projection, by transforming them.

Such is the curiously selfless experience of time adumbrated by Liz's real antagonist, McCandless, in his most eloquent critique of a modern world tragically oblivious to its own historical inertia and, therefore, blind to the self-limiting imperatives of the naively totalizing self. Toward the middle of the novel McCandless entertains his most self-consuming conception of human subjectivity by imagining a telescope so distant from earth that "you could see history, Agincourt, Omdurman, Crécy . . . [a telescope so strong that] you could see the back of your own head . . . [or] set up a mirror on Alpha Centauri, then you'd sit right here . . . watching yourself four, about four and a half years ago" (153). I have tried to show how history is the resolving focus of that telescope in *Carpenter's Gothic*. It is space mediated by time, a space crossed only by contradiction. Liz, the character to whom McCandless is speaking here, aptly takes his remarks as mockery of her own credulity, as a parody of her desires, a gap in her understanding. For Liz has mistaken Agincourt, a battle, for the name of a planet or "constellation." Yet the fulcrum of parody here is not her ignorance, not her misconstrual of the relevant constellation of concepts. Rather, it resides obliquely in the concept of constellation itself.

This is more resonantly the case if we remember that both Adorno and Benjamin deployed the metaphor of constellation to designate the most potent methodological weapon of the critical allegorist. The allegorist strips away the false appearance of totality by rendering meaning in a "juxtaposition of extremes": a conjunction of image and concept, the rationality of which is produced by the separation of concept and object exhibited in it.[14] Liz's mistake instantiates such a conjunction by virtue of the inverse logical reciprocity of "battles" (Agincourt) and constellations, which asserts its own contextual imperative here. The interpretive proposition is, in fact, not so different from the mythological constellations captured by the astronomer's telescope. These are, of course, only "reflections" of the naked eye refracted through the desire for its own objectification. The telescope embraces the contradiction between the two realms that it appears to unify, the earthly and the unearthly; it is a juxtaposition of extremes. McCandless's desire to see the back of his own head with the telescope is a similar juxtaposition of extremes whereby lucidity does not escape the threshold of contradiction, because once again it entails transition and change. It reformulates the conventional wisdom of character and reader alike such that the only undeluded reflection of human subjectivity can appear in the parodic two-way glass of nonidentical relations between subjects and objects.

Finally, parody is revealed here as that discursive genre that gains intelligibility as it proliferates contingencies (in nonidentity) rather than resolving them. It simulates the most rigorous rhetorical stricture of intertextuality. In effect, the novelist must ventriloquize his own voice to achieve a philosophical eloquence. Like the ventriloquist's displaced voice, which problematizes the inside/outside structure of thematic certainty and formal stability, Gaddis's parodic/dialogic fiction fulfills a philosophical imperative in the guise of a "carnival entertainment; he makes theme intelligible as structure, voice intelligible as vocal agency and temporality intelligible as time. Only in this way does carnival culture become more consequentially what Bakhtin aspires to but cannot attain in his more mystically minded expositions of dialogue: an active place of reflection rather than a moribund reflection of our place in history.

In the next chapter the reflective subject comes even more to the fore of my argument as a crux of form. Reflective consciousness will be seen as the cognitive fulcrum between form and theme and, hence, the enabling precept of a self-critical aesthetical totality.

5

The Burden of Thematics: Transformation and Totality in Blanchot's *Récit*

The fictitious is never in things or in people but in the impossible verisimilitude of what lies between them: encounters, the proximity of what is most distant, the absolute dissimulation in our very midst.

—Michel Foucault, *The Thought from Outside*

By revealing to each moment the whole of which it is part, literature helps it to be aware of the whole that it is not and to become another moment within another whole, and so forth; because of this literature can be called the greatest ferment in history . . . culture is the work of a person changing himself little by little over a period of time, and not the immediate enjoyment of a fictional transformation which dispenses with both time and work.

—Maurice Blanchot, "Literature and the Right to Death"

Form and Theme

To explicate literary form is implicitly to explicate the subject. Thematics has been the tool of this explication since Plato, for whom philosophy was ethical as it made the implicit explicit, that is, insofar as it thematized. Yet, in the course of the subject's long historical explication by literary criticism, theme has been polemicized into a contentious antagonist of aesthetic form. Thematic critics deem aesthetic form, by invidious comparison, to be a dehumanizing limit of particularity. Form embodies the other of thematic knowledge, the unknowing absence of the subject. By contrast, theme marks the constitutive unity of experience and so the ethical warrant for literary criticism. There is no doubt that the dialectic of form and theme persists as the motor power of literary criticism, but it will be my purpose in this chapter to note how this dialectic stubbornly begs the question of the agency that drives it.

Rather than follow the argument between formalism and thematism
into the vicious circle of mimetic and antimimetic art manifestos, this
chapter will reflect on the possibility that the agonism of form and theme
is itself organic to the dualism it springs from: thematics has repressed its
knowledge that the subject is really a presupposition of form itself, thus
implicating theme irrevocably in form as a structural condition of its own
conceptualization. Ironically, the most powerful valorization of theme
over form asserts the impotence of formalism to assign subjective agency
to the effects it occasions. Paterian formalism ("Style," 1888) offers the
definitive bad example of a formal particularity so immediate that it
reduces to pure sensation the very subjective agency of artistic genius it
is meant to actualize. By contrast, thematics typically poses itself as the
translation of form into subject and proposes that the subject is an end
rather than a constitutive means of interpretation. In this way thematics
renders the subject a bearer of teleological truths, the product of an
ennobling, ethical labor, rather than dehumanizing the subject in the
airless chambers of formalism. It is in these terms that thematic criticism
has arrogated to itself the authority of a moral dictum. Thus, thematic
criticism assumes the burden of social responsibility; it accretes the density of the Arnoldian touchstone.[1]

Yet it will not escape our notice that, as long as theme remains
oppositionally determined, its hegemony leads to the very epistemological
impasse it blames on formalism: the foreclosing of subjective agency. In
fact, where it remains predicated on an agonism with form thematics sets
itself up for a self-deconstructing analysis. The terms of this deconstruction sharply reflect modern critical theory's general suspicion of any unity
based on the spiritual overcoming of material differences. The agonistics
of theme and form call to mind the self-subverting opposition of work
and alienated labor, reference and representation, and, most notably,
reality and ideology. By invoking the context of ideology critique in this
way, we might see more clearly how the ideological character of thematics
presupposes an alienation of the subject comparable to form's alleged
derealization of subjective agency. For, by eliding the subject with thematic meaning, by repressing the constitutive function of the subject,
thematics removes itself from the ground of its self-reflection and becomes
like the reified image of ideology or the alienated labor of the assembly
line: a constitutive unity without a unifier.

Taking the analogy between thematism and the problematic of ideol-
ogy-alienation as my point of departure, I want to indicate a way of

dissolving the form-theme opposition, thereby discovering a premise for literary interpretation that comes to terms with the determinative power of subjective experience. After all, the opposition of formalist and thematic reading is itself symptomatic of our persistent displacement of the subject as an effective agency from an enterprise of literary theory that has all the while been predicated on the discovery of that subject. This paradox is deepened by our realization that in the history of the dualism of form and theme the subject is always already effectively there in the dynamic of reflection that animates it. As I have suggested, the form-theme opposition presupposes this fact in the idealizing drift of formalism and thematism toward autonomy and totality. Our task, then, is to determine a possibility of reading and thinking that renders the category of the subject conceptually distinct from the dualistic frame of reference within which criticism valorizes its activity as a *doxa* of preemptive ethical norms. Such an analysis would make it possible to set aside the thematic derivation of the subject from organic literary form and to reveal the constitutive role that the subject plays in our determinations of literary value.

For this reason I want to treat the subject as assimilable to a reflective activity that is neither preemptively reduced to intention, and therefore rendered as teleological/thematic knowledge, nor preemptively reduced to atomistic particulars and rendered as formal knowledge. Such a subject would be capable of reflecting itself as an activity rather than serving passively as the reflection of preconscious or presubjective essences.

On the contrary, thematics has typically promised a revelation of essences. Beginning with the exegeses of sacred texts, thematics has always presumed a redemptive role for the reader. Classical thematics—taking its direction from Aristotle's subtle subsuming of action to *anagnorisis* in *Poetics*—has always carried the heavy responsibilities of determining the indeterminate and universalizing the particular. Thematics takes the partial as the pretext of its specifically "ethical" reductions of form to theme. Furthermore, in its reach toward the ideal of totality it has borrowed a conspicuous moral self-righteousness from the project of work. The exegetical "work" of thematics allegedly unburdens the reader of the weighty opacity of formal particulars: the "ethical labor" here is abstraction.[2] Abstraction, then, elides the temporality that otherwise obtrudes formal particulars as impediments to reason. Abstraction is the naturalization of an otherwise ominous temporality. But the means of this abstraction (like the notoriously problematic agency of Husserlian "reduction," which purports to thematize the unthematizable) always seems to escape the temporalization of its own process in thematic criticism.

Against this epistemological current I will argue that if literary criticism would valorize thematics as an edifying labor, this labor might be formulated more productively in terms of Hegelian "work," or *arbeit*.[3] For the Hegelian regimen of work involves a scrupulous reckoning with time as the contingency of self-reflection, the very self-reflection that thematics effectively eschews. Particularly where theme presents itself as mutually exclusive of form, it is dualistically bound by a metaphysical principle of origin. Thus thematics, like the fetishistic image of ideology, courts the stasis of idealization, displaces the allegedly timeless particulars of form with its own timeless reifications of meaning. As I have indicated, this results in a mystification of the subject that is cognate with the target of ideological critique: alienated labor. Elsewhere I have argued the inadequacy of the Hegelian model of subjectivity as the basis for a theory of agency in literary narrative. Yet, where the theory of literary form seeks to elude the ideological imperative of thematic categories, the Hegelian engagement with temporality, especially at the level of its methodological rigor, offers a useful premise of argument.

In this regard it is important to observe that Hegel's concept of *arbeit* prefigures the distinction between objectification and alienation that, for Marx, would become a prerequisite to the critique of ideology. The ethical impetus of Marxist critique maintained in this distinction is the necessity to *reflect upon reflection*. *Arbeit* would, in turn, necessitate the immanent critique of ideology as a corollary to any potent phenomenology of mind or any full account of totalizing experience.

The problematic of ideology, after all, puts into question the possibility of totalization upon which thematics presumes, since it equates totality with the fallibility of knowledge. Indeed, form and theme are therefore both already deeply complicit in the problematic of ideology, as long as each proposes the completion of the other, as long as each is conceived as a remedy for the other's distorting effect. Within the form-theme opposition theme purports to be an "objectification" of objective forms, that is, an escape from contingency. Form, by contrast, purports to present the object itself, to belie the universalizing distortions of theme. In any case both conceptual operations are presupposed on the model of physical work, or production: they necessitate the transformation of objects into subjects or subjects into objects, as if subjects and objects were mutually exclusive realms of experience, both harboring the specter of alienated labor as the inverse pretexts of their opposition.[4] Hegelian *arbeit* may therefore be constructively counterposed with the notion of alienated labor. *Arbeit* proposes a removal of conceptual distortions, hence the reconciliation of subject and object.

Moreover, if we suspend the overarching trajectory of Spirit—that is, if we bracket the telos of the Hegelian system—we will foreground the fact that the work of reconciliation and self-realization entailed by Hegelian *arbeit* is not dualistically posed against a recalcitrant world of objects. On the contrary, *arbeit* is carefully distinguished from material labor whereby the material form of a worldly object determines the meaning of human enterprise or where human meaning displaces that object. While the Hegelian slave does objectify the material world in his work, he works for a master. The object upon which he works thus accrues the status of idea and, as such, inscribes upon the material world the intersubjective struggle to the death for nonvital ends, which originally determines the master/slave relation as a fundamental dynamic of human culture and value.[5]

This relation of the object to idea may at first seem simply to recapitulate the paradoxical axiom of Aristotelian identity: it posits a "form" that is ontologically grounded in a timeless realm (*eidos*). The being designated in the object is paradoxically derived from the idea by which it is designated and doomed thereby to perpetuate an endless dualism.[6] But in the Hegelian scheme this timeless *eidos*, or idea of the object, is made monumentally historical in the *transformational* effectivity of self-conscious acts of mind. Thus are they salvageable from the paradox of Aristotelian formalism and the aporia of the ahistorical. The humanity of the Hegelian subject derives from the self-transformative agency of the "objectifying" worker rather than the objectivity or reification of the object, which would otherwise statically reflect the worker in an all too venerable Kantian dualism, a quintessentially alienated labor.

In this familiar analysis we find the basis for extending the analogy between alienated labor and thematics in order to make the discussion of the aesthetics of the novel more acutely pertinent to an elucidation of subjective experience in social praxis. I will maintain that the novel, as the most profoundly thematized genre of subjectivity, is also that genre in which the mysteries of the subject remain most impenetrable. For what links non-Hegelian labor and thematics is their irresistible reification of the object, or the corollary transcendental determination of the subject. By contrast, I want to see how the freedom implicit in

Hegelian *arbeit* at least intimates, by its dereification of the object, the possibility of a nontranscendental subject, or what I have already called a positional subject. The positionality of this subject would be mobilized by the irreducibly reciprocal determination of subject and object in the dialectical momentum of *arbeit*. I take this as a strong warrant for a critique of thematics that would go beyond the terms of the form-theme opposition: it anticipates the goal of the nontranscendental or positional subject as a more epistemologically astute basis for criticism of the novel form.

Thus, our recasting of the burden of thematics, in terms of Hegelian work, would give us access to a subjectivity that is unfettered by an idealized temporality, or by an objective reality that remains resistant to the consciousness that produced it. We will not forget, of course, that Hegel himself does reintroduce the transcendental subject into the system of his *Phenomenology*, with consequences radically at odds with my own project; in the *Phenomenology* intersubjectivity is supervened upon by transsubjectivity. My argument will therefore be an inherently risky attempt to spring off Hegelian assumptions without consequently plunging into the downward vortex of spiritualism that "grounds" the Hegelian dialectic and without alternatively disappearing into the ether of utterly ungrounded speculation.

Toward a Critical Thematics

As I have already noted, the critique of thematics proposed here has particular urgency in the context of the novel because thematic strategies have so dominated the theory of the novel: the form of this genre is treated as if it were organically predisposed to the epistemological constraints of thematic knowing. This assumption abides in the account of the novel's universalist striving against those worldly particulars that divide it from the unity of epic time. Lukács represents the most pervasive influence of this assumption. It accounts, I believe, for the persistent Kantianism of novel criticism in general and, more specifically, for the impassable antinomy of form and meaning that obstructed the argument of Lukács's own *Theory of the Novel*.

Curiously enough, this hegemony of thematics appears to have its basis in the image, that most conspicuous formal particular of the novel, and the locus of its realist or mimetic pretexts. For in the novel the image, while immediately particular, is nonetheless the ineluctable signifier of a scenic whole. To assert in this way that the novelistic image marks the complicity of form with thematics is only to restate in more emphatic terms a point already long established, if often unacknowledged, in the Aristotelian formalism we have already discussed: form, identified as it is with the principle of contradiction (form's necessary articulation through *eidos*, whereby its being entails a transcendental unity outside of time), is actually already, predicated upon thematics. The duality of form and theme is inherently unstable. Consequently, the novel, in its deployment of the image, may be said to make explicit an implicit premise of any self-professedly ethical literary thematic: particulars in their immediacy pose a troublesome obstacle to the unity or identity that Aristotelian peripetic plot seems to strive for in its thematic pursuit of truth. It is on this account that the novel is an especially apt site for contemplating the dissolution of the form-theme opposition into a dialectical relation whereby a reciprocity of differences would displace the impossible struggle toward a holistic identity. In subsequent chapters this insight will entail a richer account of peripeteia. But for the moment it will suffice to accept the traditional view of this fulcrum of Aristotelian plot as a rough analogue for thematic unity.

To this end I once again adduce the criticism and fiction of Maurice Blanchot. Blanchot is that most prodigious theorist and practitioner of modern prose fiction for whom the problematic of the image deliberately thwarts the moral edifications of thematic reading by foregrounding the paradox of form predicated on theme. I want to show how his own formal practice, precisely by exacerbating the temporal paradoxes intrinsic to the novelistic image, theorizes a way out of the paradoxical impasse. Significantly, Blanchot has written prose works (*Death Sentence* [1948], *Thomas the Obscure* [1941], *Aminadab* [1943], *Les Tres-Haut* [1948]) wherein theory and practice are not antinomical, because form and theme are not configured as oppositional terms. Because the Blanchotian image does not recapitulate the form-theme dualism by presenting itself as alternately a reified particular or a general synthesis of particular sense experiences, it offers an especially productive site for rethinking the relation of theme and form. More to the point, we could say the Blanchotian image presents an opportunity to attack the dualistic modes of self-knowledge attendant upon thematic understanding whenever theme is insufficiently theorized in light of its own inherent temporalization. I take this temporalization to be the vital contingency of all novelistic form giving and the elided middle term of all inert, undialectical thematizing.

Furthermore, I believe that this temporalization, exemplified in the narrative form that Blanchot designates as the *récit*, will become an increasingly compelling imperative of contemporary literary criticism in general when we see how fully Blanchot's formal experiments have rationalized the temporality of the image. Blanchot's *récit* enables a practice of writing and thinking that can accommodate a representation of the subject fully adequate to the temporalizing exigencies of subjective experience. Moreover, Blanchot's deployment of the image, because it also confronts the epistemological risk of reification—which links it inextricably to the dynamics of self-production—may provide occasion to generalize (more polemically and more convincingly than has been done in recent narrative theories) from the identity of this literary genre to the exigencies of social reality. I have already established the relevance of ideological critique to the mutual questions of personal identity and the identity of literary forms. It will nevertheless be necessary to show how our new perspective on the burden of thematics gives us leverage to lift the oppressive weight of self from the alienated social individual. Such individuality yearns for a mode of self-realization that staves off the "unhappy consciousness" of irresolvable part-whole, form-theme dualities.

In other words, I am suggesting that literary criticism can lift the burden of thematics through a specific protocol of work. Or such is the case so long as the necessity of work is understood to be an exigency of the narrative predicament common to both literary texts and social individuals: it imposes the same interpretive demand upon each. It is not simply the demand for a nondistorted or true discourse, the weary refrain of vulgar Marxism. Rather, it is a demand for a discourse in which totalization is assimilated to transformation, wherein the synthesis of subject and object or form and theme aspired to by ideology-critique is reconceived (as Marx himself stipulates in *The 1844 Manuscripts* [1959]) as an activity rather than as an identity. Here the goal of ideology-critique is to restore not the truth but, instead, the agency of the subject.[7] Not coincidentally, this is where Blanchot's aesthetic of the image is most instructive. Blanchot's image becomes a locus of reflection that insists, as the most successful theorists of reflection always have, that reflection is an activity that does not seek its realization in completeness but, instead, always returns problematically to its origin.

So, if thematics entails a labor, we may say that when properly undertaken in terms of Hegelian *arbeit* its end is no longer tantamount to the crude self-justifications of ethical law, i.e., the self posited as a counter of exchange value vis-à-vis universal truth. It is rather a self*less* production. It temporalizes the self without dispatching time in the process. It proffers what I have been calling an agency without a telos. This agency, as we shall see, acquires its formal integrity through a principle of temporal recursiveness, which, unlike the Aristotelian telos, avoids making space and time mutually exclusive. We might say that the purportedly ethical labor of thematics is by contrast only a vicarious escape from time. It is the fulfillment of telos and *rests* in that end; it proverbially kills time that mankind might live forever in the patriarchal image of an idealized rather than an active self. The burden of thematics undertaken in my argument will acknowledge a more complex habitation of time, as an activity, not an idea/ideal. The critical thematics that I am proposing here *works* in time. In this way it will force us to see the necessity of transforming the reigning hegemony of space (the image) over time in the classical novel according to a more productively dialectical notion of space as time.

The Temporality of the *Récit*

We can now inquire into the relation of image to the concept of subject. The image is the counter of the intentional subject if only because, as a locus of attentional consciousness, it takes up the burden of thematic knowledge in the service of totality. Derrida has argued the necessity to see this totalizing imperative of theme in the context of his own critique of presence; in its totalizing momentum theme demands a phenomenological reduction. I have noted that there is a conspicuous parallel here with Husserl's predication of theme on an unthematized consciousness: a prior, nonthetic apparatus of consciousness, which theme discloses. Inasmuch as theme here denotes a topos, a place in the text where the prethetic consciousness is spatialized, the image can be deemed its signifier, the marker of its intentionality. (This place would otherwise be displaced in the determinations of thetic consciousness [the *non lieu* in Derrida's "Living On / Border Lines"].)[8] In his critical assessment of this phenomenology Derrida wants to escape the totalizing authority of theme, but not the imperative of determinate meaning projected in the concept of intention itself. The mimetic image, by nature, poses an obstacle to this desire in its refusal of temporal contingency. Derrida gives us a provocative counterexample in his account of the "inscription" of contingency as *différance*.[9] *Différance* simultaneously invokes a ground of difference *and* determination. The synthesis of every grammatological inscription is always contextually bound.[10] But each context is reciprocally determined in relation to the determinations it cannot account for. Derrida consistently looks toward a way of making the phenomena of determination and totality assimilable to the temporality of determinate consciousness.

I want to suggest that Derrida's goal is attainable if we realize that totality is not thinkable without thinking transformation. This is how we make the transition from intention to agency a determinant ground of meaning. It is the means of determining totality without a totalizer. In the previous chapter I established a basis for seeing how this proposition might be buttressed by Anthony Giddens's sociological paradigm of structuration wherein the notions of structure and action are conceived as always presupposing each other, thus making transformation plausibly compatible with totality.[11] For Giddens, who follows Wittgenstein on this point, totalization is a correlate of rule, and rules are conceived as recursive for practices. Rules recursive for practices instantiate temporality in the instance of contradiction that temporal succession imposes upon all actions. That is to say, the application of rules to a given situation entails their transformation.

Similarly, we will see that for Blanchot the critique of the image offers a pretext for reconceiving the structural imperative of the genre as neither formal self-sufficiency or thematic self-sufficiency. The image for Blanchot becomes the fulcrum for the rhetorical leverage of contradiction against static totality when it is temporalized by what Derrida himself calls "the bias of contingency." Contingency is adamantly contradictory in virtue of its structural resistance to any representation of the temporality unfolding within its purview. Agency, by contrast with intentionality, incorporates the contingency of its own determinations of meaning.

Specifically, in Blanchot's concept of the *récit* contradiction serves as a rhetorical equivalent of the temporality by which I have been distinguishing intention from agency: he posits a narrative experience that opens a temporal gap or contradiction within itself as its only mode of teleological progression. Blanchot explains the need for a distinction between the novel and the *récit* on the grounds of the latter's temporalization, such that agency takes precedence over intentionality in one's thinking. What is at stake in the distinction is best elucidated by one of Blanchot's incisive and often quoted characterizations of the atemporal visual imperative of novelistic narrative: "l'attente . . . l'oublie" (*Gaze*, 190). The novel moves by deflection, or forgetfulness from the known, the image, by a reifying negation. It finds in the image the hallucinatory mirror of itself, the beautiful figure of immediacy, the dream of teleological fulfillment. By contrast, the intelligibility of the *récit* obtains in its movement toward an unknown point. But the movement is neither random nor indeterminate because, pointed toward the unknown, it is pointed toward itself: it becomes "an allegory of itself" (*Gaze*, 191). Such was Mallarmé's self-justifying claim for his own poetic text, a notoriously dense body of writing by which Blanchot's most abstract theoretical speculations were passionately seduced. For Blanchot the allegory of the self is the fascination of unsurpassable mediations.

The *récit*, contrasted with the novel, denotes that "fascinated" contemplation of the visible that, according to Blanchot, separates speech from sight on the model of allegory. Allegory separates speech from sight by its obligatory juxtaposition of mediating differences. Blanchot contends that the *récit* establishes the ground for a rigorous critique of the image (sight) because it remembers *itself* in the articulation of the image, much as allegory remembers itself in that extremis of contradiction, which is its most immediate condition of possibility. The inadequacy of the allegorical image to the idea it expresses is, in its particulars, the threshold upon which allegory comes to a full account of itself as contradiction. We have seen how, for critics such as Benjamin and Adorno, this is the threshold on which allegory will yield the fullest account of its own historicity. In this regard Blanchot asserts that the *récit* comprehends the limits of the image better than the novel does because (to use a phrase by which Adorno distinguished historical from idealized images) it does not "fall into the image" like the novel and so demure its historical contingency.[12]

The novel "falls" and forgets itself in the image by what Blanchot designates as the detour of "visual clarity" (*Gaze*, 112, 191). Visual clarity, like the sensate particulars of the allegorical signifier, designates a nonreciprocal relation between narrational consciousness and the image. Such "clarity" would inhibit the possibility for transformations of narrative perspective, transformations that, not coincidentally, constitute the very formal armature of the *récit* itself. In other words, because the *récit* does not deflect from itself—to the implicit duality of images or the explicit duality of characters—its movements are more pointedly articulated as self-contradiction. The *récit* subsists upon a principle of transformation that the novel's visual clarity preempts insofar as its modus operandi is simple negation and synthesis.

I will begin to examine the conceptual stakes of the preceding by attempting to gloss a scenic image from Blanchot's *Madness of the Day,* a work that ventures into that liminal reality in which the conspicuous scarcity of visual images amid a verbal plenitude everywhere taunts and fetishizes our appetite for concreteness, for the certainty and stability of the visual. *The Madness of the Day* is a particularly apt text because this narrative hinges upon a first-person narrator's loss of sight—the loss of the image. It proffers a tantalizingly simple thematic gloss. The narrator's speech appears in this ambiguous "light" to be compensatory, an explanatory cause for the inscrutable effect of blindness. Yet it is a narrative that deliberately divides speech from sight, as Blanchot indicates the *récit* is bound to do, in which the idea of compensation is precluded by a deeper understanding of what is lost—a transformation of loss itself. This narrative gives us the image of the "day" lighted by the reflective shards of a fractured "vision."

At first, however, the imagery that focuses this narrative seems perversely to invite the reader to "see" an identity of the visual and speech in the manner of conventional novelistic scene. It invites us to fall into the mode of the novelistic image by forgetting the temporal contingency it obscures, to ignore the contradiction in "terms" of speech and sight. Only the elaboration of Blanchot's imagistically clear scenario makes the reasons why we cannot ignore this contradiction readily apparent. They are consonant with the so-called materialist critique of the subject. When Adorno, for whom contradiction without resolution is the impetus of negative dialectic (and effectively "historical" images), credits allegory with the power of historicizing interpretation, he correlatively critiques those methods of knowledge that are, by contrast, based on a simple negation of Nature.[13] Inherent in them is the danger of forgetting that the second nature (produced by negation) must be "interpreted" or critiqued in turn and in terms of the first Nature that passed away within it. Otherwise, the difference between first and second nature is effectively rendered as a temporal synthesis, belying its material historical conditions, eliding the terms of its agency. It is precisely the danger of such forgetfulness that lurks most ominously in the narrative purport of Blanchot's image in *The Madness of the Day,* at that moment when it proffers the identity of speech and vision:

> Outdoors, I had a brief vision: a few steps away from me, just at the corner of the street I was about to leave, a woman with a baby carriage had stopped, I could not see her very well, she was maneuvering the

carriage to get it through the outer door. At that moment a man whom I had not seen approaching went in through that door. He had already stepped across the sill when he moved backward and came out again. While he stood next to the door, the baby carriage, passing in front of him, lifted slightly to cross the sill, and the young woman, after raising her head to look at him, also disappeared inside. (10)

The apparently frivolous, though oddly elaborated image "scene" here precipitates a narrative crisis resonant with the etymological ambiguities of the Greek *krisis*—separation and judgment, movement and transformation—all of which in turn become the crucial coordinates of reading the *récit*. For this scene is immediately discontinuous with what precedes and follows. It does not come from anywhere; it does not go anywhere in linear terms. As if to preemptively thematize and so heal this diegetic discontinuity, the narrator subsequently declares, "This brief scene excited me to the point of delirium" (10). Inasmuch as it proffers an abstraction from the scene, the putative meaning of his delirium reveals Blanchot's theoretical stake in the transformational or metamorphic impetus of the *récit*.

In a dialogue called "Walking like a Crayfish" Blanchot characterizes this transformational imperative more specifically in grammatical terms as: "The speech . . . [that] is the return to this first turning—a noun we have to understand as a verb, the movement of turning . . . " (*Gaze*, 194). Delirium here marks a disruption of narrative that reveals its own grammatical infrastructure in the reversal of objective and subjective points of view: in the passage I have just quoted from *Madness* we move from the scene to the seer without the continuity of a line of sight. Thus, the scene demands to be understood as speech but "speaks" to the image (the scene described) as if to make a transition between the abstract universals of speech and the sensate particularity of the visual world via that most reductive of thematizations, the conflation of subject with object.

The transition that immediately follows the scene in the guise of a deadpan narrative exposition presents an irreducibly contradictory juxtaposition of universals and particulars. This juxtaposition has typically served as the warrant for thematic elucidation, though it stymies any straightforward thematic reading in this case. With respect to the scene that has just transpired the narrator says: "I was undoubtedly not able to explain it to myself fully yet I was sure of it, that I had seized the moment when the day having stumbled against a real event, would begin hurrying to its end." Here specifically the "end" anticipated is isomorphically related (on the level of plot) to the telos of particularity proffered in the visual image. But Blanchot's prose obtrudes an indeterminate oscillation between abstract and concrete denotations. The abstraction of the verb (*hurrying*) gathers nominal weight just as the nominal *day* "having stumbled," is derealized in its anthropomorphic particularity (in the trajectory of action), gathering in its turn a distinctly verbal inertia. Meaning here seems to "reject determination in the category of the object as well as the subject" (*Gaze*, 198), an effect Blanchot self-consciously designates as the "neuter." The *neuter* is another of Blanchot's neologisms designed to rethink the familiar terms of narrative determination, so as to avoid the reduction of formal elements to any preemptive totality that would be voiced monologistically.

Because the determinations of the visual image are sensate, it establishes conditions for knowledge that privilege completeness and limitation. But the reversal of the abstract and the concrete registers of reference observed in the previous passage, the verb veritably "turning into a noun," makes us re-view the ever more obtrusively enigmatic image of the woman and the baby carriage. This rereading gives the whole passage the appearance of an abortive thematization that, rather than relieving the burden of particularity, renders particularity instead a counter of transformation: not into other sensate particulars but, rather, into "other" particular moments of attentional consciousness. Determinateness is still the epistemological imperative of meaning, but it is not, by contrast with the classical image, determinate for any totality that is not in turn assimilable to transformation. That is to say, in reading this passage, we cannot be satisfied that we know what it means by reducing subjective to objective determinations, or vice versa. We cannot know what it means beyond the text's elaboration of the conditions for such a reduction. The elaboration takes precedence over the situation it purports to clarify.[14] The complex notion of the image coaxed by Blanchot in the concept of the neuter thus suggests the ideal of an extensive, rather than an intensive, unity. *Extension,* as we shall see, is a fundamental term of aesthetic inquiry because it denotes the activity of proliferating moments of attentional consciousness corollary to the ever more elaborate aspects of formal figuration.

Aesthetic Determination: Baumgarten into Blanchot

This foregrounding of the extensive register of determination is significantly the foundation of post-Enlightenment aesthetic formalism laid by Alexander Baumgarten in *Reflections on Poetry* (1735). Because Baumgarten inaugurates the history of idealist aesthetics with a formal paradigm that seeks to adequate aesthetic judgment with rational judgment, to coordinate the so-called higher faculties of reason with the lower faculties of sense, he offers a crucial frame of reference for the kind of argument I am making here.

Specifically, Baumgarten's criterion of aesthetic representation is pegged to the *quantity* of particular determinations configured in a sensible "object." The aesthetic object remains distinct from the rational object in that its configuration is extensively apparent rather than subject to any intensional intuition.[15] The object of rational intuition is designated by Baumgarten as clear and distinct, whereas the object of an aesthetic intuition is designated as clear and confused: it exhibits an extensive *fusion* of sensate particulars such that our cognition of it may not transcend the relational order of its composition. Or we might extrapolate with respect to the subject of aesthetic intuition and say that it is effectively indistinguishable from an *elaboration* of sensate representations and therefore inseparable from the temporal exigencies that determine them. The subject is imagined here as constitutive of the contingency of particulars rather than becoming itself a contingency of their representation.

As Baumgarten elaborates his aesthetic theory in *Reflections on Poetry*, however, this crucial distinction between intensive and extensive determinations (the foundation upon which the category of the aesthetic is built) collapses. Ironically, it collapses under the growing weight of particulars adduced by his original valorization of extension (*aistheta*). For, in Baumgarten, the proliferation of extensive particulars inexorably devolves to an insupportable temporal disjunction. We are thus confronted with a temporally open-ended contradiction, which in turn demands to be resolved by a totalizing finitude. This "end" Baumgarten designates as *theme*. With its inescapable spatialization of meaning, however, theme can only be postulated in the guise of a new transcendental ground, since it can only denote a spatial totality by an interdiction of temporality. Specifically, Baumgarten defines theme as "that whose representation contains sufficient reason of other representations supplied in the discourse but which does not have its own sufficient reason in them" (*Reflections*, 62).[16] To imply, as Baumgarten does here, that extensive particulars are grounded and unified in a relationality that transcends the temporality of their relation is effectively to transform the field of extensive particulars back into an intensive ground. This is, by his own account, the basis of rational rather than aesthetic judgment.

Ultimately, we might say the difference between intensive and extensive determinants collapses under the "burden of thematics" where that burden weighs heaviest in Baumgarten's criterion of "formal perfection." This criterion is invoked as the ultimate thematic "closure" of aesthetic judgment. Formal perfection is achieved through a proliferation of particulars such that the greatest number are unified in their variety. As I have already implied, this amounts to the contradictory grounding of aesthetic particulars in an individuality that determines the necessity of its constitutive particulars but simultaneously hides its own particular determination in them. Baumgarten's stress here on the individualizing imperative of theme indicates the most glaring weakness of his argument. For the value of *aistheta* (the constitutive elements of theme) is initially imputed to their materiality (the number of qualities they exhibit), seeming to privilege a spatial register of meaning. But the singularity of formal perfection denotes the transcendence of that materiality, seeming to privilege the register of temporal meaning. After all, such synthetic singularity could only situate itself outside the constraints of material existence and its atomistic temporal constraints.

The contradiction that obtains here is the result of the apparent interchangeability of spatial and temporal registers in *Reflections on Poetry*. I believe that such a contradiction could only be resolved through Baumgarten's conceding that the extension of the material particularity is also a temporal process. In other words the contradiction can only be productive here if it is recognized as a contradiction, if it entails a dialectical rather than an identical relation of parts to wholes. Baumgarten's failure in this regard makes it most difficult to see a way for him to preserve the integrity of both extensive and intensive registers, upon which his original claims for the analytic rigor of aesthetic valuation seemed to depend.

One way of appreciating Blanchot's innovation as a "formalist" narrative artist is to observe how, by contrast with Baumgarten, his aesthetic practice effectively preserves the distinction between intensive and extensive determination by foregrounding the intrinsic contradictoriness of the concepts of, "theme" and "formal perfection" that derive from Baumgartenian assumptions. Because Baumgarten's theme stipulates a unity that transcends particulars but that nonetheless must be rationalized on the basis of those particulars—favoring resemblances over differences in the manner of idealist reason—it vitiates the determination of aesthetic form as distinct from rational form. It furthermore nullifies the determinative vitality that Baumgarten originally claimed for an aesthetic value predicated on extension. This is the case at least insofar as extension, in its dependence on an active proliferation of qualities, expresses a self-transformative relation to contingency.

Under the terms of the present confusion Baumgarten's aesthetic form seems to be predisposed, like all identity-based theories of meaning, to the stasis of ideological posing from which we would want to distinguish it. Baumgarten's theme subsumes aesthetic particulars to a determining principle that is irreducibly reflective rather than productively speculative. Furthermore, the principle of "formal perfection," by which we are bound to thematize according to Baumgarten, is reflected only in the particulars it proliferates as observable effects without a specifiable cause. It therefore begs the question of its own agency, presupposing what it is meant to reflect. We can perhaps best see how the integrity of Baumgarten's aesthetic depends on the very distinction between intensive and extensive determinants that his definition of theme elides, if we see how the category of the aesthetic survives epistemologically intact in the practice of Blanchot's *récit*.

The Aesthetic of the *Récit*

Blanchot's aesthetic, based as it is on the critique of the optical image, wherein the image no longer reflects a totality distinct from the transformations it entails, resists the static reflexivity of Baumgarten's theme. It compromises the reiterative infrastructure of intensive determination. Intensive meaning always posits a relation with its own past abstractly by reducing the manifold to a proleptic singularity. This follows the pattern of Aristotelian plot dénouement that unifies disparate moments through the synthetic function of *anagnorisis,* based as it is on a cardinal resemblance. Hence, the ahistorical bias of intensive meaning and the resultant split between the disciplines of aesthetics and social history.[17]

It is not that the abstraction of intensive meaning is positively purged in Blanchot. Rather, abstraction itself remains contingent instead of paradoxically rendering its own ground of concrete particulars contingent—as was the case in Baumgarten's theme—and thereby obscuring its own groundedness. In this way Blanchot establishes the foundation for a traversable bridge between the orders of aesthetic and historical determination. Furthermore, Blanchot's emphasis on transformation shows us a way of critiquing theme without succumbing to the alternative temptation of idealizing a prereflective particularity, without confusing speech and sight at the extremity of absolute theme or absolute form.

We may now assert that the project of the *récit* grounds the totalizing determinations of meaning without either skeptically opposing formal particulars and thematic universals or idealistically conflating them. While the opposition of form and theme inevitably resolves itself, as we have already seen, into an ironic relation (form always already presupposed in the theme that reveals it), Blanchot reveals the necessity of dialectizing that irony. He suggests a new order of determinations. In effect, he supplants the form-theme opposition with a form-irony opposition, wherein irony does not herald a resolution of the differences between form and theme but, rather, a transformation of the formal particulars that instantiated difference in the first place.

For Lukács, we will remember, irony overcomes subject-object oppositions, but only as an ideal of detachment from the world of such oppositions. Though he credits irony with being nonreductive by comparison with symbolic or metaphoric language, Lukácsian irony reduces the reciprocity of differences that obtain between subject and object by insisting upon the universality of that opposition.[18] The price paid by this Romantic view is the metaphysical attenuation of the Hegelian, or "positive," dialectic. Blanchot obviates the antinomic relation of subject and structure upon which Lukács's theory of irony is based. The opposition of form and irony prompted by Blanchot's aesthetic would escape the inherent abstraction of narrative irony by preserving its determinations in a kind of negative dialectic.

Here I am, of course, referring to the method of Adorno's *negative dialectic,* which, counter to Hegelian dialectic, aspires to reflect the reciprocity of differences operative in negation rather than to sublate them. Or at least I believe that the negative dialectic is one way to elucidate the mechanics of the temporality that Blanchot aims at in the *récit,* when he says: "[the *récit*] is not the narration of an event, but the event itself, the approach to that event, the place where the event is made to happen" (*Gaze*, 109). Because Blanchot further maintains that "to experience an event as an image is not to have an image of an event," we are in a position to speculate how the placement of the self, with respect to the image, always *eventuates* (i.e., "the noun turning into a verb") a proliferation of differences. In Blanchot's *récit* this aesthetic principle denotes a *connectedness* that transcends the immediate sensate particulars (as theme purports to do), but by scrupulously relating them to the *process of connection* itself. It thereby intimates a formalism that is totalizing without being individualizing, in the manner of Baumgarten's ideal of formal perfection; it intimates the form of form as practice.

On this basis I think that the "madness" in the narrative of *The Madness of the Day* is now specifiable as the recursive principle that makes the process of connection in this text so conspicuous. We thus confront the question of agency, which a more uncritical thematics begs. Recursive action is implicit in the supplanting of the form-theme opposition with the form-irony opposition because it presumes an agency that is modified by its own determinations. Lukácsian irony produces an indeterminate, or Kantian, "outside," a regulative ideal that strives for the stasis of objectivity. Blanchot, by contrast, locates a determinate *hors-texte,* which by its external determinateness acknowledges its own articulation on the threshold of activity. Specifically, the process of connectedness in *Madness of the Day* is "maddened" beyond the more "reasonable" mode of representation that does not reflect the terms of its own articulation by changing them. Unlike the positive negation, which is bound to particularize in spatial terms (because it makes individuality its limiting term), the particulars entailed in the Blanchotian text are temporal. They do not transcend the extensive register because extension is extended beyond the thematizing limit of individuality and, as we will see, beyond the notion of limit itself.

Meaning in Blanchot's text is thus linked to an ambiguity that is never simply resolved in the text but is, rather, assiduously *developed.* Indeed, the term *ambiguity* becomes the touchstone of Blanchotian meaning in his critical writing. Blanchot's *ambiguity* denotes an indeterminacy that is always determined through a movement in time. To employ ambiguity as a mode of *development,* as Blanchot does, is to save it from the ontological abyss of indeterminacy. By the same token ambiguity returns us to the earlier postulate of the subject conceived as activity—wherein the temporal particularity of negation coincides with the development of, rather than the resolution of, ambiguity.

The hypothesis of the "subject as activity," so influential for Marx and other theorists of ideology identified earlier as the precursors of Blanchot's aesthetic, derives even more originally from J. G. Fichte. In his *The Science of Knowledge* Fichte theorized the subject as activity on the basis of his postulate that the "I" positing itself as an absolute totality presupposes a limit (a "not-I"). This limit entails its own divisibility as the necessary condition of its existence. Fichte licenses the assumption that to reflect upon the I is inextricable from the project of dividing one's self from oneself: "What is thereby posited in the not-self is *precisely what* that which is unposited in the self *does not* posit, or negates. The act returns upon itself; insofar as the self is not to posit something in itself, it is itself not-self" (*The Science of Knowledge*, 161). For Fichte this project looked toward the goal of escaping the universalist abstractions of Kantianism by locating the self within the predicative stance of positing itself in relation to an object. But it already foreshadowed its own counter-critique.

In his proto-Hegelian striving to unify beyond the terms of the duality that he sought to overcome, Fichte posited an "absolute self" as a regulative ideal of subjective activity. The synthesis of subject and object intimated in this famously problematic Fichtean ideal—like the Hegelian synthesis it presaged—suggests a *nonqualitative unity in difference*. Here the absolute self is presupposed as the condition of the not-self that grounds it (in particulars), thereby depriving the self *for itself* of any determinate particularity. One could thus argue that the absolute self possesses no qualities independent of the negating will through which all objective differences devolve to an identical being. It is precisely the drift of such a dialectic toward nonqualitative identity that I am arguing Blanchot resists.

By contrast, Blanchot posits an aesthetic form eminently consistent with Baumgarten's desire to distinguish aesthetic value from rational value as a knowledge based in extensive determination. In Blanchot's thematizing of the *récit*, Baumgarten's hope of conceiving art as a mode of positive determination tantalizingly approaches fulfillment in terms that also reflect the Marxist ideal of making aesthetic determinations continuous with our human activity in the world. Because Blanchot, by his attempt to salvage the particulars of self-determination through negation, renders them temporal rather than spatial (unlike the thematic narrative artists and the idealist philosophers who precede him), he advances a notion of aesthetic practice that does not tend to reify the categories of experience it so eloquently formulates.

We must now look at another example to see how the complex of issues broached here is reconfigured and clarified in the elements of Blanchot's text. The visual ambiguity we have already highlighted in the narrator's "brief vision" of the woman and the baby carriage is aptly "developed" (rather than resolved) along the lines I have just suggested, in an "episode" that ironically resembles the resolving focus of classical plot dénouement, which the strategy of "development," by definition, precludes: it is an episode that dramatizes the loss of the narrator's own sight. The irony of its meaning is explicit in the fact that this scene purports to be a cathartic revelation of the "madness of the day" in the spectacle of extinguished light. Thus, Blanchot locates us on the threshold where the image disappears—where its disappearance is made apparent— where the image articulated recursively appeals, as I have just suggested, to a temporal rather than a visual register of intelligibility:

I nearly lost my sight because someone crushed glass in my eyes. That blow unnerved me, I must admit. I had the feeling I was going back into the wall, or straying into a thicket of flint. The worst thing was the sudden, shocking cruelty of the day; I could not look, but I could not help looking. To see was terrifying, and to stop seeing tore me apart from my forehead to my throat. What was more, I heard hyena cries that exposed me to the threat of a wild animal (I think those cries were my own). (*Madness*, 11)

The ambiguity that compels our greatest interest in this passage has nothing to do with the superficial blurring of contextual markers that obscure the visual clarity of "dramatic" scene but, rather, with the insuperable distinction between extensive and intensive determinations that governs interpretation in this context. The finite boundaries of the event described here are simultaneously present and absent in an array of particulars that appear in the guise of dissimulation.

Dissimulation is distinct from negation in its ambiguous reference. Dissimulation has multiple referents by virtue of its active reciprocation between subjective and objective perspectives. As with the previous vision of the woman and the baby carriage, Blanchot here adduces spatial references—"I was going into a wall"—in a manner that evokes plotted locations on a well-mapped course of physical action. But, simultaneously, these spatial loci are attenuated to the indeterminate condition of the noun turning into a verb (which we have seen is the pretext of the *récit*): "I could not look but I could not help looking. To see was terrifying and to stop seeing tore me apart from my forehead to my throat." For the reader to see what is so terrifying he must look with his own eye through the blindness of the narrator's I, occluded as it is by the "immediate" imagery of the wildly absent beast. In other words it is the presence of the visible that marks the absence of the visual agent and so makes the visible manifestly a contingency of speech.

The register of the visible sacrificed here in the attenuation of spatial loci, is the place of the subject. It is the I (eye) of this narrator who coincidentally began the narration of this *récit* with a comparable bid for a clarity—one that nonetheless also escaped his ability to clarify, our ability to "see" him! On the first page of *Madness of the Day* we get an intimation of the present crisis. We understand that the subject in Blanchot's fiction has no place (space) in which he can objectify himself: "I am not learned; I am not ignorant. I have known joys. That is saying too little: I am alive and this life gives me the greatest pleasure. And what about death? When I die (perhaps any minute now) I will feel immense pleasure" (5).

In this opening passage and in the complementary "scene" of climactic blindness previously discussed, it is as if the incommensurability of the verbal and the visual (intensive and extensive) modalities expresses dissimulation more as a condition of further determinitive meaning than as a product of negation. As a product of negation, this incommensurability would be indictable as what the ideology critics might call a programmatic false consciousness. But false consciousness, contrary to Blanchot's text, would legislate meaning according to a preemptive subject-object dichotomy.

There is no doubt that the ambiguity of these passages from *The Madness of the Day* may be glossed in terms of the ironically self-aggrandizing "crisis of the subject" so widely reported in poststructuralist literary theory. But in the case of Blanchot we are compelled to resist the fashionable conflation of the crisis of the subject with the pure negation of the subject—precisely because Blanchot forces us to contend with the hypothesis that negation is *not* prior to dissimulation. The ambiguity of the episode of "lost sight" is exemplary for Blanchot's whole approach to the epistemology of fiction because it dramatizes the insupportability of a thematic reading on the specific grounds that the totalizing will of the I/eye, proffered by the visual image, expresses the mutual divisibility of intensive/extensive determinations.

We are not induced to see intensive and extensive determinations as mutually exclusive terms or negations of one another. For example, the loss of the image dramatized in the narrator's experience of blindness portends the loss of extensive qualities but is nonetheless articulated in energetically detailed imagery. At the same time the sensory particulars of these images are themselves ineluctably intensive in their striving toward a visual "completeness," which would thematize them. We must recall that, after Fichte established the self through the act of positing a not-self, he was in the similarly contradictory position of striving to appropriate that not-self through an activity that could never impose a limit or assign a causal principle predicated on a purely external position. By prohibiting a pure exteriority, the act of positing precluded the very interiority of self that it had aspired to in all previous philosophical systems that had sought some unconditional ground of knowledge.

In the case of Blanchot's *récit* the absence of the faculty of sight, which "tears the narrator apart from forehead to throat"—a blindness occasioned by the sharply etched imagery of the invisible beast—epitomizes the priority of dissimulation over negation, which I have just asserted, because it suggests the possibility of a referent that is not specifically independent of the referring agent. The relation between the hyena cries and the self, which is their source here, anticipates the difficulties to come. The image is not predisposed to be an image of something. It does not presume the ground of a negation, as does the classical image, which, by opening a space between subject and object, purports to master that space. It does not preempt any reflection upon its activity that could be expressed as activity, as the moment of productive speculation.

The image here epitomizes what Foucault calls, in appreciation of Blanchot's rich epistemological stance as a novelist, "the thought from the outside." Blanchot himself designates this stance as the condition of "negligence." He claims it is fundamental to writing the *récit*. "Negligence" is proposed as an alternative to the negation upon which he believes the classical image is conditioned by marking the complicity of aesthetic form with negating consciousness. Negation, by contrast with negligence, is a touchstone of the "inherent" inwardness of reflection, turning the object obsessively back into an intensive *I* of discourse, a

conceptual refuge of theme. Negligence, even in its most colloquial parlance, denoting absent attention, serves as an apt descriptive term for
what Blanchot deems a necessary corrective to the cravenly narcissistic
self (the merely reflected I).

Blanchot nonetheless gives that colloquial sense of the word *negligence*
a dialectical twist by positing in it a point of view that turns speculatively
upon the surface of the eye: denying it depth, rendering the eye a surface
upon which seeing and seen are coincident as differentials. Yet they are
not simply differentials of each other. In his special definition of the term
Blanchot stipulates that *negligence* denotes the irreducibility of the space
between the representation and what it represents. This phenomenon is
no longer conceived as a dynamic of subject-object relations but, instead,
as a condition of determinate consciousness itself. Negligence is a constitutive dissimulation (as opposed to a merely regulative principle, à la Kant,
Schlegel, Kierkegaard). It is located at the core of individual being, where
the notion of the self as a limit is coincident with the notion of the self
as a purpose, or determination. Again we are reminded of Fichte's premise
that the I presupposes activity because, as a determinative whole, it is
limited, and, as a limit, it excludes what posits it (purposiveness). The
Blanchotian image, by preserving the distinction between intensional and
extensional determinations, has the effect of raising the concept of determination itself to a level of concreteness that cannot be thematized: theme
in this case is effectively rendered a telos of determination achieved only
through the progressive manifestation of the determinants of that telos.

The juxtaposition of the two meanings of limit and purpose that is
imposed in Blanchot's concept of negligence once again echoes Baumgarten's use of the term *determination* to specify the extensive register of
aesthetic form.[19] In both cases the spatial must reciprocate with the
temporal if it is to preserve its power of determination. Or, as I have
already suggested, in both Blanchot's and Baumgarten's attempts to conceptualize aesthetic form, extensive particulars are temporalized rather
than thematized. Blanchot makes explicit what remains implicit in
Baumgarten. Theme, for Baumgarten, implies spatial totality, because
singularity, the singularity of the individual, is the index of aesthetic
determination in *Reflections on Poetry*.[20] Therefore, in the organic individual (which is specifically Baumgarten's paradigm for aesthetic totality)
extensional clarity would manifest itself as the principle of difference in
unity. I have already intimated (with response to Fichte's absolute self)
that such an account of aesthetic particularity consigns our thinking to a

Kantian/Coleridgean metaphysic of the beautiful, for which the interpenetration of the universal and the particular preempts an account of the determination of the particular *as* universal. Such thinking consequently valorizes a mystical Being, the very antithesis of the extensive determination in which Baumgarten originally sought to ground the significance of *aesthesis*.

By contrast, in *The Madness of the Day* the stipulation that the narrator be reconciled with the world through a state of negligence instead of negation is dramatized as a persistent ambiguity of Blanchot's narrative plot: the narrator himself is always on the brink of disappearance. It is a threshold whereupon appearance is presented as a temporal crux. Again the problematic of the image figures as an important framework. The classical image *is* its appearance. Precisely because the appearance of the classical image is reciprocally bound to negation, as truth is bound to falsity, Blanchot is obliged to constrain his images within a negligent perspective. But he must do this without at the same time putting negligence itself into an oppositional relation with negation and thereby replicating the dualistic modality of thought he otherwise seeks to escape. Following this scruple, the narrator's disappearance must eschew any nostalgia for appearance. Accordingly, we are led by Blanchot to a redefinition of the image as a resemblance, not to a thing but, rather, to itself.

In an essay entitled "Two Versions of the Imaginary" Blanchot says: "the category of art is linked to the possibility objects have . . . of abandoning themselves to pure and simple resemblance behind which there is nothing—except being" (*Gaze,* 84). Contrary to appearances, this formulation need not be confused with the ontological verge of Heideggerian Being. For the image denoted here does not dis-simulate in the manner of the subject, which self-deludedly instantiates itself through a negation of the thing it objectifies. The being of the image may only be approached here as an activity that can reflect itself by transforming itself, by remaining within the matrix of reciprocal determinations.

In a conspicuous footnote to his analysis of the *récit* in "Two Versions of the Imaginary" Blanchot reveals what is staked in this *seemingly* radical notion whereby the image ceases to be a locus of purely subjective determinations. The emphasis on dissimulation implicit in Blanchot's refusal of the classical image is revealed to be not a flight from determination per se. Rather, it entertains a confrontation with the paradox of any determinate meaning that would, by opposing ambiguity, simply recapitulate the dualism of being and nothingness, in effect binding them in a static identity.[21] As we have anticipated, he now postulates that ambiguity is not opposed to being. Rather:

> ambiguity expresses being as dissimulated; if it says that being is, insofar as it is dissimulated . . . ambiguity, then no longer consists only of the incessant movement through which being returns to nothingness and nothing refers back to being. Ambiguity is no longer the primordial Yes and No in which being and nothingness are pure identity. Essential ambiguity lies rather in the fact that—before beginning—nothingness is not equal to being, is only the appearance of the dissimulation of being *or else that dissimulation is more original than negation.* (89; emphasis added)

In a narrative where dissimulation is regarded as "more original than negation" we can assert with more rigorous confidence the possibility that extensive determination is neither reducible to thematic singularity nor attenuated to infinity. Because Blanchot rejects the equation of being and nothingness, the best account of the world "imaged" in Blanchot's fiction would testify that the things of this world have the status of what we might call *personifications without persons.* Blanchot's practice of the *récit* suggests that, if the figure of personification could be invoked without the regulative concept of person, it would signify the notion of dissimulation as a transformation whose formal lineaments conform only to the necessity of its unfolding. Indeed, the most potent ambiguity of *The Madness of the Day* is inextricable from Blanchot's relentless personification of the conceptual abstractions, which so oddly populate this *récit.* As we have seen, this strategy is precisely what induces the indeterminate determinability of the neuter. It no doubt makes the process of determination itself seem ominously interminable.

The most paradigmatic of all these personifications in *Madness of the Day* is the personification of the law, who "sees" the narrator in terms that are inaccessible both to the reader and to the narrator: "She [the law] would show me a part of space between the top of the window and the ceiling. 'You are there,' she said." This pedantic *deixis* does not point away from itself, nor does it denote itself. Whereas personification programmatically takes the measure of intensive states by dressing them out in extensive qualities, Blanchot's "personifications without persons" exfoliates from the "outside" as if to preclude any such hypostatic interiority, as if to posit an ascription of extensive qualities that forces us to attend that much more scrupulously to the ascriptive agency itself. We are led to think of it as taking the measure of mental acts from the very limit of mental attention, which by nature defiles the limit. This tells us something more about the vicissitudes of the subject relative to the burden of thematics in the *récit*.

Specifically, the law denotes the limit. It is like the "rule" of spatial coordinates, which gives existential dimension to the image. But in Blanchot the personification of the law portends the limitlessness of the limit. Appropriately, the law here "appears" to the narrator as a kind of syntactical entanglement whereby "her" presence in a series of self-perpetuating paradoxical encounters taunts the intuition of the visible: as if its "rule" could be made to appear and she could be finalized in accordance with that rule. In an illustrative passage the narrator remarks: "I knew that one of her aims was to make me see justice done" (*Madness,* 15). The punning locution here, which is neither fully determined in subject or object, as noun or verb, epitomizes how the visualizable in Blanchot always redounds to the verbal contingencies of the desire to visualize. This in turn devolves to an elaboration of the situation of the visualizing subject.

The law here is, to use Blanchot's own example, like that mysterious intuition that denotes a resemblance to life in the human cadaver.[22] For Blanchot intuition of the being of the cadaver recalls the interpretive rigor of Mallarmé's formal ideal insofar as it purports to be an allegory of itself: it is neither a reflexivity of consciousness nor a negation of consciousness because it entails a transforming recursiveness. As Blanchot explains in "Literature and the Right to Death," our relation to the cadaver is immediate but empty of any immediate determinations that are not themselves transformed by the necessity of there being no "thing" there beyond the circumstance that modifies it. Just so, personifications without persons implicitly configure a relation to the moment of determination that is transformative of that determination.

Having said this, we could perhaps press home the earlier point that form in *The Madness of Day* (because it so emphatically does not totalize on any intensive—thematic—ground) is most clearly elucidated by presupposing its conditionality upon a dialectic with irony: irony concedes the lack of simultaneity between intensive and extensive determinations, which, as we have already seen, the form-theme opposition eschews to hapless ironic effect. The form-irony dialectic expresses the incommensurability of intensive and extensive determinations, which theme typically makes commensurable, even at the price of instantiating a theological limit of objectifying perspectives that preemptively ends time. Blanchot, by "ending" the limit, instead, reinscribes the temporality of human experience in the form of activity. Thus, unlike the irony resultant from the form-theme dialectic (which portends the atemporal unity of intensive and extensive determinations), the irony in Blanchot's aesthetic is neither reductive nor aporetic.

Or we might say that what irony expresses here is the principle of transformation, which makes the recurrence of contemplative consciousness to an object the object of consciousness itself. In this way it renders the formal dimension of the artwork a more productive form of work in the Hegelian sense of *arbeit*. Once again to speak of form in this way is to think totalization and transformation together. Furthermore, to follow the narrator's "progress" in the pages of *The Madness of the Day* is to adopt the principle that form is wedded to time through the contradictions latent in temporal succession, provided that succession is not itself dissimulated in the specter of false identity. From the point of view we have now established such a dissimulation would be too conspicuously a product of negation rather than a condition of negative judgment, as Blanchot has stipulated it must be in the *récit*. It is precisely in this regard that we might head off the premature conclusion that the temporality of Blanchot's *récit* simply concedes to a mindless succession of moments. Rather, it posits a coherence that is based on the notion that difference *is* change and that change respects the ever more particularized incommensurability of intensive and extensive moments.

Closing the *Récit:* Opening the Aesthetic

In Blanchot's *récit* the work of reading now plausibly reconciles Hegelian *arbeit* and Fichtean activity, offering in turn a new way of meeting the rationalistic demands of thematic unity without making that unifying principle abstract from the situation of life it addresses. The Blanchotian terms *negligence, the neuter, dissimulation,* etc., become more shrewdly instrumental to this purpose in the curiously liminal dénouement of *The Madness of the Day*. The most hypostatized of all moments in the classical Aristotelian narrative, the dénouement is annunciated here in a question put to the narrator by his doctors: "Who threw glass in your eye?" Like personifications without persons, this question becomes a self-perpetuating, self-transformative activity for the narrator, who essays to answer it. Aptly, the question calls for a personal identification that conflates person and cause. In turn, it evokes both the telos and the teleological subject, which are reconstituted in Blanchot's aesthetic in terms of dissimulation not negation. In fact, the concluding passage of the *récit* conspicuously enacts the dissimulation upon which the split between the novel form and the *récit* is originally predicated, in order to call subject and telos both to critical account. After all, the doctors' question turns out *not* to be important for the answer it summons. No answer is forthcoming. Posed like so many intractably nonvisualizable images in this work, the question occasions its own temporalization in the ever more astutely foregrounded act of reading itself.

Confronted by his doctors, who want a *story* about the injury to the narrator's eye, the narrator counters in the final line of the *récit* with: "A story. No. No stories, never again" (*Madness*, 18). This refusal has the force of a self-parodying negation rather than the self-reifying negation eschewed by negative dialectics. The narrator's refusal of story parodies the negative absolute of idealist aesthetics (upon which the transcendental self is founded) because the refusal itself is conveyed in the form of a story. It is, even more disconcertingly, a story we have heard before, an exact repetition of the opening lines of the *récit:* "I am not learned; I am not ignorant. . . . " This story is literally a re-seeing of the already "passed" beginning (of the story) as present, with the knowledge that the present now entails a dissimulation that puts past and present into a reciprocal relation. The sense of reading as work comes through here in the prevailing transformational exigency of the passage, which eludes any moment of recognition that is not also a moment of re-cognition, of re-positing. Blanchot thus contrives a unique textual density by conflating the formal "autonomy" of the text with the activity of reading it. Form is not spiritualized by reading, as it would be in the process of thematic reduction. But neither is it hypostatized into a concrete particularity. For each moment "speaks" recursively to what it transforms, with the effect of restaging its own contextuality as a kind of temporal extension of subjective consciousness.

Blanchot's most elucidating contrast with a classical thematization in *The Madness of the Day* is evoked in the portentous configuration of speaking characters that sets up this final scene of the narrative: the patient (the narrator) confronted by the inquisitorial doctors. There are at first two doctors: an eye doctor and a psychiatrist, near-comic allegories of the visible and the verbal. Yet as the narrator attests: "because there were two of them, there were three and this third remained firmly convinced, I am sure, that a writer, a man who speaks and who reasons with distinction is always capable of recounting facts that he remembers" (18). With all the Hegelian foreshadowing of this text we can see the appearance of the "third" as compelled here by the instability of the dualism of the visual and the verbal (eye doctor and psychiatrist). This allegorically recapitulates the instability of the subject-object opposition driven as it is in the idealist tradition toward a synthesis beyond the limits of opposition. In this way the limit becomes an unselfconscious ground of meaning. But because in this final episode of *The Madness of the Day* the question posed by the doctors is precisely not answerable, the hitherto unacknowledged limitlessness of the limit obtrudes as a textual determination that leads back to the beginning of the text without circling back on the itinerary of a merely reflexive subject.

Needless to say, it is precisely at the point of the narrator's refusal to cooperate with the inquisition of the two/three doctors (whose conversation has the character of "an authoritarian interrogation, overseen and controlled by a strict set of rules") that Blanchot's own narrative ceases to be a story and becomes most definitively a *récit*. For here we are compelled to observe a sudden contraction of the distance between writing and reading as the most conspicuous formal pressure exerted by the text. The invitation to the reader to go back to the "beginning" of the text has the authority of an authorial revision, which is nonetheless contingent upon the temporality of reading. Blanchot reminds us: "[the *récit*] only 'narrates' itself . . . it cannot exist as a narration unless it writes what is happening in that narration . . . " (*Gaze*, 110). Indeed, the presence of a third becomes a counter for the mode of dissimulation that mitigates the writing/reading distinction as it simultaneously mitigates the form/theme distinction: it obviates the possibility of getting sufficiently "outside" the text that one can posit its unproblematically meaningful interior.

It is impossible to come to the end of this text in the way that we conventionally "finish" reading. In the episode in which the narrator refuses the "reading" of his doctors, more than anywhere else in the text, dissimulation is manifestly prior to negation. This is true in the sense that the negation of form, which would effect closure according to the dictates of Romantic irony, is itself temporally complicit in a "third reading," so to speak: in the imperative to reread the text from the beginning, i.e., "I am not learned. . . . " Yet this third rereading, because it precludes the possibility of repetition as much as the narrator's own refusal of stories, inhibits any individualizing, totalizing of the text that does not return us strangely and incompletely to the beginning. This third rereading is differentiated without being transumptively different. The triad of beginning, ending, and repetition presents a profound contrast with the triadic schematization of the Hegelian telos—thesis, antithesis, synthesis—insofar as Blanchot's third term here has no representational force beyond the concrete extension of its temporal effectivity. In the next chapter this triad will figure again as the triangulating armature of Jamesian syntax and in that regard will even more decisively elucidate the generative principle of a narrative subjectivity that transcends the limit term of Romantic irony.

Romantic irony in the novel (as we have discussed it via Lukács) is inextricable from the asceticism of self-abolition, since it makes the self always a measure of its own insufficiency with respect to the universalizing labor of representation. Temporality in this respect is banished to a kind of absolute externality vis-à-vis narrative desire. The possibility of conceiving of the self in narrative terms at all is precluded by this externality of time, forcing us to accept, in the purview of the novel at least, the ideal of a contemplative rather than a practical self. The *récit* redeems the construct of the self from the self-deconstructing regress of Lukácsian irony or, rather, posits the self as a constructive agency that recurs to the situatedness of its self-construction for its only claim to essentiality: for contingency is the only constraint upon that situation.

Thus, with Blanchot asceticism can become aestheticism in Baumgarten's sense of an exfoliation of extensive qualities whose unity is determined temporally. This condition obtains specifically insofar as the proliferation of the particular aspects of this text sustains our attention by repositing the circumstances of attentional consciousness. "No. No more stories . . ." is the most propitious beginning for a *récit* because the putative beginning that it impels us toward, as we reread the "opening" lines of this particular *récit,* is thematizable only in a way that transformation allows: by so individualizing its determinations that they are perpetually turning into one another, thereby making determination itself an untranscendable ground of subjectivity. The reprise of the opening passage is neither an adequate beginning nor an adequate ending because its "return" takes the form of a repositing rather than a simple reappropriation.

The narrator obliquely testifies to the lucidity of this knowledge: "I had become involved in their [the inquisitional doctors'] search. We were

all like masked hunters. Who was being questioned? Who was answering?
One became the other. The words spoke by themselves. The silence
entered them, an excellent refuge since I was the only one who noticed it"
(*Madness*, 17–18). If we are reading astutely, we will notice that the
narrator is *not* the only one to notice. Rather, such notice becomes the
ethical burden of the reading experience per se. By contrast, the external
temporality of Romantic irony, imposed by the insufficiency of form-
giving consciousness to the world (an insufficiency that by definition,
precludes the work of self-transformation in the Lukácsian novel) renders
form and ethos mutually exclusive. This temporality is internalized and
rendered ethical in the *récit* if we accept the premise that Blanchot's
aesthetic form is assimilable to the subject of Fichtean activity: in other
words if we accept that the fulfillment proffered by activity is an augmentation of its field of reference rather than its completion.

Significantly, Blanchot's impatience with the inexorable completions
of story may furthermore be elucidated by observing the opportunity it
presents to go beyond the paradoxical impasse that Fichtean subjectivity
carries within its own trajectory of thought. For, as we have noted, the
Fichtean self, torn between a theoretical or conceptual aspect that freely
posits (the object world, the other) and an empirical aspect that strives
to overcome that object world, guiltily presupposes its own third aspect,
the absolute self. This absolute self is like the narrator's imaginary third—
insisting upon the unity of the duality through which we discover it. As
I have suggested already, the absolute self potentially compromises the
whole epistemological thrust of Fichte's theory. Because it must be deduced from activity instead of manifesting its own active constitutive
powers, it posits a totality distinct from transformation, thus vitiating
the theory of the subject as activity per se.[23]

The problem for the Fichtean subject, as for the Hegelian subject after
it, arises from its inability to resist totalizing beyond that very asymmetry
of positing and striving according to which the original privilege of
activity over identity seemed to be granted. The opposition of the positing
self and the striving self is specifically paradoxical because it presupposes
the unity of the positing self *before* it divides itself. Constrained as we are
by the understanding that the opposition between the two cannot be
logically deduced from the principle of unity, because what opposes the
self (the other it posits) necessarily also excludes it, we face an even more
difficult problem. On the one hand, the positing self stands for finitude
and totality, which we passionately aspire to in the concept of the subject,

but which is patently unreal. On the other hand, the striving self, which is undeniably real in the resistance presented to it by the empirical world, is just as undeniably infinite.[24]

We might now say that the subject in Blanchot's fiction remains faithful to, but unconfounded by, the paradoxical premise of Fichtean activity because it insists upon a more radical reflection of self than the concept of the absolute self yields up to close scrutiny: conceding the infinity of activity—but not the indeterminateness of infinity.[25] The Blanchotian récit gives us an aesthetic warrant for the subject that is neither formalist or thematic. Alternatively, it preserves the determinative force of formal agency without hypostatizing that agency—specifically, without making it a site for reconciling the finite and the infinite. The recursive principle inherent in the "madness of the day" then obviates the necessity of this reconciliation because finite and infinite are inevitably seen as constitutive of one another.

The récit is strikingly at odds with story because story, by thematizing the infinite, vitiates the vital ambiguity of the event. By contrast, the récit is just as strikingly not at odds with narrative because it demurs the specular attraction of the finite image. Rather, it gives us significant epistemological leverage against the burden of thematics because the infinite, totality, history (all of which weigh so heavily in the balance of thematism) are rendered narratable without being narrated.

In this regard the récit might be characterized as a figuration of contingency promulgating an aesthetic practice that is, in the Nietzschean/Foucauldian parlance, historically effective (wirklich historie).[26] The "effective history" of genealogical method does not hypostatize causes but, rather, causes itself to be reconfigured according to the effectivity of its own finitude. Like the most authoritative post-Enlightenment aesthetic theories, the aesthetic of the récit arises from the impulse to close the gap between ethos and form, to naturalize time and make it iconic by antinomically particularizing the universal. But, unlike post-Enlightenment aesthetic theories, the récit seeks not to represent time so much as to express time in the determination of ever more complex relations to the exigencies of temporal experience.

What Blanchot proffers in the récit, then, is what I will at least tentatively call an "expressive aesthetics." This expressive aesthetics instantiates the subject in a self-reflective activity that does not redound to a Lukácsian crisis of contingency, of inauthenticity, of the insufficiency of form to experience. Because what the récit expresses is not the intentional self. Rather, the *récit* follows an extensional trajectory of self-realization exhibited as a structurally recursive proposition: language more fully determines its conditions of possibility as it transforms them. The work of literature undertaken in the name of expressive aesthetics transforms the world because it accedes to the transformational pressure of worldly desires over which no other world holds absolute precedence. It would be conceivably the most historically committed form of criticism because it recognizes that its work is never done except as it is being done:

> Literature is that experience through which the consciousness discovers its being in its inability to lose consciousness, in the movement whereby, as it disappears, as it tears itself away from the meticulousness of an I, it is recreated beyond unconsciousness as an impersonal spontaneity, the desperate eagerness of a haggard knowledge which knows nothing, which no one knows, and which ignorance always discovers behind itself as its own shadow changed into a gaze. (*Gaze*, 50)

In the next chapter we will follow the speculative line of sight projected here in terms of a nonnegating irony. Thus, we will try to make out an even clearer image of the expressive aesthetic as a syntactical armature of narrative, as a centering of the ironic subject that is neither radically idealized nor radically contingent.

6

The Figuration of Contingency:
The Subject beyond Irony

Nothing deserves to be called an artwork that keeps the contingent
at bay.
> —Theodor W. Adorno, *Aesthetic Theory*

. . . if one is always doing, he can scarce, by his own measure, ever
have done.
> —Henry James, "Preface," *The Golden Bowl*

Figuring Irony

The idea of an "ironic center" is the deeply paradoxical centerpiece of the
aesthetic system figured forth in Henry James's preface to *What Maisie
Knew* (1897): it is the plan of a novel wherein

> the child [Maisie] becoming a centre and pretext for a fresh system
> of misbehaviour, a system moreover of a nature to spread and ramify:
> *there* would be the "full" irony, there the promising theme into which
> the hint I had originally picked up would *logically flower*. No themes
> are so human as those that reflect for us, out of the confusion of life,
> the close connexion of bliss and bale, of the things that help with the
> things that hurt, so dangling before us for ever that bright hard medal
> of so strange an alloy, one face of which is somebody's right and ease
> and the other somebody's pain and wrong. To live with all intensity
> and perplexity and felicity in its terribly mixed little world would
> thus be part of my interesting small mortal . . . (7; emphasis added)

The conflation of irony and centrality in James's "terribly mixed little
world" constitutes a ground of determination that confidently embraces
contradiction as its condition of possibility. It could be said that the figure
of the ironic center thus proffers the key piece of the puzzle that James's
critical prefaces pose for us as we strive to decipher in them the intention-

141

ality of the works. For the notion of a centering irony, by its evocation
of the "full flower" of meaning under the sign of lost meaning, does seem
to apprehend the complexity of James's notoriously attenuated aesthetic
totalities: they are forms wherein ironic reversal prevails as the most
salient consistency of dramatic structure. Yet, quite to the contrary, it
could also be argued that the figure of the ironic center, rather than
solving the puzzle of Jamesian style, animates our most complex involve-
ment with the puzzle-solving activity qua activity in James's writing,
precisely because of its detotalizing imperative. The subtle irony released
in the oxymoronic drift of the ironic center potentially detotalizes the
formal integrity it otherwise seems to confer. Thus, it jeopardizes as well
the broader project of making this author's theory and practice cohere as
interlocking figures of a totalizing pattern of thought.

The metaphor of patterned thought has, of course, served eminently
as our touchstone for appreciating James as the exemplary aesthetic formalist of American fiction and, by extension, for characterizations of the
modern novel that seek to distinguish it invidiously and on a formalistic
basis from its more naively realist precursors. The most common formulation of this distinction avers that the modern novel yields a fuller reflection of the determinate possibilities of reflective consciousness than its
precursors. Such art, formalist theorists argue, is our strongest defense
against the fatalistic determinations that are otherwise imposed upon
consciousness by a monstrously impersonal history. The beneficence of
patterned thought—of "leitmotif," "symbol," "controlling metaphor"—is revealed in the canonical accounts of critical formalism
(Wimsatt and Beardsley, Frye et al.) to be the human antagonist of an
inhuman determinism.

In this context it is not surprising that the most incisive "pattern of
thought" etched by James upon the modernist cornerstone of Anglo-
American narrative aesthetics is the trope of irony. Irony purports to
make the difference between determination as agency and determination
as fatality. In the modern ethos that James so conscientiously bequeaths
us in his prefaces, irony proffers the mobility that makes point of view
an active trajectory of consciousness instead of a mortal weight of unconscious determination. In unconscious determination the lisible mind submits to the gross demands of the body politic, the prodding finger of
ideological hegemony, the fatal hand of historical tragedy. Against this
threat irony evolved into the master trope and theme of high modernist
narrative from Joyce to Pynchon.[1] According to the critical mythos of

this tradition, modern narrative fiction forms itself heroically through its recognition of an oppressive contingency. Irony mirrors the fact of contingency, reproducing the gulf between subject and world, and by that subversive mimesis appropriates the gulf as an aspect of its own activity.

Yet on this premise irony, perhaps too cleverly, renders the mimetic gesture the most profoundly self-reflexive gesture of all. The gist of human identity comprehended in the ironist gambit remains one of the most problematic themes of modern literary theory precisely because the self animated by ironic will seems at the same time to move paradoxically toward its own abolition. Under the sanction of ironic consciousness the self-professedly heroic posture of modernist formalism very quickly withers into the self-annihilating gesture of unmasking the poseur in every posture. Thus do we precipitate the cataclysmic break between aesthetics and history that renders the authorial subject an exile from the world of all consequential acts—acts that depend after all upon those consciously posed stances toward the world that inevitably belie the authority of their own being. The vulnerability of those stances was precisely what the authorial subject of ironic epic sought to escape on the wings of absolute irony, only to incur a comparable epistemological liability. A kind of sympathetic magic, ironic form actively severs us from our past that we may not be involuntarily alienated from the self-recognition that otherwise resides so passively within it. But I want to consider that ironic form thereby makes us over again into creatures of another, perhaps more intractable contingency. This is only too devastatingly the contingency of the Hegelian skeptic caught indecisively between freedom and totality, each choice haunted by the tragically unrealized specter of its agonistic other. Ironic form precipitates a crisis of the subject, which ultimately drives the subject into the permanent exile of unhappy consciousness.

What purports to "center" irony and thus seems to endow its epistemological autonomy in literary formalism, is, as I argued in the previous chapter, a faulty conception of the subject. For irony proffers a subject that is denied agency insofar as it ignores, by merely imitating, that demonic operator of contingency itself: temporality. To make irony a center of consciousness, as James seems to propose, is to be compelled to see one's self in two places *at the same time*. Thus, it is precisely the experience of time as temporality that such ironic form demurs. The internal contradiction of this proposition is more starkly apparent when we see that irony, understood as the negation of a prior moment in time, constitutes a structurally morbid nostalgia. Nostalgia allegorizes the difference that time "makes" in the primordial fact of particular consciousness, which is change. Sadly enough, it is precisely the fact of ceaselessly changing consciousness, wherein we are decisively separated from one another, that necessitates the conceptualization of subject as agent in the first place. Agency implies the change of state that irony precipitates. But irony, when it is prevailed upon to become a "centering" device, belies that change by sublimating in turn the specific contingencies of the representational act itself. Thus does it compel identification with the pathetic sadness of time passing rather than with the processes of consciousness that change in the course of such passionate temporality.

Notwithstanding James's will to center ironic consciousness, I propose that aesthetic form and James's aesthetic form in particular, gives us a more historical grasp of our situation than the trope of irony otherwise permits. This is particularly the case if we treat aesthetic determination as the assimilation of contingency to the enterprise of self-reflection, rather than as an unreflective identification with the ironic distance that form opens between self and contingent world. Any notion of form founded upon the transcendentally centering or unifying function of irony separates out the fact of contingency from the phenomenon of formal determination and resurrects a Kantian two worlds system. As we shall see in the final chapter of this work, such is the conceptual impediment against which Lyotardian theory stumbles in its ambition to reconcile aesthetic value with the realms of the historical and, even more ambitiously, the political. The transcendental imperative of the trope of irony thus obscures the true referent of narrative mimesis, which is human action: the determination of act as a corollary of contingent existence instead of as a *self*-aggrandizing antagonist of that contingency.

Not surprisingly, syntax, that most conspicuous stylistic feature of Henry James's fiction, prompts my thesis and for me makes his work an especially rich site for contemplating the shifting distance between aesthetic and existential determinations. James is the practitioner of a style of syntactical elaboration that, by characteristically disjoining subject and predicate, makes the process of predication turn back upon its parts as the fullest contemplation of the whole. James employs a syntactical strategy that obtrudes temporality. It figures the temporal gap upon which reflection depends if it is to become speculatively productive. In James's narrative the semantics of action, which upholds the paradigmatic order of Aristotelian plot, is supplanted by a syntactical mode of action. This syntactical modality stresses the relationality of subject and predicate over the transcendental unity of subject and predicate.[2] In this understanding of Jamesian syntax I believe we overcome the objections to ironic centering as a transcendental enterprise by reconceiving the Jamesian practice of irony as critique. We must see the deployment of irony as a means to critique the diffuse perspectives precipitated out of ironic displacement.

My purpose in reading Jamesian style, then, is to open a field for speculating upon the temporal aspect of aesthetic form without making the concept of time a threshold of a phenomenological purity, as many of James's contemporary critics are tempted to do. The temporality of narrative action in James is not focused on any abstract totalization of experience. The relationship between subject and world, configured in these terms, does not imply an intuitive claim to resolve the temporal aporias attendant upon every argumentation of totality, each so time-consuming in its desperation to consume the time. The claim of aesthetic form is not, in this way, haunted by a Kantian totality whose language it cannot speak except by conceding the indeterminacy of its own linguistic constituents or by subordinating a conscious to an unconscious register of human experience. Rather, it is the eloquence of linguistic determination itself that is at stake in the notion of totality that James' aesthetic practices entail.

Interruption: A Conceptual Schema for Jamesian Style

In order to establish a convincing groundwork for such claims I must proceed to close readings of Jamesian style. But I do so mediately—by way of my own syntactical detour through what I consider to be a compelling theoretical synthesis of the modalities of narrative logic and subjective agency. Only by this detour, through what we now commonly call the philosophy of the subject, will we be able to see how any account of James's fiction as syntactically complex can be made simultaneously instrumental for a critique of subjectivity. Such a critique is immanent to the innovation of aesthetic form I am identifying with syntactical complexity in the Jamesian novel.

For me the key theorists of this philosophical/analytical context are Paul Ricoeur, Anthony Giddens, and Theodor W. Adorno. These three thinkers are united by a common field of speculative inquiry that transcends both the diverse disciplinary provenance of their ideas and the genre distinctions between prose and poetry, novel and history, that have hitherto inhibited literary criticism from the kind of inquiry they undertake. All three implicitly share and develop W. B. Gallie's well-known contention (in *Philosophy and Historical Understanding*) that what relates narrative action to history is the dynamic of determination and contingency, where the goal of analysis is neither solving the aporias of time nor accepting the aporia as a threshold of indeterminacy.[3]

Both Ricoeur, in the tripartite theory of mimesis worked out in *Time and Narrative,* and Giddens, in his already discussed theory of structuration, are critically alert to the formal problem that obtrudes in any effort to theorize the "autonomy" of the artistic creation: the temptation to concede a dualism that can be resolved only by entertaining an effectively spatial reduction of other to self. The discussion of aesthetic form in modernist literary criticism, perhaps because it always proffers a revelation of essence, is ruled unapologetically by this standard of autonomy. But, because such autonomy is equated with self-actualization independent of social contingency, it stoically falsifies its own historical genesis. It reifies the category of self, transcending the very phenomenon of historical determination that makes the self qua self originally articulable.[4] Both Ricoeur and Giddens reconceive the goal of autonomy as antithetical to any reifying authority by revealing the complicity of the "autonomous" self with the sociological contingencies of all temporal experience. For Ricoeur and Giddens the ideal of autonomy is constrained by narrative desire and, hence, remains inexorably temporal. In this spectrum of experience all narratives are narratives of time. But time is never approached as a threshold of phenomenological purity from which subjective agency would necessarily be eclipsed.

The virtue of juxtaposing the work of a preeminent philosopher of narrative aesthetics and the work of a preeminent social theorist with my own analysis of James is strikingly indicated by their mutual recognition of the fundamental reciprocity of structures (forms) and actions (subjects)—binding both to an irreducible and therefore conceptually potent temporality. Furthermore, my strategy of superimposing theorists upon artists (the case of Henry James) implies, by its very troping of the superimpositions of temporal succession, an apt premise for insisting upon the impossibility of segregating aesthetic valuations from the facts of social transformation. After all, the common assumptions of both Ricoeur's narrative aesthetics and Giddens's social theory arise from their even deeper continuity with the Kantian and Hegelian tradition that underwrites the hegemonic claims of literary formalism since the advent of Romantic consciousness. This is a philosophical tradition that acknowledges, at least initially, that formal autonomy, whether it is credited to artistic intuition or social agency, is never a self-sufficient act.

For Kant himself the conflict of duty and desire is not psychological but sociological, appealing to a universal maxim of human conduct. Similarly, Hegel's critique of Kantian duty insists upon the self-actualization of a "collective subject," which is presupposed in any individual self-reflection of reason upon the conditions of its own existence. Within this tradition, as Seyla Benhabib has pointed out in her excellent account of the history of reflection philosophy, *Critique, Norm, Utopia* (1986), the "bond between critique and autonomy, between the self-reflection of reason and the realization of freedom . . . is maintained" (186). Upon this bond hangs the possibility of political action that preserves the agency of the historical individual without reducing the scope of historical action to a solipsistic island of subjective intentionality.

It is precisely the bond between critique and autonomy, then, that undergirds my hypothesis that there might be a crossable bridge between aesthetics and history in the formalities of Jamesian prose. I have already indicated that syntax is the structural armature of this bridge because it makes the mediated status of subjective knowledge the basis of self-reflection rather than making self-reflection the limit of mediated experience. It may be viewed in this sense as a functional corollary to Adorno's positing of the aesthetic quality per se as our only avenue of escape from a dangerously furtive identity logic. Such logic, according to Adorno, would otherwise subvert the initial integrity of the Kantian subject as a socially mediated agent. It would lead to the fatalistic severance of critique from autonomy.

Adorno sees that both the Kantian and Hegelian paradigms of self-reflection, despite their initial predication upon the mediations of an other, arrive in the course of their historical ascendance in Western philosophy at a tautological proposition: they seek the subsumption of the self under the law of the other, or vice versa. Adorno concludes that, despite the initial valorizations of a moment of authentic reflexivity in German idealism, where self meets other on the threshold of material contingency, both Kant's and Hegel's philosophies of the subject concede to regressive tautology by virtue of their increasing dependence upon the idealism of reason: either transcendental or historical reason. Alternatively, Adorno insists that the realm of the aesthetic constitutes the self in an otherness that is not transcended (*sacrificed* is Adorno's term). This is a self that may be thematized only under the methodological exigencies of activity or transformation. The activity entailed by a nonsacrificial otherness always brings the subject back to the temporal threshold of its self-recognition. And this, for Adorno, is the only acceptable idealism of art: "If art were to discard the long demystified illusion of duration and incorporate into itself its mortality out of sympathy with the ephemeral which is life, then it would live up to a concept of truth at the core which is time rather than some enduring abstract essence" (*Aesthetic Theory*, 42).

I have already intimated that the phenomenon of syntactical determination gives us an even more well-marked threshold for this disclosure of Adorno's aesthetic realm because it makes the temporality of succession (the predicate) itself integral to the reflection of the grammatical subject. It thereby preempts the possibility that the subject (the propositional whole) will ever become a simple reflex of the predicate. According to Adorno, such a reflex nature inhibits the transformational possibilities instrumental to speculative growth. Without such possibilities the ideal of autonomy is stillborn in the phenomenon of a reflective will that remains stubbornly narcissistic. The subject's inability to realize its being in otherness is linked by Adorno to a mimetic paradox that parallels the paradoxical predicament of formalist irony discussed earlier: it resorts to a displacement of the temporal as its only representational mastery over temporal experience.

In Adorno's analysis the subject's desire for self-certainty or rational autonomy springs from the glaringly painful apprehension of one's uncertain existence compared with the conspicuous certitudes of organic Nature. The concomitant desire to negate Nature, to gain freedom from contingency, is however undertaken by the idealist subject through a furtive identification with Nature. Adorno points out that this "suppressing of nature for human ends" is revealed to be "a mere natural relationship, which is why the supremacy of nature controlling reason and its principle is a delusion" (*Negative Dialectics*, 179). The subject's identification with Nature is therefore an internalization of the drive to repress Nature. This mentality, intelligible in the terms of Nietzsche's resentful moralist and the Freudian superego, empowers the self only to annul itself, that is, to free itself by divesting itself of its own desire to annul the Natural. This is what we might call, following Benhabib's lead, the "paradox of autonomy,"[5] inspired by mimetic desire. The impetus toward autonomy paradoxically incurs the relative anomie of the subject in the manner of Hegel's stoical consciousness. It portends the impossibility of any mimesis that could sustain the static self-reflection toward which mimesis traditionally aspires. It would preclude the possibility of a self unfissured by the discrepancy between its formal and thematic imperatives: once again it severs autonomy from critique.

The syntactical phenomenon I have identified with James' aesthetic becomes even more compelling as a correlate of desirable speculative growth in view of the foregoing exposition of the mimetic paradox / paradox of autonomy. For the subjective determinations foregrounded in syntactically elaborated periods induce a specular otherness that, complementary to Adorno's insight, is *not* reified or made finite (stripped of agency) in the act of self-apprehension. In syntactically extended periods, as we shall see in our close readings of Jamesian prose, the structural disparity between subject and predicate—intrinsic to the temporal vitality of syntactical determination—induces a degree of self-forgetfulness as its condition of intelligibility.

This phenomenon has a historical precedent in the controversy surrounding the Senecan or anti-Ciceronian prose styles of the seventeenth century, specifically in the stylistic performances of Sir Thomas Browne and Robert Burton. Modern critics seeking a thematic schema for rationalizing the anacoluthic density of Senecan prose, with its apparent eschewal of secure grounds for predicative intentionality, frequently resorted to the explanation of psychopathology. But, as Morris Croll has famously observed, the predicative intentions of this syntax are best understood in terms of psychological effects that are proliferated through them. Thus, such syntax precludes any free thematizing that might divorce itself from the processual aspect of psychological states (79–128). This processual aspect displaces the thematizing stance that would seek to identify it.

The syntactical effects perceived to be scandalous in Senecan prose constitute precisely the threshold of formal difficulty lamented by the more thematically minded readers of Jamesian prose. For such readers these are works in which the reading subject programmatically loses his or her place in the act of reading. Yet it is precisely the discipline of refinding one's place that makes such texts vehicles for a self-reflection that is not merely a narcissistic reflex of the situation that inspires it. For Adorno the aesthetic quality of the work of art animates just this experience of self-forgetfulness to guarantee a more vital reflexivity than could be actualized in any mimetic gesture—e.g., memory. The status of the aesthetic in relation to time is self-transformative on the models of allegory and cipher, both of which also signify through an obtrusive temporal gap.

As we have already noted, allegory and cipher are forms that for both Adorno and Walter Benjamin exemplify the temporality that is so essential to my founding assumption: that James raises the question of formal autonomy through an implicit critique of irony.[6] Like allegory and cipher, the critique of irony reinstates rather than removes a temporal gap as a condition of intelligibility. Since I am identifying syntactical complexity as the stylistic hallmark of Jamesian prose, it will come as no surprise if I link this syntactical register of the text with the minimal condition for the critique of irony itself. Thus, the critique of irony is causally implicated in the status of the aesthetic object. Aptly for Adorno, the status of the aesthetic object is in turn most fully realized in the antimimetic effect of what he calls "tour de force" (*Aesthetic Theory*, 155–57).

In tour de force Adorno stipulates that the meaning of a legitimate artwork will remain "illusory" as distinct from expressive. He is invoking the Hegelian nuance of *schein* (*erscheinung*) in order to designate an illusion (in emphatic contrast to *de*lusion), which is itself conditioned by a "working through" of essence, where revelation of essence is mediated by transformative action. Hegel is Adorno's source for this, despite the apparent invidious contrast he makes with Hegel's own "expressive" bias. In his *Science of Logic* (1812) Hegel stipulates that "illusory being is essence itself in determinateness of being" (398). Because the essence of an illusory form is rendered opaque, the form draws our attention to the conditionality of expression (temporal gap) rather than to the expression itself. Form thus sets off the terms of its own self-relation in such a way that any atemporal, mimetic identification between the form of aesthetic expression and the object world is precluded. Despite the fact that essence is not representable, however, Adorno's view does not push us, as his critics often claim, to that precipice of indeterminacy from which the self-professed aesthete is obliged to leap into political-historical oblivion.[7] Rather, the emphasis on the mediation of essence confines analysis to the process of change itself.

James's syntactical style in *What Maisie Knew* specifically traces the pattern of thought I have outlined here in my attempt to link what might otherwise be commonly perceived as deeply incommensurable fields of reference: the philosophical and the literary. Conspicuously enough, the form of this brief novel is complemented by a thematization of the mimetic paradox dramatized in its plot. Schematically, at least, the prose "narrative" of *Maisie* entails the struggle of a subjective mind to reconcile itself determinately with a specular other: Maisie with her father, with her mother, with Mrs. Beale, with Mrs. Wix, and, finally, with Sir Claude. The thematics of mimesis, upon which the possibility of the aesthetic unity of the work seems to depend, founders upon a syntactical overdetermination: the telltale preponderance of long syntactical periods, multiple pronoun references, proliferating subordinate constructions, and the like. The thematic corollary of this subversion of thematic lucidity is the problematic triangulation of Maisie's desire within the dyadic framework of each of the aforementioned specular relations.

In other words the duality of the theme of mimetic autonomy (pitting self against Nature) is challenged in James's aesthetic practice by what I would characterize as a triadic order of syntactical mediations in the prose. Syntax mimes the "love triangles" that consequently proliferate rather than rationalistically reduce the relational imperatives of meaning. Thus, meaning seems to devolve to the indeterminacy of purely contingent time: precisely the mode of temporality that would seem to belie that possibility of mimesis conceived as autonomy in the first place. Such opacity of meaning is nonetheless perversely suited to the specific cognitive experience of reading a text like *What Maisie Knew,* which so powerfully conjures the dream of mimesis/autonomy in its plot and theme. For the possibility of thematic reading itself is ultimately put into question by a temporal disjunction (determination vs. contingency) that is integral both to the theoretical model of mimetic autonomy (mimetic paradox) and to any aesthetic form that aspires to autonomy under the sign of syntactical complexity.

Oddly enough, it is because *Maisie* imposes a protocol of reading that brings the reader's attempted resolution of the form-theme opposition to a threshold of inexhaustible activity through syntactical complication that it exemplifies so well Adorno's ideal of tour de force. For it thereby perpetuates the "illusory" status of its own artifice without valorizing that illusion. Tour de force, so constrained as it is in this context by activity, is thus expressible exclusively in the determinative particulars of change as opposed to any abstract indeterminacy, which would, if we accept the inevitability of the mimetic paradox, fall prey to similar temporal vicissitudes in its bid for autonomy.

As we might have expected, the thematics of mimetic paradox cannot be represented thematically in *What Maisie Knew* because its syntactical form deconstructs the theme of mimetic autonomy. It is a theme that, in its own right and as we have already seen, resigns us to an irreducibility of form and theme. But with quite an unexpected irony, and for the reasons just given, I believe that this work does proffer a mimesis that escapes the mimetic paradox, at least if we are prepared to continue an Adornian line of thought.

Adorno himself refurbished the concept of mimesis in his *Aesthetic Theory* by invoking an invidious comparison with mimicry: Adorno's positive understanding of mimesis acknowledges that its object is an imitation and is thereby complicit in the contingencies that it displays. Just so, the self-deconstruction of the thematic subject in *Maisie*, which takes the mimetic paradox as its theme, mimes its own inevitability here.

We cannot, however, ignore the fact that Adorno's emphasis on contingency once again raises the specter of indeterminacy, which the concepts of mimesis and tour de force were both meant to banish from the field of aesthetic practice. Still, the threat of indeterminacy that lurks within the bracketing operation of Adorno's mimesis is put into an ameliorative perspective when contrasted with an earlier posing of the same problem by Husserlian phenomenology: phenomenology, acknowledging that theme is conditioned by an unthematizable essence, or *intentum*, of consciousness, tempts us to conclude that our methodological commitment to deciphering the unthematized is de facto a commitment to undecidability. We would thus court the regress of indeterminacy by putting our project beyond the bounds of predicative lucidity, voiding absolutely the material agency of the subject.

On the contrary, however, because the paradigm of syntax would constrain my analysis of the Adornian mimesis exemplified by James within the laws of predication, we might proceed along an alternate speculative path. If, in our pursuit of a thematization of Adorno's mimesis, we seem to commit ourselves to the unthematizable, the *purely* contingent, I would suggest that there is nevertheless scope in Adorno's thinking for a more productive construal of contingency as analogous to the way in which consciousness is "committed" (in the energetics of Freudian/Lacanian ego theory) to the unconscious: syntactically, via the activity that subsumes them both. Again, I have invoked the concept of "syntactical relation" here to designate just that reciprocity of determinations that attends upon action as long as the concept of act is *not* made mutually exclusive of the concept of structure. Such is the case, especially in the Lacanian schematization of the unconscious, which, as we will see shortly, is applicable here because it is articulated through its *relationality* with the conscious mind. It thus preempts any essentializing of act or structure. Specifically in Lacan, Freud's somatically mediated, reductive dualisms of life/death, love/hate, are supplanted by the linguistically mediated, proliferative, triadic order of the "symbolic," "the imaginary," "the real."

As I have already indicated, however, the tripartite mimesis elaborated by Paul Ricoeur in the first volume of *Time and Narrative* (1984–88) provides our most compelling context for moving the discussion of the syntactical determinability of Adorno's mimesis (the locus of aesthetic quality) toward a new practice of literary formalism. For Ricoeur's task of reconciling time and narrative closely parallels the task implicit in understanding syntactical determination as a counter for the aesthetic quality in James's text: syntax carries the burden of reconciling the phenomena of determination and contingency. Such a reconciliation is immanent to all conscientious temporal experience because it has its complementary schematization in the opposition of act and structure. Ricoeur asserts that the "poetics of narrativity [structure] responds and corresponds to the aporetics of temporality [immanent in act]" (*Time and Narrative*, 1:84). In this thesis I believe we have the essence of that order of syntactical determination that surpasses irony as a generative paradigm for narrative in James. It both represents time and incorporates the time of representation into the representational act.

Ricoeur helps me to press the point home with an elucidation of the concept of narrative mimesis wherein the poles of action and structure are emphatically commensurable rather than mutually exclusive.[8] He begins by contrasting two classical paradigms that ordain a mutually exclusive ordering of time and narrative structure: Augustine's *Confessions* and Aristotle's *Poetics*. Book 11 of the *Confessions* gives us an experience of time without a structural unity: it is a *distentio animi*. Aristotle's *Poetics* gives us a structural unity of experience (a possibility of aesthetic unity) purged of its temporal exigencies. In Ricoeur's account Augustine's notion of *distentio animi* comes to terms with that experience of time that is bound by the contradiction of a consciousness always attending upon the passage of time in order to account for its passage through time, thereby sacrificing the totalizing power of its conceptualization. The relation of past, present, and future can only be explained, as Augustine stipulates, by accepting that the referent is in the mind, not in the "world" of temporal experience. In the mind these times are commensurable with one another only in terms of change (action / change of state), not structure: the mind's experience of time is therefore definitively aporetic in its structural exigencies. Temporality cannot be totalized within the compass of its own passing away.

For Aristotle, by contrast, it is the coherence of moments of time passing (beginning, middle, end) that ordains human actions such that they are intelligible preeminently in their totality. Aristotle's ideal plot is a totality that memorializes rather than actualizes the moment of change or reversal (peripeteia). Catharsis literally remembers or recalls the moment of reversal as immanent to the inciting moment of dramatic action. The act of memory unifies. Thus, it is unlike the Augustinian act, a moment out of time, a moment that Augustine would characterize as *intentio,* that eschews *distentio.* For Aristotle the aporia of Augustinian time is supplanted by that invidious dualism of formalist aesthetics that privileges the work's time over the world's time. Here is the inception of the aesthetic formalism that we have already seen to be suspect because it breaks the bond between autonomy and critique by severing act from structure.

Nevertheless, because Ricoeur describes *distentio* as "nothing other than the *shift* in the *non-coincidence* of the three modalities of action" (*Time and Narrative,* 1:20; emphasis added)—past, present, future—it is no surprise that his speculation about how narrative emplotment might transcend the antinomy of the Augustinian and Aristotelian paradigms (one is discordant, one is concordant) solicits the terms of Adorno's negative dialectic. Adorno's "nonidentity" is the epistemological complement of Ricoeur's "non-coincidence." Ricoeur's schematic triad of mimesis 1, 2, 3, entails figuration, configuration, and refiguration as component elements of a temporal unity that does not totalize but nonetheless preserves the structural imperative of "making" so emphatic in Aristotelian *mimesis-praxeos.*[9] Beginning with the idea that all thought is already "figured" or presignified in the cultural practices that annunciate it, Ricoeur holds with the impossibility of a signification that could encompass its own conditions of possibility within an unbroken temporality. That is to say, Ricoeur insists upon the impossibility of a pure phenomenology of time. With this cautionary he means to discredit "an intuitive apprehension of the structure of time which not only can be isolated from those procedures of argumentation by which phenomenology undertakes to resolve the aporias received from an earlier tradition, but which would not pay for its discovery with new aporias, bearing a higher price" (1:83).

By contrast, tripartite mimesis articulates temporality through its scrupulous reckoning with aporia. For the place of aporetics is preeminently the place of the text. Narrative understanding is structured insofar as the configurative agency (mimesis 2), by which the reader recognizes her own figurative complicity in the text of language (mimesis 1), already bears within it the obligation to a future moment that solicits her self-understanding of the text as an explanation per se, as a threshold of sociality. Such a structure of expectation must be assimilable to the subsequent refiguration (mimesis 3) of a reading audience. This is inevitable for Ricoeur since he wants to stipulate: "it is the time of action [itself] that is refigured in the configurational act" (*Time and Narrative*, 1:83).

In other words, what the Augustinian paradigm lacked in structural terms and the Aristotelian paradigm lacked in existential terms the Ricoeurian paradigm makes up for by subsuming both to a field of activity: structure and time mark the interdependent coordinates of a prevailing structural activity. Ricoeur's point, as already noted, is that narrative poetics both "*responds* and corresponds to . . . aporetics" (*Time and Narrative*, 1:84; my emphasis). Rather than either solving the aporia of Augustinian time or tragically identifying with it, poetics engages the Augustinian dilemma dialectically as an enabling ground of self-generation or Aristotelian *sustasis*. Ricoeur emphasizes that *sustasis* or *sunthesis* designates the organizing of events into a system, not the system itself (1:48).

So, despite the fact that Ricoeur's tripartite mimesis purports to bridge aporetics and poetics, it nevertheless, like Adorno's aesthetic quality, resists inadvertently producing an identitarian synthesis *in the process*. Ricoeur conceives mimesis as act without conceding the meaning of action to an idealized and preemptive telos. Such a conception would plausibly offer the threshold for the revisionary formalism we are seeking: one that would not succumb to functionalist or idealist totalizations. Such a conception of mimesis would thereby be exempt from the antiformalist critique of aesthetics that results either in the hegemony of idealized history or in an ahistorical irony.

In turn, Anthony Giddens shows us even more starkly that the impetus toward a negative dialectic (the critics of the Frankfurt School notwithstanding) need not result in an effete aesthetics bound to disguise its nihilism beneath the tragically ennobling mask of indeterminacy. The principle of "nonsacrificial" otherness[10] in Adorno's aesthetics has a complementary precept in Giddens's paradigm of "structuration," despite the fact that Giddens's work has neither an explicit application to aesthetic phenomena nor to the category of the literary. As we saw in chapter 3, Giddens defines structuration in terms that constrain us to think of structure as a relation to action. His stipulation that "structure is . . . the mode in which the relation between moment and totality expresses itself in social reproduction" (*Central Problems,* 71) indicates that the structurational register of social analysis conforms to the temporal register of experience, which both Adorno and Ricoeur maintain is pivotal for aesthetic valuation. In both cases, social totality and the totality of the aesthetic work, we are impelled toward the recognition of a contingent (aporetic) moment that relates part and whole without conflating them symbolically or analogically. This irreducibly temporal contingency reciprocally determines what it is related to. Indeed, Giddens likens the social whole—heuristically represented in every contingent moment—to the conspicuously absent set of syntactical rules that authorizes any instance of grammatical lucidity as an expression of the totality of the language system. The operative moment of individual agency constituted in the rules and resources available to social actors within the scope of social interactions is itself significantly reconstituted in the course of those interactions (71). Such is the basis of Giddens's insistence that structure be absolutely distinguished from the stasis of reified form and that form, inscribed in any rule-governed activity, is inherently transformational (*Constitution of Society,* 64).

Extending this line of thought, Giddens appropriates Erving Goffman's term *copresence,* from *Frame Analysis,* to describe that condition of overdetermination implicit in structuration that nonetheless does not sacrifice its determinative vitality. This is the case so long as the recursive reflex, which binds each moment of instantiated agency to another, transforms it as well into another determinate moment. Specifically, copresence designates that orientation toward others upon which the self is predicated: where all significant contexts of action are deemed to entail a transition from one spatiotemporal state to another. This is the way in which the principle of *co-presence* reveals an affinity with the "nonsacrificial" otherness of Adorno's aesthetic value.

Even more aptly for my purposes, it mirrors a stance from German Romanticism concerned with grounding aesthetic value in some formulation of part-whole relations that might accommodate the temporal exigencies that stretch isolate perceptions beyond the moment of their instantiation or enactment. The term copresence figures prominently in Lacou-Labarthe and Nancy's *The Literary Absolute* (1978), an appreciation of Friedrich Schlegel's ideal of fragmentary writing. Here the assumption is that fragments and the fragmented rhetoric of Schlegel's *Atheneum* pieces implicate the totality of the experience denoted in them not as a mere notation but also as a veritable syntax of transformations that respond to the inherent temporal elasticity of perception. Lacou-Labarthe and Nancy indicate the motive for Schlegel's philosophy of the fragment, insofar as it connects the concept of totality with the transformational imperative of action, as follows:

> That the totality should be present as such in each part and that the whole should be not the sum but the co-presence of the parts as the co-presence, ultimately, of the whole with itself (because the whole is also the detachment and closure of the part) is the essential necessity [*nécessité d'essence*] that devolves from the individuality of the fragment: the detached whole is the individual and "for every individual, there are an infinite number of real definitions." (*Literary Absolute,* 44)[11]

Because the conception of the whole is presented here not as "the sum of its parts" but as a principle of relatedness immanent to the parts, it can only be made intelligible through the relational process itself. This indicates the usefulness of *copresence* as a term to help us close the gap between aesthetics and action. For it gives renewed emphasis to the register of particularity in human experience, which has been so consistently at stake in the course of my argument to this point. In this respect Schlegel's use of the term *co-presence* recalls A. G. Baumgarten's characterization of the aesthetic as a proliferation of particular extensive qualities. Both Schlegel's and Baumgarten's accounts of the relation of part and whole have recourse to what we might call a synecdochal process whereby the revelation of aesthetic "unity" in the part entails a proliferation of parts, of new qualities determined recursively through their reflection of their own contingency. Significantly, the *newness* of such qualities is a function of the determinative vitality that they sustain as particularity.

Accordingly, the syntactical style of Henry James, which I have described as problematizing the thematic unity (holism) of his works, gives us the warrant for a literary aesthetic that deliberately challenges the ground of thematic abstraction: it mandates a reconception of the constitutive agency of the subject, which theme purveys as the agency of a changing particularity. The particularity of experience is above all else what the concept of agency denotes. This protocol of aesthetic formalism compels us to treat the form as interdependent with the formative agent, i.e., as a mode of *co-presence*. We must now, however, distinguish this copresence from its Romantic precursor, which, like Baumgarten's "theme," postulates a veritable Kantian premise of unity in difference, elevating the phenomenon of transformation ("changing particularity") to the status of a transcendental signified (the "closure of the part"). To the contrary, I want to show how Jamesian syntax expressly maintains the potency of the transformational principle as a signifier. Unity does not transcend difference. Difference articulates unity: the transformative principle remains an activity, not a punctual product of labor/work. Aesthetic "unity" here is more active than contemplative. It is an *energia*, not an *ergon*. Yet it is an *energia* with an expressive trajectory.

Another way of formulating my position is to think of an analogy between Jamesian syntax and the trope of metaphor where we understand metaphor to be a distinctly symbolic, rather than a schematic mode of representation. This is a distinction elaborated to great effect in Paul de Man's account of Kantian hypotyposes.[12] Schemata do not mediate what they represent, de Man explains. Symbols function metaphorically when they assimilate the concept they denote to the representational matrix that thereby confers their denotative value. Thus, in the symbolic matrices of metaphor there is an implicit transformation of denotative content on the principle of analogy. This follows the pattern of the Kantian sublime, which prevails upon an analogy between imagination and reason instantiated as the mind's failure to unite apprehension and comprehension. Metaphor and the sublime both issue in an unreserved particularizing of experience conditioned by the gap between represented and representing consciousness. As we shall see, this gap may be productively construed in accordance with much of the foregoing analysis as an effective *transition* rather than a temporal *aporia*.

But now we must connect this transformative principle specifically with James's own formidable transformation of the novel, in which syntactical determination foregrounds the symbolic function of narrative desire as distinct from the schematic purport of thematism: for such thematism always alludes (albeit inadequately) to a transparent relation between particulars and universals. In the distinction between symbolic and schematic representations we should be reminded of Herder's important challenge (in *On the Origin of Language* [1772]) to more naive expressivist theories of language current at the end of the eighteenth century. We will recall Charles Taylor's claim that against the expressivist model, Herder demonstrated speaking to be not only the expression of a reflective capacity but also its fullest realization.[13] This is very much the epistemological path to which we are led by James: the encroaching syntactical imperative of his narrative may be said to reformulate the conditions of thematic intelligibility that inform reading competence. Certainly, Herder's claims about the origin of language show a strong affinity with the system of language ordered by James under the sign of syntactical determination. What is at stake for James's reader is the possibility of reflecting upon the text without reifying the self-image of readerly competence through which the text is made available. James proposes a rethinking of the relation of the reader to the text that precludes the tautological reflection of intentional agency promulgated by those mimetic theories of language against which Herder reacted. Thinkers like Condillac ("Essai sur l'origine des conaissances humanes"), for example, who sought the origin of language within an individual intuition, in effect presupposed what they were looking for by positing a mirror relation between expressive agency and the identity it expressed.

Herder's point about that constitutive function of language, which defers to the intersubjective space of speculative reason, is particularly resonant within the context of recent theoretical speculation about narrative logic. Such speculation, conducted under the influence of Ricoeur and W. B. Gallie, insists upon distinguishing narration from logical deduction. We have seen that for Ricoeur, particularly, the distinction is made on the premise that narrative is a configurational act conditioned by an Augustinian temporality. In this view narrative events are intelligible not insofar as they are deducible from a prior unity, whose totality they reflect (on the model of scientific truth), but insofar as they can be "made acceptable" to the contemplative mind, which always implicates what it contemplates in its own temporal contingency. Ricoeur makes this point with particular sharpness by comparing narrative totality to a Kantian reflective judgment in which the unifying rule is a constitutive function of the mental attention animated within its purview. Once again we are approaching the notion of unity or totality through a recursive principle activated in the recognition of contingency: contingency itself is, in effect, the animus of recursive mind. Or we could say that it is contingency rather than any a priori principle of reason, which drives narrative development. For contingency compels a revision of the standard of intelligibility whose horizon it otherwise threatens to blur.

I have anticipated that in this context the relation of reader to text can be seen as recapitulating the psychoanalytical genesis of the ego or subject. Especially in Lacan's exposition of "the symbolic," syntax eclipses semantics as the determinative agency of the unconscious,[14] since the

subject is always incommensurable with the Other that reflects its presence: "Speech is moving towards nothing less than a transformation of
the subject to whom it is addressed by means of a link that it establishes
with the one who emits it" ("Agency of the Letter," in *Ecrits*, 114-17).
Lacan characterizes the specifically syntactical terms of the relation between self and other here with the designation "unconscious." For Lacan's
unconscious "is not a type defining within psychic unity the circle of that
which does not possess the attribute of consciousness" (*Ecrits*, 82). Rather,
like symbol, the unconscious manifests the *belonging* (through repression)
of the signified to a specific system of signifiers.

James's text works to foreground precisely this modality of the unconscious in its dramatization of the mimetic paradox. We have already seen
how the mimetic paradox anticipates the Lacanian unconscious, where it
precludes a belief in any prereflective unity of the subject that could be
captured through reflection. This impossibility is explicit in the self-
repression that epitomizes the most elemental form of the mimetic paradox. The mind that is compelled to find itself elsewhere, like that of
James's protagonist Maisie, is propelled into a centrifugal momentum
toward the object world.

In Lacan, of course, this subject is not vitiated by the impossibility
of its own self-reflection, because self-reflection appears within the dynamic of what Lacan calls the *"objet petit a."* This is a phenomenon of
identification that binds the subject to its own self-lack according to the
performative, not constative, terms of this lack. As Lacan says: "The objet
petit a is something from which the subject has separated itself in the form
of an organ, the phallus. It functions as the symbol of a lack, that is to
say the phallus, not as such, but insofar as it is lacking" (*Four Fundamental
Concepts*, 193). The subject sees the threat of total self-annihilation loom-
ing in the acceptance of castration, in the lack of the phallus, and thereby
acknowledges the impossibility of finding itself in the symbolic order.
To foreclose that threat the subject sacrifices a part of itself—that part
that is objectified in the object that reflects it, but only incompletely. For
the object cannot reflect the otherness upon which such subjectivity is
predicated except by excluding the subject, which is presupposed in its
own objectality.

The *objet petit a* is a roughly Fichtean concession to the structural
incompleteness of self-reflection (occluding what conditions the particular
otherness of the Other), thus relating the self syntactically to what *ex-ists*
beyond its own self-reflection in every reflective act. In other words the

reflective act, subsisting as it does upon a partial reflection (its *co-presence*), binds itself metonymically to its ex-centric conditions of possibility and thus predisposes itself to that syntactical exposition of its meaning, which gives us a useful analogue for the Lacanian symbolic. In sum, the self is irreducibly active so long as the positing of any self-reflection entails an elaboration of its own predicative grounds.

Resumption: Interruption Is Transition

Now I would like to suggest that it is just such complexity in Jamesian syntax that renders *What Maisie Knew* an especially lucid account of its heroine's inescapable, because intersubjective, situation. The poet John Ashbery is one of the few readers who has come to terms with the transitional/predicative métier of Jamesian style on the threshold of its syntactical complexity. In the next chapter I will follow out Ashbery's elaboration of this formal project in his own *Three Poems* (1978). But for the moment it is significant to observe that his comment on James is itself mediated through the syntax of another American novelist whose prose might be said to verge on a syntactical sublime for which indirection remains the trajectory of thought. Ashbery invokes "Jamesian style" as a codex for reading Gertrude Stein's *Stanzas in Meditation*.[15] In a review of that work entitled "The Impossible" Ashbery acknowledges the risks of unintelligibility taken in such enterprises. He characterizes both James and Stein as practitioners of a style that enacts "the endless process of elaboration which . . . seems to obey some rhythmic impulse at the heart of all happening" (252). In this way I believe Ashbery alludes to the elaboration of predicative grounds, which I have just equated with the recursive principle operating narrative subjectivity. The elaborative syntactical reflex of Jamesian prose (like all parenthetical discourses) is bound by a formal contradiction. Elaboration, in its supplementary capacity, denotes the incompleteness of the thought it expresses and thus makes the recognition of the insuperable limits to self-control a conspicuous aspect of the problem of self-representation. Yet elaboration, which is perforce interruption, simultaneously denotes the prospect of completeness, the adumbration of a self so modified by the supplementary gesture that it can, through its identification with the infinite, begin to believe in the possibility of absolute self-control. So, the notion of interruption exposes the internal dynamism of elaboration.

James's exquisitely *unformed* protagonist in *What Maisie Knew* oscillates between these two possibilities of self-expression. James himself seems presciently to confirm Ashbery's judgment of the relevance of this dynamic to the art of the novel in general. In identifying the flaw in the fiction of his contemporary, Anthony Trollope, as an excess of self-control, he links self-control to an ideal of completeness that is ultimately self-transformative.[16] Trollope, according to James, lamentably makes no effort to disguise the manipulative hand of the artist in the work. In other words James sees Trollope as too active a presence in his fiction. But James is not, as we might suspect, indicting the obtrusive artifice of Trollope's omniscient voice. Rather, James objects that in Trollope's case the authorial identification with artifice confers an identity upon the artist that would purport to be independent of the ideologically binding artifices of everyday life. This argument actually disputes the duality of art and life upon which James stalwartly grounds his own fiction in the prefaces to the New York edition, as if only art, not life, were conditioned by an ideal of totality. On the contrary, in James's critique of Trollope the concept of totality is the bridge, not the chasm, between art and life.

It is on this basis I believe that we are encouraged to see a family resemblance between Maisie and the Jamesian artist, at least insofar as the artist is the self-confirmed antithesis of Trollope's self-assured narrative persona. It would appear that both character and author exist within the purview of Adorno's rationalistic "illusion." This is in lieu of any self-understanding that would purport to escape contingency into the *de*lusion of absolute self-control. Adorno's suspicions of "vulgar aesthetics" (*Aesthetic Theory,* 157), which disguises illusion as natural, prompts the thought that illusion implicitly abandons the possibility of expression, which is its self-proclaimed and self-proclaiming goal. Thus, self-control, when it purports to be expressive, supplies an inadequate premise of self-understanding, if only because the absolute, or total, self is exactly what is presupposed in the quest for it.

We might then aptly characterize the more honest alternative premise of self-knowledge as "interruptive" or "parenthetical," precisely insofar as the syntactical coordinates of interruption take their meaning from the subject as activity. Herein self and not-self are conditioned by each other's predicative determinations. I am echoing my original claim that the best formal exemplification of the exigencies of human subjectivity demands a formal complication: the most potent complexity of form entails an apparent disjuncture of meaning, in which the project of self-knowledge exceeds the tropes of self-control. In such cases this excess constitutes a transition between different discursive registers. This, of course, is the conceptual efficacy of trope itself, to make a transition.

In *Maisie* James dramatizes the growth of the self in terms that mimic the dialectic of self-control without fixing the criteria of selfhood within either the subject or the object. *Transition* is the ground term of growth. Transition is inherently a slide from resemblance to contingency, from metaphor to metonymy. This slide is inevitable insofar as metaphor and metonymy are both intelligible only in terms of a resemblance between them, which makes them reciprocal for each other. Every metaphor, by virtue of its placement on a syntactical grid, has a metonymic register. This is another way of saying that form is always substantially transformative.

Following this logic of transformation, Maisie's development as a character (which James encompasses in a deceptively organicist simile as "the growth of the 'great oak' from the little acorn" [5]) evokes the mimetic principle of Aristotelian identity, only to reveal its incommensurability with the plotted action of this novel. In this case the acorn falls quite far from the tree. For Maisie's reflective capacity, the motor of her character, actually thwarts the organicist proposition. What she sees and what she knows are progressively divorced from each other over the course of the narrative action. Divorce, after all, is the incitement of action in this novel. Marriage, by contrast, is the most suitable trope for Maisie's struggle to unite apprehension (seeing) and comprehension (knowing). And in Maisie's capacity as the mediator of her parents' differences (through all their marriages and divorces) we are invited to see how the play of opposites might yield to a transformational exigency of expression rather than a simple contradiction. Such expressivity warrants a strong comparison with that threshold of expressive identity implicit in Herder's notion of language acquisition and Fichte's notion of the self, whereby the medium is both the agency and the outcome of its articulations.

In any case we see here that Maisie is the transitional figure or the figuration of that transitional imperative, which is needed to carry any inequality beyond the impasse of contradiction. Maisie serves as a counter for the resentful wills of her divorced parents simply by moving between them. In the preface James anticipates her function as "rebounding from racquet to racquet like a tennis ball or shuttlecock" (50), as if her alternative moments of self-knowledge and alienation are explicable in terms of a frivolous play of differences.

But the plot invention that James himself takes to be the key to

Maisie's technical efficacy as a character, thus animating her character with an agency all her own, is not the divorce of Maisie's parents. Rather, it is the remarriage of each to another and hence the impossibility that Maisie can realize, in her capacity as "shuttlecock," a reflective consciousness that attains fulfillment in a virtually static reciprocity of differences. What is proposed here is the supplanting of a two-term relation, whereby a simple mediation of differences obtains, with a three-term (hence a more dialectically open-ended) mediation, whereby differences proliferate in a determinate way. In fact, when James recounts the genesis of this plot invention (the device of remarriage), he juxtaposes it with his pointed characterization of Maisie as simultaneously an agent of change and an index of change, i.e., the shuttlecock. Judging from his preface, the agency James postulated here is explicitly linked in his own mind with the exfoliation of "a full ironic truth" (6). If we follow the logic of Jamesian plot, ordained under the aegis of an ironic center, it should bear thematizing only as long as the theme of the fiction demurs from any overtly reductive closure.

It should already be clear that what I am interested in here is the collocation of "irony," "theme," and "agency" in James's preface to *Maisie.* I have been trying to fasten these concepts to the syntactical armature of human action and to discern the potential for aesthetic valuation therein. As I see it, James seems to assume that such linkage entails the paradoxical knowledge that agent, theme, and irony are homologous with the parts of the syntactical period (subject-agent, verb-theme). Such parts possess integrative meaning only insofar as they are linked to another predicate, through changing contextual imperatives (the matrix of irony). Similarly, we have seen how the initial paradox of making *Maisie* an ironic center is now resolvable only if the contradiction originally propounded in it could be shown to go beyond negation, thus adumbrating a novel mode of subjectivity. What I am proposing now is that James's syntactical practice offers the most secure grounding for the reflection of that subjectivity.

Specifically, Maisie's own growth as a character is catalyzed by the contradiction between her alternatively subjective and subjected wills. She is alternately knowing of and known by (objectified by) her parents. But this alternation is not treated so much as a logical contradiction as it is a lever of plot transformation whereby each instantiation of the opposition subject-subjected eschews the "logical" reduction of one to the other by making the postulate of the opposition itself disclose its own ever more recessed and ever more propulsive determinations. This thematic motion explicitly mimes the syntactical elaboration of Jamesian style. Because such syntactical elaboration might be glossed thematically as the postulate of a nonintentional agency, it fits our description of Maisie only too well. The hypothesis of a nonintentional agent is precisely the "cause" we are led to postulate, where the meanings of the sentences of this fiction are more and more apparently a function of their sufficient elaboration rather than their predicative necessity.

Here is the general pattern of syntactical elaboration: a main propositional clause is extended and attenuated in a succession of typically anaphoric qualifying phrases to the point of reversing the predicative polarity of the sentence; what seemed the subject is transmuted to an object. Here, for example, Maisie's mother, Mrs. Farange, contemplates a flaw in her daughter's character: "It was of a horrid little critical system, a tendency, in her [the daughter's] silence, to judge her elders, that this lady [the mother] suspected her, liking as she did, for her own part, a child to be simple and confiding" (27). In this case what begins as Maisie's irksome quality is transmuted from the potent volition of the child to the arresting judgment of the mother, in a way that confuses reflexive movement with transformation. Despite the apparent self-subversion of this syntactical gesture, I must point out that James evokes a deeply moralistic precedent for the appearance he gives of surpassing intentional logic without vitiating subjective agency in the process. I am thinking of Aristotle's insistence that *phronesis* takes priority over logic. As opposed to *episteme* (knowledge in the abstract), *phronesis* is a "doing" whose meaning does not escape the terms of its transitivity. It is this doing to which knowledge is rigorously subordinated in the moral structure of Aristotelian tragic drama.

Nevertheless, before we can fully appreciate the problematic this kind of knowledge fosters in James's texts, we must acknowledge that the telos of change implicit in such knowledge is superficially at odds with the most familiar conceptual topoi of Jamesian style. So, before we consider the consequences of granting my reading of Jamesian syntax as "interruptive," we must note all of the continuity-bearing signature features of Jamesian form: (1) the binary poles of phenomenological consciousness thrown into relief by the devices of the "ficelle"; (2) the "center of consciousness"; (3) the totalizing imperative of formal complexity-completeness as contrasted with the diffuseness of "real life"; (4) the "centering" effect of irony. Finally, there is the epitomizing of all of these gestures at totality in that most venerable crux of narrative plot, the recognition scene, which James deploys to punctual effect and which stands for the pinnacle of his artistic success in his most exemplary "masterpieces," *The Ambassadors* (1903) and *The Golden Bowl* (1905).

If we now ask why does James's own syntactical style seems to frustrate the goal of thematic unity announced so clearly in each of these "epitomes" of aesthetic form, we might answer by pointing out James's implicit agreement with another Aristotelian postulate (at least as Ricoeur interprets Aristotle) that hints at erasing the boundaries between form and theme: the aim of literature is to convert ethics into poetics. For Aristotle ethics is teleological, on the model of fateful character. Virtue guides action. Poetics, by contrast, coordinates aspects in multiple-relational terms: "It serves as a counterpoint to ethics" (Ricoeur, *Time and Narrative*, 1:46). Teleology is thus deconstructed in the temporalizing of its own logical trajectory. I will show that it is this aim that ultimately puts James's syntax into some harmonious accord with a thematic trajectory of literary meaning, albeit one that does not permit any thematic gloss that is not itself part of this activity of *putting things into accord*. As Ricoeur forcefully reminds us, the connection between ethics and poetics "remains dependent upon contingencies" (1:241). For Aristotle the ethos of theme is inaccessible to the reading subject until it is palpably formed into an urgent contingency of subjective experience. In other words poetics is the fulfillment of an ethical imperative when it puts rational universality within the reach of temporal particulars. This, by definition, can only be achieved through an ethos that is trans-formative, that achieves its formal self-expression through a transitive/transitional modality of self-reflection.

And, of course, the central issue in *What Maisie Knew* does formulate itself as the baldest of ethical questions: Are people good or bad? But James poses this question in terms that are strikingly antithetical to the human Nature that originally staked its identity in such a question. Maisie must choose in this fiction between right and wrong in such a way that the choice represses the desire that prompted the question. It is, after all, the desire for a purity of experience, which her own existence powerfully belies. She seeks a good that is mitigated by the bad only in the oppositional logic that keeps good and bad apart. Here, as in the paradox of autonomy, every effort to secure ethical warrants through an identitarian logic is qualified by the necessity of appreciating how the scope of identity must encompass that which is not (as in the Lacanian paradigm of the unconscious). This is most devastatingly the position Maisie is in at the end of the novel, when she must choose parsimoniously between something and nothing: life with the Count and Mrs. Beale in bad faith or holding faith with a possibility of goodness that inheres exclusively in the knowledge of what is not good, the latter choice embodied in Mrs. Wix.

What is most significant, however, is that, while Maisie's choice is posed dualistically between Sir Claude and Mrs. Wix, the account of her choosing, at least on the syntactical threshold of the narrative, foists what I have characterized as a triadic or dialectical structure of choice upon the reader's construal of dramatic plot. We have seen this already in our discussion of how syntax mimes the triangulation of the love relations of the novel. As we have only just anticipated, however, the difference between the two-term and the three-term mediation may now be usefully characterized as a transition from ethics (identity) to poetics (transformation) or a transition through nonidentity to a new identitarian knowledge that subsists in reflecting nonidentity to itself. Nonidentity now epitomizes the constitutive function of the dialectical third term.

As the Adorno of *Negative Dialectics* observes:

> Totality [by which he means narcissistic/ethical identity] is to be opposed by convicting itself of non-identity with itself—of the non-identity it denies according to its own concept. . . . Thus, too, it [the concept of totality] remains false according to its identitarian logic: it remains the thing against which it is conceived. (147)

Thus, he concludes, "Non-identity is the secret telos of identification" (149). In other words this identity/totality is the nonidentity of identity with nonidentity. Or, to put this issue in the more instrumental context of Maisie's function as a transitional figure (shuttling between two different counters of identity), we might assert that nonidentity is itself, and perforce, a mode of transition rather than a mode of negation. Once more this recalls how the Fichtean self (Fichte's concept of the absolute self notwithstanding) obviates the need to reconcile ideal and real selves.[17] For the self cannot tolerate the self-limitation (not-I) imposed in recognition of the other, a recognition that nonetheless is the ground for its self-reflection. In this context self-activity, which instantiates the opposition of self and not-self, is predicatively grounded only in the augmentation of its own predicative ground. It is not grounded in the transcendental postulate of any "absolute self," which would be abstractly inclusive of both ideal and real.

What we have here is a notion of identity that dovetails with my earlier gloss on Baumgarten's formulation of thematics: where the theme can be said to contain the rationality of its parts but is unable to discover its own rationality in them.[18] As we saw in the previous chapter, theme is bound to proliferate parts in its pursuit of that identity that is not itself. Furthermore, and not surprisingly, it is at this stage of analysis that Baumgarten's thematics might be seen to elide into Baumgarten's aesthetics. For the intuition of formal identity under the rule of Baumgarten's aesthetic entails a proliferation of extensive particulars such that their unity is discernible only in determinative activity. I have been characterizing such configurations as dialectical (as a triadic mediation) because, like Baumgarten's aesthetic object, the clarity of their determinations would obtain not in a specular unity of discernible parts but, rather, in the active principle that articulates its unifying causes in its effects. The more effects, the more determinate is the synthetic agency of those effects.

Taking this discussion back to the agency of Maisie's character, we must now see once again that, while Maisie perceives the choices (between either parent or either of their lovers) as binary, the sentences of this novel systematically diffuse the binary trajectory of any such simple predication, and to increasingly dramatic effect. They do so in the manner of what Louis Althusser has Spinozistically called a "structural causality," in which the cause of the structure is deemed to be immanent in its effects. Its intuition, therefore, is inseparable from the determining motions of the mind that is preoccupied with it.[19]

In the Prefaces to the New York Edition of his works I believe that James himself gives the schema for such a structure. In explicating the concept of novelistic form, he has explicit recourse to a binary distinction that, as a function of its own syntactical disposition, precipitates a dialectical momentum. His definition of form in the preface to *The Portrait of a Lady* (1881) is among his most unequivocal manifestos:

> Here we get exactly the high price of the novel as a literary form—its power not only, while preserving that form with closeness, to range through all the differences of the individual relation to its general subject-matter, all the varieties of outlook on life, of disposition to reflect and project, created by conditions that are never the same from man to man (or, so far as that goes, from man to woman), but

positively to appear more true to its character in proportion as it strains, or tends to burst, with a latent extravagance, its mould. (*Art of the Novel*, 45—46)

I take this to be a characteristic Jamesian sentence, the interpretation of which helps us to characterize the "aesthetic dimension" of the novels without alienating theory from practice and without relinquishing the concern for character to any nonnarrative or purely thematic propositions. The pattern of binary choice already acknowledged to be a structural frame of *What Maisie Knew*, and that is featured here as a choice between structural stasis and organic kinesis, is recapitulated in the digressive, interruptive syntax of this single complex period. This complexity forces us to think the binary choices only in terms of the effects rather than the cause of their opposition. The subordinating contingencies proliferated in this sentence thus animate a predicative not a recuperative mode of reflection, which has repercussions that implicate the reader methodologically in the situation of James's characters: "having to range through all the differences of the individual relation to a general subject matter" in order to totalize them.

Yet this would not be a totality in virtue of some resolution of the duality it seems to be predicated upon (stasis/kinesis). Rather, we "pay the high price" of the novel when we must read it through our recognition of a totality that is only discernable in the coherence of its incoherent moments. For example, the phrase "its power only . . . ," serving as a kind of anaphora (but with a decidedly verbal and transitive purpose) for "the high price of the novel form," is almost immediately a disruption of the nominative plenitude it announces. The explicitly "interruptive" phrase "while preserving," by its syntactical departure from the nominative mode that sets it up, thus presciently instantiates "the differences" (which threaten identity) before they are named generically "[in] relation to its general subject matter" or enumerated in the specific syntactical dependencies that differentiate the sentence from itself in the course of its meandering development. Its meaning, apprehended here as a proportion of its incoherence ("the bursted mould") accords with my earlier characterization of aesthetic form as an asymmetrical relationality that is governed by the self-transforming parameters of context. The specific agency of this transformation, thus far undefined, must now be precisely delineated.

To begin with, we must observe how the suspensive syntactical structure of the sentence under consideration speaks directly to the thematic gist of the protagonist's shuttlecock existence in *What Maisie Knew*. In what looks like a parody of Freud's Oedipus complex, Maisie appears as the fragmented part of the familial whole in which the adult characters of this novel seek to reflect their highly individuated integrity, an ironic counter of the integrity of the family. For Beale and Ida, Maisie is a medium for an idealized self-recognition. Such self-certain identity is explicitly denied them in marriage by the intractable fact of the very physiological differences that marriage is intended to spiritualize. Because the very concept of matrimonial union belies the duality it presumes upon for its intelligibility, it demonically hastens the return of primordial difference with the vengeance of all repressed knowledge. The idealized speculary existence that the parents enjoy at Maisie's expense depends on Maisie's involuntary movement for its rationality. For her mobility, in itself, frees them from any reckoning with a self-evident (albeit repressed) reality: what is *in motion* is emphatically not *in itself*. Contrary to the oedipal paradigm of subject-formation, where the child discovers his or her contingency in self-fracturing contemplation of the mother's body— this always escapes the contemplative gaze—here the parents preserve the totality of their own narcissistic world by making the child's place into a deliberately fractured "play" of surfaces, by sending her back and forth.

If we in turn see this mobility as the pattern of the author's own predicative progress through the narrative, we, as readers, can aspire to know what Maisie knows precisely by traveling the same convoluted path. Thus, we will appreciate how, by remaining within this syntactical imperative, we may come to an idea of an aesthetic totality that applies equally to James's theory and practice of art. If our reading of *What Maisie Knew* keeps to the formal discipline implicit in the self-critical passage quoted above from the Prefaces, we will anticipate the convergence of form and theme in a syntactical matrix that preempts their distinction.

Here is an example, a passage in which Maisie's relation to her mother is articulated as much by the syntactical rigors of James's prose as by any thematic gist of the dramatic encounter conferred by the concept of character:

> Her visits were as good as an outfit; her manner, as Mrs. Wix once said, as good as a pair of curtains but she was a person addicted to extremes—sometimes barely speaking to her child and sometimes

pressing this tender shoot to a bosom cut, as Mrs. Wix had also observed, remarkably low. (70)

The thematic gist, the totalizing principle of this sentence, would seem to depend upon the dualistic knowledge of analogy: "Her visits were as good as an outfit." The brevity of the statement is exaggerated by its symmetry. It invokes a structural relationship that bridges two worlds by collapsing one into the other, implying precisely the kind of resolution that thematic reading typically effects in the service of closure or generalizing thought.

Presuming upon the metaphor of interruption, by which we have gained a handle on Jamesian syntax, we may now observe that, to appreciate fully the conceptual stakes of this sentence, we must contrast it with the more characteristic suspended, multidependent sentence that immediately precedes it and "opens" the scene of this episode:

It must not be supposed that her ladyship's intermissions were not qualified by demonstrations of another order—triumphal entries and breathless pauses during which she seemed to take in everything in the room, from the state of the ceiling to that of her daughter's boot-toes, a survey that was rich in intentions.

In the context of this opening sentence we can savor the comparative succinctness of "Her visits were as good as an outfit" as a necessary corrective to the less well-ordered aspects we have just read, as if the two styles/modes presented a balanced equation, the conceptual symmetry of complexity and simplicity.

But, if we now resume our reading of "Her visits were as good as an outfit," the dualism is immediately transgressed in the interruptive motion of the ensuing syntax. The second analogy, "her manner . . . as good as curtains," draws the curtain over the window of perspective that framed the "view" of her "visit" (outfit). The one analogy compounded upon the other constitutes an interruptive moment in our intuition of the symmetry of their structures. There is a further asymmetry (in the guise of symmetry) in the metaphoric embodiment of the child as a "tender shoot." Again the pattern of extending the syntactical structure to include antithetical parts is the compelling formal injunction here. The tender shoot pressed to the maternal bosom is juxtaposed with the metaphoric *cut,* which moves our attention in two directions at once: the metaphoric bearing of the shoot is beneficent toward Maisie, but the cut of the bosom, which guides our eye to the literal image of Ida standing before her daughter, resonates back to Maisie on the metaphoric track of our understanding that, for Ida, Maisie is another outfit cut to her dimensions. She is a flower cut for her mother's adornment.

Furthermore, in each case Ida's treatment of Maisie is cut by James to fit the competing patterns of association: the shoot is a new metaphoric context, in contrast with what precedes it, but, insofar as it is cut like the mother's décolleté, it is a continuation of an old one. Even this doubling is doubled by the contextual slipperiness of *gathered* in the final clause. In the context of the dress Ida is "gathered up" into an image for Maisie's contemplation. But in her manifest desire to be elsewhere, her presence is gathered in an altogether different point of view. The fact that there is, coincidental to this realization, a shift of perspective (from the omniscient point of view to Mrs. Wix) only reaffirms the correctness of privileging transition and movement over image and intuition, as the determinants of aesthetic value in this narrative.

It is for this reason that we must discuss the most conspicuous feature of Jamesian syntax in terms of the disparity between form and theme and the destabilizing irony that conventionally follows upon that disparity. As I have been suggesting, contrary to James's own assertion of its "centering function," the irony in James's syntax is conceived more instrumentally as a supplanting of the theme-form opposition with a form-irony dialectic, whereby we see the inevitable self-deconstruction of the first opposition as a threshold for our intuition of the latter. Or, we might say, the latter stands in relation to the first as the realization of its own (repressed) figurality. The negation of form in theme or theme in form presumed in their opposition curiously eschews the very relationality that in fact conditions the rationality of both. By contrast, figuration sustains a movement between opposing terms, rather than any conflation of opposites that would stubbornly perpetuate dualistic perspectives. Figuration articulates its contingencies as its only mode of self-presence. Contrary to appearances, nonidentity is more articulate than identity.

More precisely (and true to the force of transition/transformation in Jamesian syntax), we can reiterate that figuration here is the acknowledgment that nonidentity must be understood not as negation but, instead, as a mode of transition itself. In this perspective identity is always mediated by a third term: the shifting contextual boundaries that transition denotes. Furthermore, transition, as conceived here, is inherently recursive through the principle of nonidentity, since nonidentity itself is a retrospective view of identity. The implicit reasoning by which we are led by Adorno to accept nonidentity as transition and led by James to accept this capacity as a foundation of the aesthetic may now be schematized in a way that brings together several different strands of our discussion so far: we start with the premise that self-identity, because of its figural ground, is never merely the reflection upon an existent self-image. Rather, it is a "doubling" (though this doubling is illusory and stands for a splitting, a self-repression). But this doubling of the self in the self-image can only be expressed as the imperative to make the correlation between self and self-image ever more exact. This is inevitably to undermine the ground of correlation. After all, what enables the doubling in the first place is some criterion of identity that remains nonidentical to whatever image may be summoned as its reflection. I think we can now say more confidently that this transition has its best paradigm in Fichte's dialectic of positing and striving, from whence this discussion of subjectivity began: the positing self presupposes the striving self, thus transforming it. In any case it is our most emphatic recognition of this problematic that I am calling for when I invoke the form-irony dialectic as both a corollary of nonidentity *and* of Jamesian syntax.

Furthermore, in this context we see the full significance of the concept of transition as a constitutive feature of aesthetic form: it frees us from making the distinction between morality and aesthetics so profoundly intimated in the dualistic drift of the form-theme opposition. In other words, because we are specifically led to recognize the reciprocity of form and theme in the access of a dialectic of form and irony, we are released from the necessity of choosing between the individuated autonomy of form (the aesthetic) and the intersubjective, or social matrix of totalizing, thematizing knowledge (morality). According to the transitional imperative at work here, aesthetic value gathers the force of Adorno's assertion that "non-identity is the secret telos of identity." As it is theorized by Adorno and formalized by James, this notion of the aesthetic is original in that its traditional gesture toward totality is tied signally to change, not to stability, transcendent or otherwise.

Indeed, James's aesthetic, contemplated in this context, does seem obedient to just such a transitional movement *between* different interpretive registers: making a change of meaning rather than the reification of meaning the burden of narrative development. We have seen how Jamesian prose stubbornly solicits rationalization beyond the thematic glosses that its formal density invites. The more detailed those glosses are, the greater the attention to formal detail they warrant and the more apparent becomes the incommensurability between form and content. This in turn prompts the need of an *other* mediating term. Such prompting to a further entailment of knowledge in my view epitomizes Jamesian style. James's themes are, after all, deceptively social, all too easily mapped onto the expositional and totalizing coordinates of verisimilar scene and action. But, just as conspicuously, James's forms are animated by the detotalizing consciousness of a contingency that escapes any timeless representation of time and place. The exigency of such reading is ineluctably conditioned by the shifting predicative frame of Jamesian syntax. It is no surprise, then, that James's commentators have been traditionally divided between doctrinaire formalists such as Percy Lubbock and doctrinaire moralists such as F. R. Leavis, each recognizing the impossible contingencies of the other without any means of passing through them.

The contingency that escapes representation is, however, precisely the object (rather than merely the unconscious condition) of James's representational aims in the novel genre. It is equally the "knowledge" at stake in Maisie's actions as an emplotted character. Or, resisting the temptation to see such a self-transformative form as an allegory of its own unreadability, we might say that in James we are meant to see how theme is always figural in the extremity of its nonidentity with form.

I believe that James's intentions in this respect are best illustrated by observing how Maisie's desire to impose an allegorical reading of the relation between meaning and image mirrors James's account of problems encountered in his search for appropriate frontispiece images to adorn the first edition of the "collected works." The work in the novel and the work on the novel both converge in a critique of illustration and the simple specularity that inspires it.

The publication date of *Maisie*, 1897, falls notably close to the compilation of the standard edition of James's works (completed in 1909), in itself a challenging feat of self-identification. But the problematic of identification becomes particularly telling for James in his fastidious commissioning of photos by A. L. Coburn to serve as pictorial complements to the written text. The "aesthetic" question that guided this search for James was precisely the one that now elicits our own efforts to understand the syntactical particulars of his style: What are adequate terms of representation? More important, how can adequacy be assessed without preempting itself in a tautology of reference, by making the standard of adequacy a mirror of what it purports to analyze, in effect, nullifying its analytical aptitude? Regarding the adequacy of the frontispiece photos, James declares that Coburn's pictures must refuse the purposiveness of illustration and/or resemblance. The ideal photograph would be one

> the reference of which to Novel or Tale should exactly be *not* competitive and obvious, should on the contrary plead its case with some shyness, that of images always confessing themselves mere optical symbols or echoes, expressions of no particular thing in the text, but only of the type or idea of this or that thing. (*Art of the Novel*, 333)

Representation thus is a reckoning with the desire for a reflective identity that precludes simple specularity as the ground of self-knowledge. It puts the activity of grounding in the place of a ground. The "appropriate" image would disclose that relationality that can only be dictated by the necessary incommensurability of the image with any "standard of adequacy" by which it is originally representable.

The same "solution" to the problem of representation strikingly asserts itself in the unfolding plot action of *What Maisie Knew*. It converges upon the reader's recognition that what Maisie wants from Sir Claude is not possible so long as she depends on a dyadic rather than a triadic protocol of reflective consciousness. She wishes for herself and Sir Claude to be a couple (the witty pitfall of all of the marriages in this novel). This implicit critique of dyadic truth, like the critique of the illustrative image, is reminiscent of the choice between thematic and syntactic imperatives that was posed earlier as a structural pivot of the novel—if only insofar as it was problematized within the novel. We have already seen how the problematizing of such a choice, where it facilitated a redefinition of the aesthetic, led precisely to the nullifying of the dualism from which that choice seemed to spring.

Now we must go a step farther by observing how (as was the case in our earlier view of the syntactic overdetermination of theme and the analogous overdetermination of image) the entirety of the plot in *What Maisie Knew* ultimately turns on Maisie's comparable inability to make her consciousness coincide with itself through a specular reflection vis-à-vis Sir Claude. Put very simply, Maisie seeks everywhere to reduce triads (broken marriages) to dyads. Correspondingly, she can see herself only in dyadic terms. If Sir Claude would choose her to the exclusion of Mrs.

Beale, Maisie's dream of self-identity would be consummated in the mirror of his affection. But, as James specifically avers in his preface to *What Maisie Knew,* the key to Maisie's character is the absence of terms to express her being (9), the absence of mirroring presences. In this way he intimates a paradigm of identity that solicits change, not stasis.

In keeping with this insight, we must note that the most propitious coincidence of image and world, the most propitious mirroring reflection in *What Maisie Knew,* obtains not between Maisie and her self-image but, instead, between the formal matrices of the text and the cognitive development of the character as she comes inevitability to the threshold of what we might now call "triadic desire." R. P. Blackmur alluded to this coincidence as the "trumping of the formalism-moralism opposition," which we have already judged to be prerequisite to any nontranscendental premise of aesthetic value: one that does not depend on the sublime oblivion of autonomous subjectivity. This observation accords well with James's own slowly building assertion, in the preface to *The Golden Bowl,* that the aesthetic is inherently a structure of action.[20] As he explains in the preface to *The Golden Bowl,* the "aesthetic vision" warrants a prose that is "in the conditions of life,"[21] by which he seems to desire an annulment of the distinction between the act and its consequences.

Accordingly, every contingency of predication would become a new aspect of that predicative power, in effect a transition to a fuller contextualization of meaning. Such an annulment of the distinction between act and consequence is for James nowhere better exemplified than in the activity of revision, which he has conspicuously undertaken as the pretext for these prefaces—prefaces that, in turn, resemble nothing so much as fictions themselves in their masquerading as beginnings rather than conclusions, whose function they resemble most closely. Under the pressure of so much recognition they are cast in terms of a virtual ethic of self-transformation, turning criticism into art and art into criticism. This stance is conceivably even more radical than that which seeks to dissolve the distinction between act and consequence. It becomes increasingly apparent that James is ultimately asserting that the status of act, under the aegis of "revision," obviates altogether any need to distinguish what one *does* from what one *thinks*.

Because action is the dominant theme of my own argument, we should not be surprised to find James concluding that the standard of aesthetic value implicit in the act of revision takes its strongest motive from the fact that it translates more directly into "the conditions of life"

(*Art of the Novel,* 347) than aesthetic credos that sequester thought from action in the manner of a transcendental or autonomous subject. As he says:

> All of which amounts doubtless but to saying that as the whole conduct of life consists of things done which do other things in their turn, just so our behavior and its fruits are essentially one and continuous and persistent and unquenchable, so the act has its way of abiding and showing and testifying, and so, among our innumerable acts, are no arbitrary, no senseless separations. (37)

I believe that this line of thought leads us back to Adorno's discussion of the dialectic of nonidentity in general and to the specific assertion that "cognition of non-identity [rather than constituting a negation of identity] lies not only in the fact that this very cognition identifies—[but] that it identifies to a greater extent and in other ways than identitarian thinking" (*Negative Dialectics,* 149). The logical trajectories of this "greater extent" and these "other ways" point, for Adorno, toward the contention that identity and nonidentity elaborate each other rather than cancel each other. Just as important for us, if we want to see Adorno's theoretic stance as illuminating James's practice, we should say that these remarks postulate a link between the concepts of act and structure. Such a link gives force and definition to James's own homiletic conclusion to the prefaces, in which he appears to admonish the artist to eschew any notion of totality (structure) that is not also transformation (act). The dictum of the prefaces is: "Thus, if he [the author] is always doing, he can scarcely by his own measure ever be done" (*Art of the Novel,* 348). What is salient in this notion of activity is its emphasis on completeness as a predicative contingency or, as he goes on to imply, a connectedness that can be meaningfully characterized, according to our preceding discussion, as structurally recursive.

Such is the case insofar as its intuition is bound up with the necessity to articulate terms that traditional "creative aesthetics" and "consumption aesthetics" reduce through logical oppositions either to a generative subject or to a fatal object, respectively. Or, rather, we could say that the dissolution of the difference between act and consequence achieved in James's inducement to a virtually unceasing activity is itself the palpable link between act and structure: a structure determined (like the triadic syntax that epitomizes James's "style") by its relation with its own contingent or nonidentical conditions. This understanding is most decisively an aspect of the structure of *Maisie* in the conclusion of the narrative, so heavily freighted as it is with the proverbial "great expectation" of bildungsroman plot: the knowledge of character revealed in the form of a fully realized being. This expectation of the union of knowing and being reveals, in the manifestation of its own impossibility, the conditions of possibility for an even more existentially worldly aesthetic.

Conclusion: Aesthetics in the Mirror of Contingency

Inasmuch as Maisie's identity is proffered in the prospect for a new constellation of "family" relationships, one that could transcend the otherwise mutually exclusive or contradictory choice between the pairing of Sir Claude and Mrs. Beale, or the pairing of Sir Claude and Mrs. Wix, its realization would seem to depend on the disappearance of a difference between them. Either Mrs. Beale or Mrs. Wix will bow out. But, quite to the contrary, James's reader is confronted with a dénouement that *produces* a difference instead. It is a difference that undermines the identity of Maisie's character, not because the narrative vitiates her point of view as a vital coordinate of intelligible action but, rather, because it obscures the reflection of the reader's identity in her character.

In the famous Brechtian parlance of materialist aesthetics this is an "alienation effect." For Louis Althusser, who to my mind elucidates this concept better than Brecht himself, the alienation effect is the production of an "internal distance" within the work of aesthetic representation. This distance is instantiated in the difference between a quality and the concept that it is transformed into. It is a gesture toward acknowledgment of aesthetics as a "modality of worked matter" (*Lenin and Philosophy,* 222). Althusser contends that art is "a certain specific relationship with knowledge . . . [a relationship] of difference not identity" (222). In the dénouement of *What Maisie Knew* such difference is punctual (especially in the last sentence) but also dilatory or "interruptive" in its deferral of the recognition it seems to deploy. The much anticipated recognition heralded here is that Maisie will be finally formed according to a formulable principle: "she is someone who. . . . " But again, interruption is tantamount to transition, because the apparent closure of the narrative performs the same double gesture we have already witnessed in the syntactical tensions of the Jamesian aesthetic.

Here is how things unfold. In the last lines of the novel Mrs. Wix embarks with Maisie, having recruited her to the service of her own highly touted "moral sense," only to realize at the last moment that "[Mrs. Wix] still had room for wonder at what Maisie knew." The word *knowledge* in this instance is both a bearer of consciousness as well as a representation of consciousness as the bearer of knowledge. Even more important, Maisie's moral sense, as soon as it is acknowledged as such, warrants comparison with James's aesthetic sense because representation and representing, noun and verb, are juxtaposed in the passive/active modality of the word *knew*—from Mrs. Wix's point of view *knew* is a noun, from Maisie's it is a verb—in such a way that a transition from the moral to the aesthetic is solicited. It is a transition facilitated in much the same terms that Ricoeur says are necessary according to his reading of Aristotle: ethics entails an ascription of qualities ("the person being imitated is a person according to ethics" [1:47]), while poetics entails a predicative agent of such ascriptions. Ethics is a reduction of action to constative nouns, while poetics is an expansion of action to the exigencies of activity qua act. But, like the twin guarantors of Aristotelian *muthos* (surprise and necessity), ethics and poetics are for Ricoeur a necessary pair guaranteeing that every predicate instantiates what Ricoeur calls a "fusion of the . . . paradoxical and the causal" (1:44), a motion toward stasis, a *sustaisis*. This is a term that permits Aristotle and Ricoeur both to specify "the operation of organizing . . . events into a system, not the system itself" (1:48).

Concomitantly for James, the pair ethics/poetics sets up a relation within the predicative order of the narrative that once again pushes our intuition of form into the modality of transformation. Any invidious choice between ethics and poetics is thus obviated by the recursive principle (the conjuncture of the "paradoxical and the causal") that is here revealed to have conditioned our ability to differentiate ethics from poetics in the first place.

Such recursiveness is, in effect, *the figuration of contingency*. It inheres in that qualitative status of the ethical that cannot be expressed, except as the intuition of a quality altered in the trajectory of its self-reflection. We must accept here a notion of quality as a virtual aspect of a process that is realized only in the transition to another quality. Such, after all, is the case with Maisie. Or such is the case in James's deployment of Maisie as a conceptual prompt for the reader's most rigorous thinking.

James's reader must think of Maisie at the end, much as he or she has thought to negotiate the syntactical baffles of the novel throughout: with the understanding that nonidentity is transition and figuration both, a recursiveness instantiated in the recurring of totality to transformation. In the last sentence of the novel ("She still had room for wonder at what Maisie knew") Maisie's presence displays the full contingency of an incomplete predication. But what saves this conclusion from self-mystification is that its contingency is rendered an object for reflection rather than an obstacle to reflection. For reflective capacity is what is at stake in James's style and what links his form to his theme. In the preface to this novel his stated ambition boils down to nothing more than a "just reflection." This reflection, however, unlike its counterpart in philosophical idealism, expands rather than delimits identity by locating identity on the differentiating threshold of limit itself. As I have said, this may be usefully imagined as a Fichtean striving. In Fichtean striving the effort to achieve increasing autonomy, which is the imposition of a limit, entails a difference (what is beyond the limit) that turns out to be paradoxically a *self-perpetuating difference*. In this regard the last sentence of James's novel stands thematically as a mirror of the formal artifice that has precipitated it. *What* we know about Maisie here leads back to a consideration of *how* we know it.

Jamesian reflection expands identity by assimilating its contingency to its agency: such is the only meaningful fusion of the horizons of character and reader that obtains as a grounding of novelistic reality for this author. This account of Jamesian aesthetic practice makes an interesting contrast with the fusion of horizons envisaged within phenomenological formalism. In the place of a more phenomenologically minded *trans*ubjectivity, James's Fichtean appeal to an irreducible inersubjectivity obviates the "pure figuration of consciousness" upon which the phenomenological reading of a critic such as John Carlos Rowe otherwise depends.[22] While my account of figuration as linked to transition and transformation precluded any such timeless "purity" of consciousness, Rowe alleges that formalism and phenomenology are united in the dream of common humanity. Such a view seeks to pigeonhole James as a phenomenological realist insofar as he may be said to present an authentic structure of experience, the moral authenticity of which would be deemed to be self-evident in its phenomenological immediacy. I would counter, following Giddens, that the structuration, not the structure of narrative, is all that can offer a moral purview because it does not grant the authority of the terms of experience in the mere fact of their presentation. In other words the chief liability of phenomenological idealism as a gloss on Jamesian aesthetics is its obviating of the threshold of activity upon which I have been arguing James's aesthetic practice is predicated.

In this context James's famous remark to H. G. Wells, "It is art that makes life . . ." begins to sound more like a deliberate solicitation of Wells's otherwise circumspect reply: "I can only read sense into it [James's formulation of art as making life] by assuming that you are using 'art' for every conscious human activity."[23] Indeed, the reflective activity animated in Jamesian form is not consonant with the concept of totality, even an absent one, as is suggested by critics like Rowe (234) (in consideration of Wells's riposte to James). Taking the smooth rhetorical surface of the prefaces as a mirror for the creative act, Rowe asserts that James's prefaces are about "the desire for an [absent] author," i.e., a phenomenological totalizer. I believe instead that the more apt analogy for James's achievement in the prefaces and the novels has to do with recognizing the need to assimilate the unintended consequences of an action to the agency of that act. This, I want to assert, constitutes a now viable instance of ironic centrality.

In his preface to *The Tragic Muse* (*Art of the Novel*, 90) James is specifically led to contemplate the desire for thinking irony and centrality at the same time. But he underwrites this formal enterprise by valorizing a strategy of "alternation" instead of totality. Alternation, adduced as a "multiplication of aspects," is linked to unintended consequences by the inevitability of our recognizing in each new horizon the unseen limits of its predecessor. I believe it would be wrong to characterize this as a simple perspectivism, as a simple decentering activity gyrating into the orbit of Nietzschean cynicism. Rather, as James elaborates, "alternation" is precisely "a different *placing* of the centre" (my emphasis).

Here we return to the topos of ironic center but without worrying the apparent paradox that launched this chapter and without suffering the contradiction between alternating centers as an aporetic threshold of narration. Rather, I want to conclude that, because, in James's style, the modality of transition negotiates the impasse of immanent contradiction, the author's emphasis on active "placement" may now be construed as an even more persuasive counterlogic to the phenomenological readings of his novels. For "alternating placement" both instantiates and modifies the phenomenological subject. Totality is linked to transformation in a way that reminds us how "placement" elicits the *setzen* of the philosophy of reflection. In Fichte and in Hegel the placement of the self at the center of things is precisely understood as a transition to the terms of that centering activity so that consciousness of one's placement entails displacement, a reconciling of self with its own causal impetus, which is simultaneously self-limiting and self-instantiating. *Setzen* is the coincidence of the theoretical and practical inasmuch as the displacement of the self remains part of that self's own predicative structure.

By contrast, I believe, the "different placings of the center" enacted by Jamesian syntax are misconstrued by those phenomenologically minded critics who see ironic displacements of the center as an absolute freedom, a freedom conferred upon the reader by the instability of contexts. Such freedom would be empty as long as it was only an index of pure mobility. The mobility of aesthetic determination as I am formulating it here (and as I believe James intimates in the idea of re-placement) is not a directionless movement. In fact, it is only a movement at all insofar as it is the *production of a difference,* in the sense that Althusser gleans when he characterizes the unique work of aesthetic determination (as a "modality of worked matter" rather than as a category of objects): the aesthetic differentiates between different appearances of the same object. Althusser's difference is specifically the difference that a concept makes in relation to its object.

In *Imaginary Relations* (1987), Michael Sprinker has succinctly captured Althusser's point by indexing it to Marx's observation in *Grundrisse,* that both the ape and the human have an opposable thumb (275). But only the human has a concept of it. In that conceptual lever the human is sprung "free" from the prereflective experience of the physical world. Accordingly, I would like to suggest that in James's novel Maisie herself instantiates a difference understood as the production of a concept. Notably, Maisie is neither the galvanic center of a totalizing perspective nor the gaping hole in an otherwise tightly woven fabric of causality. She is more precisely a counter for a transformative capacity inherent in the contradiction marked by her ambiguous presence among the other characters. This, like Althusser's distinction between two different appearances of the same object, is a postulate of differential relationality exclusively determined in the possibility of contingent error. The difference between Maisie's knowing and not knowing is profound as an acknowledgment of a necessity for reflection that can here be called aesthetic, not because it is indeterminate but, rather, because it speculates upon the limits of determination.

So ultimately it is not merely freedom but also knowledge that marks the threshold of Maisie's intelligibility in the last line of the novel. Yet it is a knowledge whose integrity is nonetheless its freedom from the constraint of any necessity of knowing that is not narratable and therefore self-transformative. The Jamesian aesthetic in this view impels a recognition of the transformative impetus harbored within self-reflection. His syntax maps this imperative onto the coordinates of plot and character in a way that strictly thematic modes of construing dramatic intelligibility cannot account for: theme cannot account for what prompts it, just as intentional accounts cannot take into account unintended consequences, except as a woefully undialectical irony. Such unintended consequences thereby remain merely a foreshortened perspective that collapses upon the self with all the weight of mortal tragedy.

By contrast, in Jamesian syntax theme becomes a crossable boundary of reflected identity, a looking glass through which one approaches the constitutive circumstances of the self. The notion of the aesthetic that emerges from the other side of that mirror is emblematic in Maisie's stance at the end of James's novel. Specifically for Mrs. Wix and hence almost ominously for the reader, Maisie is no longer so much a quality to be predicated as a predicative agency in her own right by virtue of the mobile horizon of predicative intelligibility she marks. More than any of James's titles, *What Maisie Knew* is a solicitation of the predicative mode (i.e., "What Maisie knows is . . . "). It is no accident, then, that we have found the basis for a reflection upon how the aesthetic is bound to the formation of the subject in the syntactical register of this novel's aesthetic practice. Here, in fact, we see that the aesthetic bridges the gap between value and experience. For in this thinking the notion of aesthetic quality has been effectively conflated with a notion of agency and rendered a satisfactorily transitive modality of human self-presence. There is, I believe, no more secure basis on which we can assert that predication is the expressive register of the nature we predicate of ourselves.

In the next chapter I will outline the dimensions of this narrative aesthetic more fully in order to indicate its cognitive scope and its consequence as a register of expressive action.

7

Determining the Aesthetic: Beauty Beholds the I

> words that were not words but sounds out of time
> —John Ashbery, *Three Poems*

> Impossibility of finite determination may carry some suggestion of the ineffability so often claimed for, or charged against the aesthetic. But density, far from being mysterious and vague, is explicitly defined; and it arises out of and sustains the unsatisfiable demand for absolute precision.
> —Nelson Goodman, *Languages of Art*

Narrative and Aesthetic

In order to propel the argument of the previous chapter, I must return to a first principle of this work, thereby describing a temporal circle that will be crucial to its completion. To speak of narrative aesthetics is to trouble one's speaking with the contradictory imperatives of transformation and totality. Narrative impels transformation. Aesthetics totalizes. What is worse, the conflict between transformation and totality seems inescapable, since it would appear to be already internal to the structure of narrative emplotment: narrative simultaneoulsy subsists upon and contests the terms of Aristotelian teleology. *Peripeteia* strives for reversals, while *anagnorisis,* or recognition, strives for totalities. Aristotle himself resolved this conflict only in the unsatisfying strategy of alternating perspectives that so tangles the narrative line of the *Poetics*.

In this chapter, therefore, I begin with the following idea. Because literary theory, out of Aristotle, presides over the aesthetic effects of narrative, the notion of the aesthetic as a term of literary-critical judgment (especially in its drive for universality) has served too often as a strategy to ameliorate or to mask the internal conflicts of narrative. Literary aesthetics consequently has obscured the conflictual infrastructure of narrative by conflating its means with its ends, by collapsing the vital contingency of episodic action into the absolute value of thematic unity—or, to keep this in strictly Aristotelian terms, by intimating the necessary subsumption of reversal to recognition in the mechanics of formal emplotment.

Yet it is only in the inexorable and historically manifest failure of this conflation, in the ever obtrusive incommensurability of form and theme—particularly in the novel genre—and, hence, in the dogged return of the narrative-aesthetics split, that I believe we may finally appreciate the degree of their interdependence. Paradoxically enough, I propose that the interdependency of narrative and aesthetics is predicated on the simultaneous necessity of their distinction and the denial of their difference.

In one respect, of course, this point merely rehearses the hoariest irony of "modern" and "postmodern" subjectivity, one that has pestered standards of rationality to no end, thereby seeming to make of logical thought an endless and consequently inconsequential game. This point is a fainter and fainter echo of that ontological big bang that split being from knowing in the Cartesian mind. In this chapter, however, I will assert that the intimation of an arid paradox in the theorizing of narrative aesthetics may be avoided. We can do this by reconceiving the apparent contradiction between narrative and aesthetic values in terms of a syntactical or predicative relation that obtains between them rather than as a logical proposition that subsumes them. In this way we may attempt to tackle the conceptual problems intrinsic to each. We may be able to rescue the concept of the aesthetic in order to guarantee the purposiveness of a determinate narrative will without universalizing its determinations. Furthermore, we may be able to dispose of the overly facile dichotomy of practical and the aesthetic "ends" upon which the original conflict between narrative and aesthetic value subsists.

Aesthetic knowledge has been almost proverbially opposed to practical knowledge on the basis of its seemingly precipitous reduction of experience to a sensuous register of intensified moments. This leads to the fearful "beyond" of Romantic sublimity from which no practical purposiveness ever returns to tell a coherent story. On the contrary, and as we noted in the case of Blanchot's *récit*, however much the representational impetus of the aesthetic seems to rationalize time away, time ever more consequentially conditions our recognition of the aesthetic. Furthermore, I want to assert that aesthetic theories that refrain from negating temporality may succeed in making action the driving imperative of aesthetic intelligibility. By thus linking the notion of the aesthetic to the notion of action, we may see the intrinsically narrative dimension of aesthetic judgment and thus begin to discern the dynamic that determines aesthetics and narrative together. As I have suggested, this would be an expressly syntactical dynamic insofar as the linkage between aesthetics and act would entail the transformational trajectory of time.

For the reasons just stated, any attempt to demonstrate the narrativity of aesthetics must begin by revealing the failure of aesthetic theory itself to satisfactorily transcend the exigencies of nonartistic narrative experience, as it purports to do in its commonplace presumption of an atemporal determinacy. Here I am thinking of the tradition of Shaftesbury, Kant, Croce, and the New Critics, which in one way or another takes "purposiveness without a purpose" as the reflective ground of aesthetic determination. In the course of modernist aesthetics we have seen only too clearly how such transcendence invites an effective indeterminacy of meaning. I want to show that in the failure of aesthetic transcendence, or rather in what remains of aesthetic aspiration on the misty threshold of pure indeterminacy, we might discover the firmer ground of a hitherto obscure subjective agency. Precisely because this subjectivity does arise on the threshold of a contradictory knowledge—the determinate aims of the aesthetic, the indeterminate effects of the aesthetic—we will see that it adumbrates the kind of rationalistic reckoning of narrative with aesthetics we anticipated in previous readings of Baumgarten.

To sum up: I am alleging that the aesthetic inheres *in* narrative but is uniquely expressible under that quasiteleological constraint as subjectivity. Thus, in the apparent contradiction between the narrative and the aesthetic we observe an emergent subjectivity that more fully articulates them both. In this view the concept of subjectivity would give the aesthetic a determinate agency that restrains it from dissolving into pure sensation. Reciprocally, the aesthetic would lend to the concept of Enlightenment subjectivity a capacity of self-consciousness that is historically productive: neither transcendentally self-reifying or skeptically self-annihilating. The determination of the aesthetic and the determinate agency of the narrative subject would thus be bound symbiotically in a way that preserves the practice of each against its inherent theoretical fragility. The self is a more complicated proposition than either narrative by itself or aesthetics by itself is able to unravel.

In fact, this self entails the very dimension of formal (as opposed to abstractly logical) complexity, which was the original warrant for the category of the aesthetic promulgated in Baumgarten's *Reflections on Poetry* (1735) and *Aesthetica* (1750). We have already discussed how Baumgarten's aesthetic sought to redeem the so-called lower faculties of sense to the Enlightenment project of rational self-improvement. But it was precisely Baumgarten's emphasis on the determinate complexity of sensuous form that nineteenth- and early twentieth-century theory purged by supplanting the idealism of form with the idealism of truth, epitomized, for example, in the shift from a Coleridgean formalistic aesthetic to an Arnoldian moralistic aesthetic to a Crocean lyric aesthetic. Hence, the divergence of aesthetic from narrative determinations. In following this course, Anglo-American aesthetics in particular abdicated the very cognitive agency that originally endowed aesthetic complexity as a legitimate province of philosophical inquiry rather than as a relatively passive field of sensuous play.

We may not forget here that such cognitive agency was the ground of experience from which narrative originally derived its own explanatory impetus. Aristotelian narrative is impelled by its trajectory of catharsis to simplify complexity. The albeit uneasy privilege given to the dynamism of praxis in *Poetics* is reversed in the course of literary theory's long assimilation of Aristotelian knowledge to the more clearly universalist but formally more abstract norms of ethos. Perversely enough, literary theory itself seems to have invited the encroachments of *sophia* upon the ground of *phronesis*, yielding the relatively production-oriented principles of *Poetics* to the more legislative principles of the *Nichomachean Ethics*.[1] The speculative force of this chapter will thus be to suggest that, just as the failure of aesthetics is linked to the dissipation of narrative, so the resurgence of narrative might portend a reinvigoration of the aesthetic.

I will take exemplification for these claims from *Three Poems*, an ambitious narrative prose work by the distinguished American poet John Ashbery. There are several reasons for this apparently wayward path of inquiry that adduces neither aesthetic philosophy or the "great tradition" of the novel for its analytical coordinates. Most important, however, is the reason annunciated by the equivocation respecting genre that is so self-consciously promulgated in Ashbery's title. *Three Poems* conflates the time-tempered narrative paradigm of beginning, middle, and end, with the timeless purport of lyrical *poesis*. This is to say that Ashbery's text presupposes, in its very title, a substantive reconfiguration of the axes of narrative and aesthetics. Furthermore, I will show that this reconfiguration is specifically ordained under a syntactical principle. Such a syntactical rule, I already indicated in my reading of the Jamesian aesthetic, is prerequisite to any theory of narrative aesthetics that would reconcile contradiction with coherence. By *syntax* I am, of course, designating once again both a totality *and* a transformation, or, specifically in Ashbery's case, a predicative power reciprocally coordinated with a reflective capacity. It is key to Ashbery's technique that he renders what we would ordinarily take as the "aesthetic quality" of the work virtually indistinguishable from its syntactical effectivity.

But, before we can gauge the exemplifying power of this stance toward the aesthetic, we must entertain a broader theoretical context. I therefore want to adduce Nelson Goodman's well-known formulation of the aesthetic as the supplanting of quality by cognitive function in *Languages of Art* ([1968], 138), grounded, as I believe Goodman's thinking is, in the very cognitive activity that animates Ashbery's syntactical practice. For the purposes of my own argument I want to characterize Goodman's valorization of cognition in terms of "the subject as action," since I believe that what facilitates the transition from quality to function necessitates a sublation of the structure of identity into the structure of act—even if it is preeminently the act of reflection. Goodman, in stipulating how formal (syntactical and semantic) density constitutes a signal "symptom" of the aesthetic in a work of art offers an important reference point for my narrativizing of the aesthetic. For Goodman, unlike those other connoisseurs of complexity, the American New Critics, formal complication in art is not ecstatically driven toward the sheer excessive determinateness of the ineffable. Rather, Goodman's complexity is inextricable from particular subjective agency because it entails a protocol of selection or choice of criteria by which particulars are discerned to be counters for reference by exemplification. *Exemplification* is Goodman's term for the way in which a work of art not only instantiates a particularity but also invokes the discursive categories by which that particularity can be "picked out" as a significant difference (52).

Goodman's theory of reference by exemplification constitutes a widely acknowledged breakthrough in the theory of representation. But here I only want to emphasize the way that, for Goodman, differences are significant as they proliferate reasons for observing them, i.e., by presuming the transformation of contextual parameters that we associate with syntactical predication. Such choices are indexed by Goodman as the relative "repleteness" of the art object (*Languages of Art,* 253; *Of Mind and Other Matters,* 136–37). Goodman's term *repleteness* denotes a function of the number of dimensions within which differentia are in turn functional for sustaining attentional consciousness. We will see how this notion of repleteness is thus especially useful for specifying the narrative development of Ashbery's prose. It articulates the conceptual matrix within which Ashbery's prose launches a narrative trajectory without falling into the preemptive purview of teleological judgment and, even more important, without presuming that immediacy of consciousness that is commonly granted as the basis for distinguishing prose narrative from lyric poetry. Such a distinction, as we have seen, and because it contains the narrative-aesthetics dichotomy within it, is already an endangered species in the titular purview of Ashbery's project.

Specifically, I want to show how Ashbery articulates a narrative realm by recourse to a proliferation of contextual dimensions within which *differentia are expressible as choice*. So, the repleteness of Ashbery's text may ultimately be said to be its ample means for compelling choices in such a way as to augment the analytical resources of our choosing nature. Not surprisingly, then, my strongest claim for the artistic value of *Three Poems* will bear upon its aptitude for crossing the boundary between art and criticism, which otherwise constitutes a barrier between appreciative and judgmental modes of artistic consumption.

Of course, anyone who has lived through the conceptual wars of the past twenty-five years of literary theory is liable to object that this is already a too well or too badly worn path of speculation. Nevertheless, I would argue that Ashbery takes us in a new direction: toward a redefinition of the aesthetic subject that expresses itself as action—the action par excellence, of crossing boundaries. We will see how, in *Three Poems* particularly, the aesthetic subject serves as an instance of self-reflection (a confluence of appreciation and judgment) that can *persist* rather than merely *consist* in its formal injunctions against all that shapeless temporality with which it must otherwise unceasingly (which is to say uncomprehendingly) struggle. This crossing of the boundaries may therefore issue in a more historically responsible contemplation of the dimensions of the aesthetic subject than we have yet enjoyed.

The Cognitive Bearing of Aesthetic Value:
Goodman, Adorno, Sartre

Nelson Goodman's diagnosis of the aesthetic in terms of repleteness is particularly adaptable to my desire to reconnect narrative and aesthetic determinations under the, at least potentially, ethical auspices of cognition. Goodman maintains an uncompromising commitment to match the specificity of aesthetic experience with the needs for conceptual precision. His standard of judgment is "cognitive efficacy" (*Languages of Art,* 262; *Of Mind,* 146-50). With the phrase "cognitive efficacy" Goodman means to put the aesthetic experience on a par with other determinative phenomena that yield to analysis on the basis of the ratio of difference and resemblance (or, as he says, "recognition and discovery" *Languages of Art,* 261). Here again we need only recall Aristotle's valorizing of recognition and reversal in *Poetics* as the salient coordinates of classical narrative emplotment in order to appreciate the degree to which thinking about narrative is always recursive for the activity of thinking. The coordinates of classical emplotment constitute the very tension of resemblance and difference that theorists like Todorov aver to be the key to the transformative power of narrative, the very motor of narrative cognition.[2]

Implicit in Goodman's exposition is the belief that, as long as the term *aesthetic* functions in the noncognitive register of its more traditional art-historical cognates—taste, genius, beauty—it sacrifices knowledge of the particular purposes of artistic "symbolization" to schematic recognition of their merely formal purposiveness. As we have already noted, Goodman chooses to anatomize the particulars of aesthetic form as functions rather than as qualities. He furthermore relates those functions to the task of analyzing the aesthetic under the terminological rubric of "symptom" rather than under the rubric of a Kantian-style "judgment." Unlike judgment, symptom is neither "a necessary or a sufficient condition" (*Languages of Art,* 252).

I believe that Goodman speaks so circumspectly in terms of the "symptoms" of the aesthetic because he is so suspicious of the self-inhibiting predilection of more positive assertions to function legislatively rather than productively. He resists any subsuming of the specific discriminations of meaning within the work under already generalized laws. Rather, he would maximize our sensitivity to the possibility for proliferating discriminations within the work. This capacity is for Goodman the significant guarantor of the constitutive "density" of the work of art. Goodman wants to restore content and hence consequence to our understanding of the practices of aesthetic symbolization. But he would achieve this end without granting, in the very definition of the aesthetic, the monumental obstacle to aesthetic thinking qua cognition that seems to be propounded by Kant's analytic of the beautiful.

Superficially, much of what Goodman says gets its polemical torque by comparison with Kantian "finality of form" (*Critique of Judgment*, 195). In finality of form, whereby an object appeals to understanding in the absence of a concept, such that it occasions an accord between understanding and imagination, the formal object is already entailed by the contemplative mind rather than exposing that mind to the hazards of cognitive contingency. The alternative would be to make cognition a more effective—which is to say a less idealistically subsumptive—enterprise.

By contrast with the Kantian metaphysic, Goodman's symptoms pertain to a more sumptuous body of knowledge. The body of the artwork persists through Goodman's interpretation of its symptoms rather than disappearing into the diagnostic language that would otherwise attend upon it under the sacramental spell of concepts such as judgment, beauty, and, most notoriously, aesthetic merit. In this context we could say that symptoms are deemed to be more organic to the cognitive life of the art object. This would be the case to the degree that symptom articulates the contingency of the work in relation to consciousness. Contrastingly, I would say that aesthetic qualities are an artifact of what has passed away under the remorseless sanction of artistic judgment. Goodman stipulates that the gist of cognition in such cases has to do with "delicacy of discrimination, power of integration . . ." (*Languages of Art*, 261). These are conspicuously activities of mind that bind it to the objects it works upon, rendering the "nature" of that work an ever more complex relational proposition. Consequently, for Goodman the aesthetic object is always impelled on a temporal course toward other objects that are constituted in relation to it. He says:

> What a Manet or Monet or Cézanne does to our subsequent seeing of the world is as pertinent to their appraisal as is any direct confrontation. How our looking at pictures and our listening to music inform what we encounter later and elsewhere is integral to them as cognitive. The absurd and awkward myth of the insularity of aesthetic experience can be scrapped. (260)

So, in Goodman's theorizing we are coming to unusually scrupulous terms with the problem of making the category of the aesthetic useful without obliterating the conditions under which the human agency denoted in its anticipated usefulness might be actualized.

Under this assumption the relation of that agent to his or her own experience of the aesthetic may now plausibly become a source of information about how we might act at any future moment. Under the power of cognition we may conceivably *choose* that future no less than, by sentience alone, we mindlessly hasten its arrival. Contemplating the function of the museum in this regard, Goodman indicates the degree to which a preoccupation with the temporal path of mental activity in the aesthetic elides the nominalistic tenor of the word *work* qua *artwork* with the transitive, verbal aspects of *work* qua *labor*. The notion of the art "work" consequently assumes more than knowledge of an object, even an object meticulously reflective of a competent subject. As Goodman says: "Works, work when they inform vision; inform not by supplying information but by *forming* or *re*-forming, or *trans*-forming vision; vision not as confined to ocular percepts but as understanding in general" (*Of Mind*, 180). The generality of conceptual understanding is no substitute for the particularity that instantiates it as act. But it is precisely the redundant generality of Goodman's appeal to generality that makes it hard for us to see how it could issue in any particular act. Goodman's discrediting of the use of an artwork as a "visual aid for use in seeing what lies beyond it" (180)[3] evokes a world of experience that would seem to be accessible only according to some more specifiable linkage between the weak agency of the unformed viewer and the relatively stronger agency conferred by the aesthetic form.

To this end we might observe how Goodman's appeal to a standard of "understanding in general," arising as it does from the postulate of form as re-formation, invites comparison with the project of Adorno's *Aesthetic Theory*. We have already seen how Adorno's work also seeks to situate aesthetic experience within the field of "understanding," thus challenging "the absurd and awkward myth of the insularity of aesthetic experience." Adorno, like Goodman, is a conscientious theorist of the aesthetic whose troubling with the term aspires to more than a careful adequation of subject and object. Adorno, like Goodman, seeks to make of the aesthetic something more than a weak echo of the most voluble ideals of Enlightenment epistemology. Though Goodman seems to owe no specific conceptual debt to Adorno, it is nonetheless impossible to ignore the terminological convergence of such diversely determined aesthetic theories upon the phenomenon of cognitive determination. Adorno's touchstone for the aesthetic is what we might call a notion of "cumulative cognition." In *Aesthetic Theory* he stipulates: "one thing must be conceded immediately, and that is that, if cognition proceeds by way of cumulation at all, it is in aesthetics" (474). The invidious distinction Adorno subsequently draws between the manifestations of the aesthetic and what he calls the "pre-aesthetic" gives us our most secure grip on the conceptual efficacy of this "cumulation" in determining the aesthetic.

Adorno characterizes the pre-aesthetic in baldly psychologistic terms as *projection,* a confusion of the identity of the viewer with the object, while the aesthetic proper denotes *movement,* a displacement of the subject in relation to the object. Despite the nominal resurrection of a time-honored distinction between life and art, the meticulously observed temporal lag of the so-called pre-aesthetic mitigates the apparent incommensurability of the respective fields of reference—of projection and movement—rendering the incipient antithesis of these terms more reciprocally dynamic.

Hence, it is not surprising that Adorno generalizes his point about the cumulative cognition of the aesthetic experience by putting it in the terms of a self-negation that is more differential than negative (a convergence of stasis and kinesis). Again, in *Aesthetic Theory* Adorno avers that "real aesthetic experience is a movement against the subject for the sake of the subject and its *a priori* primacy. Real aesthetic experience requires self-abnegation on the part of the viewer, the ability to respond to what art works say and what they keep to themselves" (474). Furthermore, Adorno encapsulates this analysis under the subheading "Aesthetic experience as a form of objective Verstehen" (473), thus reviving Dilthey's standard of hermeneutic knowledge—the connectedness of events in their particularity. *Verstehen* is relevant for Adorno's aesthetic in conspicuously inverse proportion to its long-standing discredit among philosophers. The *verstehen* of aesthetic experience is its war with philosophical abstraction. Thus does Adorno resonantly declaim the credo of post-Enlightenment materialist critique: "Aesthetics is a living protest against abstraction" (491).

At this point we might provisionally generalize that it is the particularity of the aesthetic experience that, for both Goodman and Adorno, seems to mandate its grounding in mediate, even agonistic, subjectivity. Furthermore, this mediation, conditioned as it must be by the objects it attends upon, presupposes an agency that is neither preemptively teleological nor inexhaustibly intuitive. In Adorno's case this succinctly explains the turn to a Diltheyan "connectedness" that articulates consciousness as a process without negating its temporal specificity. And, indeed,

such connectedness, denoted as cognitive process and instantiated as subjective agency, is precisely what Adorno's aesthetic theory seems to grasp
by recourse to the dynamics of cognitive cumulation.

Nevertheless, we cannot ignore the degree to which Adorno's notion
of cognitive cumulation thus marks an opacity as well as a highlight of
his aesthetic theorizing. Because Adorno does not explain how we get
from the ostensibly kinetic mode of cognition to the punctually passive
mode of cumulation, his exposition of cognitive cumulation fails to expose
the roots of the distinction between the pre-aesthetic and the aesthetic
that we have already been asked to accept. He has set himself the challenge
of showing that the necessity of their relation is claimed to be as much
the condition of their mutual intelligibility as it is the disjuncture between them. Furthermore, because the term *cumulation* seems to be driven
by cognition, it is hard to see *how* cumulative consciousness can gain any
self-reflective purchase without dissipating its identity in an endless proliferation of cognitive determinations. This would, in effect, constitute
the loss of subjectivity as a meaningful vantage point of human perspective. In other words we are now bound to ask more rigorously, *How* is
cumulation cognitive? *How* is the subject against itself, a subject that can
see itself in any purposive terms that are not ultimately self-annihilating?
Or, *how* does the aesthetic help to realize human identity under the
increasingly significant exigencies of time and change?

Because these questions interrogate the prospectus of human reflective
capacity, I want to complement Adorno's deployment of the term *cumulation* (and in the process to sharpen the focus of Goodman's notion of
cognitive efficacy) with an emphatically speculative "look" at Jean-Paul
Sartre's philosophy of reflection in *Being and Nothingness*. In this way I
want to accommodate the augmented breadth of human agency valorized
in both Goodman's and Adorno's theorizing of the aesthetic, without
sacrificing its reflective depth. Such a sacrifice would amount to a critical
hypocrisy: invoking the name of the aesthetic in order to ennoble the goals
of human subjectivity, while depleting the means for achieving such
goals. It would, in other words, rehearse the most futile episodes of the
history of aesthetic theory. Once again, I am thinking here of the eighteenth-century theories of Shaftesbury, Hutcheson, and Johnson, which
autocratically subsume productive agency to an ultimately self-mystifying
legislative will.[4]

Specifically, if we begin with the question "How is cumulation cognitive?" we can look at the concept of choice in Sartre's analysis of the circle

of desire and see that, for him, choice embraces agency, transformation, and temporality all at once. This is, roughly speaking, the kind of work Goodman and Adorno want the aesthetic to do. The significant difference between Sartre's discourse on desire and Goodman's and Adorno's discourses on cognition is most simply that Sartre does not purport to be making aesthetic theory. Nevertheless, Sartre's theory, more than the others, is so intrinsically narrative that it brings us into closer proximity with the material substrate of aesthetic judgment than the discourses of the aesthetic proper.

In *Being and Nothingness* the coordinates of Sartrean reflection are plotted on the familiar axes of self and other. But they are now projected into the more palpable dimension of sexual desire. The narrative dynamics of sexual desire insure that Sartre will not fall into the trap of a phenomenological reduction that renders either self or other absolute contingencies of one another. On the contrary, sexual emplotment is marked by the structure of reversal whereby what "is" reveals itself inexorably to be that which it "is not."

For Sartre sadomasochism epitomizes the striving for a human identity expressed as desire. The sadomasochistic poles of the sexual bond bear some comparison with the apparent antithesis of cognition (active) and cumulation (passive). Bodily existence is the fulcrum of this seesaw dynamic inasmuch as the would-be sadist aspires to freedom from the contingency of the body. The sadist desires to realize himself as freedom in his objectification of the other as a body qua contingent body. But the body serves simultaneously as the object and the pretext of that desire, what Sartre calls "the desire for desire." Thus, the reversal of relations between sadistic and masochistic bodies is revealed to be the very animus of consciousness itself.

That is to say, the sadistic free will founders upon the realization (contrary to sadistic intentions) that the tortured body manifests a limit as well as an expression of the sadist's objectifying self. This can only be transcended in the painful habitation of the victimized body. It is a feature of what Judith Butler, in an astute account of the genealogical links between Sartrean ontology and Hegelian dialectic, has called "the perspectival character of corporeal life" (139).[5] The body is the marker of contingency—but it is coincidentally the proof that contingency is never pure or absolute and hence harbors no threat of relativistic or totalistic (metaphysical) abstraction. On the contrary, to acknowledge that contingency inheres in the body's status as a medium for desire is to realize that contingency is always manifest as signification, as the body's insuperable affectivity toward the world. Because bodily contingency signifies in its affectivity toward an other, it signifies perforce as narrative, as an order that obtains within the constraints of temporal successiveness. It can therefore only gain self-expressive power through transformation.

Appropriately, the narrative plot of sadism has its most climactic climax in the access to physical pleasure, which reasserts the very body that the sadist struggled to deny. This impels the reciprocity between sadist and masochist. Contrary to classical precedent, however, this need not be a catharsis of tragic dimensions. For the agency of recognition in Sartre's scheme is deemed to be "prereflective." The prereflective consciousness, by contrast with the reflective consciousness of objectifying sadism, is expressly a consciousness of the inadequacy of objectification. More important, it is a consciousness that the realization of inadequacy itself constitutes a choice *to be another way*. After all, being is sustained negatively by dint of its not being *there,* thematized in the object. From this realization there follows the knowledge of the necessity to choose being. Thus, the prereflective consciousness, like Adorno's pre-aesthetic, does not denote a simple temporal priority or succession. Furthermore, it exceeds the explanatory powers of those too simple notions of narrative or aesthetic totality that depend upon a strictly teleological catharsis—in which reversal, a perspectival inversion, is presumptively conflated with the constative as opposed to the performative values of recognition. We have seen such teleologies discredited by Goodman and Adorno in the interests of a cognition that enlarges the determinative province of subjectivity rather than reducing it preemptively to the terms of its lucidity, or worse, dissolving its lucidity into an intensity of bodily feeling.

By contrast, in the case of the prereflective consciousness the critique of teleology does not altogether dispense with *peripeteia* and the perspectival imperative implied in teleological emplotment. The choice that is instantiated in prereflective consciousness obtains as an acceptance of the limit of reflective consciousness. This is so with the strict knowledge that the acceptance of a limit is a movement beyond the limit and that the prepositional force of this "beyond" has syntactical more than semantic bearing on the agency whose vector of motion it is. Just as the body, caught in the circle of sexual desire, is manifestly a hinge between alternating self-recognitions (objectified and objectifying, free and embodied), so prereflective consciousness depends upon a perspectival point of departure only to contemplate it as the expansion of the distance that it seemed to delimit. In this regard Sartre says of the body, the locus of prereflective consciousness, that it "is a point of departure which I am and which at the same time I surpass toward what I have to be" (*Being and Nothingness,* 326).

Here I believe we are speaking of the prereflective consciousness as if it might be tantamount to an expressly cognitive internalization of contingency. But, contrary to the self-annihilating momentum of pure contingency, consciousness in this case remains coherent through the necessity that each moment of cognitive attention is bound within the state or situation of frustrated reflection (which is the threshold for revelation of the prereflective consciousness): one knows one's self through the reflected object but realizes therefore, and perforce, that one does not know one's self as the knower. But this need not present an aporia of knowledge. In a sense this coherence follows the Aristotelian logic of peripetic reversal, stipulated as praxis in the *Poetics*.

There is implicit in Sartre's exposition precisely the Aristotelian emphasis upon choosing one's nature within the exigencies of a situation that exceeds one's apparent knowledge. In Hazel Barnes's appendix ("Key to Special Terminology") to *Being and Nothingness* we note that for the prereflective—or unreflective—consciousness "there is no knowledge, but a consciousness of being consciousness of an object" (630). I have already alleged that for the Aristotle of the *Poetics* the gist of action in tragic drama is a self-realization realized through the peripetic displacement or transformation, of an intentionalist logic. In this regard the reversal of fate is not an absolute discontinuity except in terms of what Sartre would call simple, reflective consciousness, e.g., Oedipus' throne reflects a loss of being as compared with the indomitability of his persevering will. This points up the difference between the loss of being of objects and that self-loss that may now be considered constitutive for the self. In its irreducible temporality *peripeteia* may be construed, in a Sartrean sense, as the continuation of being, as a decision-making process within which difference is inexorably made relevant to what one was. Here we accept a curious recognition that "what was" must be treated as a variable of "what is" rather than vice versa. *Peripeteia* is therefore a transformation accumulated about the temporal moment of its instantiation rather than a renunciation of that moment through an ecstasy of ironic abandon. In this regard *peripeteia* is a virtual cumulation of being.

I am deliberately evoking Adorno's cumulation here in its capacity to articulate the nonidentitarian logic of the negative dialectic. Because for Sartre too this line of thought asserts that *not* all experience falls dumbly within the polarity of subjects and objects, whereby consciousness of things is exclusively immediate or mediate. Sartre intimates that the prereflective consciousness is neither immediate nor mediate. In effect, he entertains the possibility that experience can be both. Or this is the gist of a famous retort to Jean Hyppolite concerning the question of whether or not cognitive experience obtains exclusively in conceptual reflection: "[The prereflective is] all the originality and ambiguity which is *not* the immediacy of life and which prepares this act of consciousness which is reflection."[6] Here I think Sartre adopts a basically Fichtean stance (Butler points out that Sartre is to Hyppolite as Fichte was to Hegel on this matter) insofar as the contradictoriness of successive moments of self-development is integral to the self and not projected outward toward a collective, universalizing consciousness.

In *Being and Nothingness* the body itself becomes the ultimate reference point for Sartre's prereflective consciousness:

> the body is the contingent form which is taken up by the necessity of my contingency. We can never apprehend this contingency as such in so far as our body is *for us*, for we are a choice and for us, to be is to choose ourselves . . . this inapprehensible body is precisely the necessity that there be a choice, that I do not exist *all at once*. (328)

The choice to be, as conditioned by the knowledge that "I do not exist all at once," legislates a law of differentiation. More important, it is expressly a solicitation of the world in its particularity since the choice to be is constrained by the tripartite structure of temporal succession (past, present, future). This temporally embodied self thus emerges through a transformation that must in this case be deemed referential without being denotative. Thus, I will assert that its value obtains as a virtual syntactical rather than semantic/conceptual bond in the sense that syntax too is both connective and dissociative. Or we could say with Sartre that "every consciousness . . . supports a certain relation with its own facticity" (*Being and Nothingness*, 386–87)—a relation with its own temporality that is forged through the syntactical vicissitudes of identification and differentiation and that renders factic contingency an articulate medium of thought in the first place. In Sartre it is as if *peripeteia* denoted the cognitive efficacy of every moment instead of a reference to the quintessential moment out of time.[7]

Or, even more pointedly, we might say that, by locating the prereflective agency *as*, rather than *in*, the body ("consciousness exists its body"), and thus saving himself from the abjection of an utterly metaphysical inwardness, Sartre is insisting that the prereflective is intelligible through semiotic matrices. After all, for Sartre the body is never experienced outside an interpretive field: "consciousness of the body is comparable to consciousness of a sign" (*Being and Nothingness,* 330). Following a truism of semiotic analysis, we must agree that consciousness of the body "as a sign" would entail the surpassing of the body toward its meaning, which makes it, in Sartre's words, "a lateral and retrospective consciousness of what consciousness is without having to be it (i.e., of its inapprehensible *contingency*, of that in terms of which consciousness makes itself a choice) and hence it is a non-thetic consciousness of *the manner in which it is affected* " [emphasis added].[8] If contingency is, according to Sartre, "that in terms of which consciousness makes itself a choice," then the prereflective agency, the home of choice, must be the condition under which these terms (the terms in which consciousness makes itself a choice) are bound to proliferate in a headlong semiosis.

This is the case since the body cannot *but* signify in its ineluctable "affectivity" (Butler 163). As we have noted already, the subject, in the "attitude" of its own affectivity, is already in the world. It thereby discovers itself to have already exercised choice. But this is not to relegate choice to the status of an unconscious motive or a Heideggerian "thrownness." In fact, Judith Butler characterizes this choice as only too consciously answering the question implicit in the sheer duration of our facticity: "How [is one] to be in one's situation?" The situation here, as in Hegel, is the necessity of recovering one's self from an ecstatic estrangement. But the indissoluble connection with other beings, with the world, which is discovered to be a prior unity in Hegelian *Geist,* is what must be *actively established or enacted* by Sartre (Butler 132). By contrast with Hegel, Sartrean temporality does not resolve its contradictions in the course of its passing but presents occasions for doing so, for doing something, for positing ends that are not already foregone conclusions.

More to the point, by his deference to the affective "situatedness" of the subject Sartre adds another measure of lucidity to the agency of prereflective choice. He indicates the degree to which the being of this consciousness, because it is already a connection to the world, must have its own predicative thrust. And its status, as "already there," suggests that this predicative thrust is once again bound by a recursive logic. For we might imagine that such choice is indexed in the specific consequences that make it known to itself. This is the structure of motivation that Sartre portentously calls "project" rather than intention. A project is an activity of consciousness that escapes the solipsistic fate that would otherwise threaten subjectivity under the restriction of an intentionalist teleology. Butler acknowledges this insofar as she points out that "the body is a restricted perspective as well as a perspective that constantly transcends itself towards other perspectives" (144). By contrast, intention would render the concept of perspective tautological for subjectivity.

We must be careful to note that where Sartre discusses affectivity and the perspective it imposes on the world, he somewhat contradictorily calls it a "transcendental intention towards the world." But to head off any confusion he quickly distinguishes this intention from its teleological counterpart. Its manifestation in prereflective choice would seem to allow for the possibility that, as we have already noted, it is both immediate and not immediate: "Since affectivity is a surpassing it presupposes a surpassed" (*Being and Nothingness*, 330–31).[9] Again I believe the same could be said of the "chosen" perspective of Aristotelian catharsis, combining, as it does, a retrospect (*peripeteia*) and a prospect (*anagnorisis*) without an inevitably or necessarily hegemonic succession—i.e., peripetic reversal does not break its connection with the past so much as it transforms the past by revealing its fit with new coordinates of experience.

Anthony Cascardi, attempting to distinguish the transformative inertia of narrative alluded to here, from the value-bereft and rationally incoherent realm of infinite transformations, has usefully pointed out that: "narratives are able to establish the validity [value] of ends by a series of transformations that require as little as the recontextualization of initial terms" (282). This is a rationalization of narrative desire that valorizes its potential for a rich diversification of human motives via transformative self-consciousness; I believe that Sartrean prereflective consciousness invites us to take the same cognitive path by the emphasis it places upon the role of choice in articulating that consciousness. It would seem that choice here has an expressive register inasmuch as the choice to be, by its acutely contingent bearing on the world and the ineluctable signifying momentum of that contingency, inevitably chooses *to be something else*. This is specifically the mechanism of its reflective scope. Thus, prereflective consciousness does not constitute a suspension of ends so much as an acknowledgment of the degree to which ends and the discourse of value that they sustain depend upon a self-conscious recontextualizing of beginnings.

Furthermore, I believe that the effort to grasp Sartre here once again implicitly returns us to the consideration of syntax as a key to narrative understanding. This is specifically compelling in the transformative/cumulative impetus of prereflective choice as we have just outlined it. For choice, construed within this constellation of concepts, makes us think reflection and prereflection as coincidental in the phenomenon of contextual transformation just as syntactical ordination makes us think subject *and* predicate as transformation. Or, more precisely, we think them alternatively and together, despite the predisposition of paradigmatic syntax to subsume the parts rather than to integrate by distinction.

From this vantage we might now see how our digression into Sartrean ontology has brought us back epistemologically to the point of departure from which this argument took off: I believe we could now say that choice proffers a temporal bridge between cognition, which we might now identify with reflection, and cumulation, which we might now identify with the prereflective. Choice is that bridge insofar as it expresses reflective consciousness by its very entailment of prereflective agency. Reflection is cognitive in its *being through negation*. But the being of reflection *is* only itself when free from the being of objects. This freedom is only attainable in the succession of objects of desire that renders prereflective agency per se, an exemplary cumulation. In effect, we might say that the being of reflection is only itself when it is turning into something else. We will remember that, for Adorno, cumulation (like prereflective agency) is explicitly a counter for the subject's surpassing the terms of "simple reflection." The art object for Adorno is distinct from ordinary conceptual objects precisely insofar as it *is already a sign,* and, so, whatever cognition attends upon it will be understood to be a "second reflection." Second reflection mitigates that propensity for reifying abstraction that otherwise prevails in the more dogmatic subjectivity of simple negation (*Aesthetic Theory,* 490).

On these grounds choice would also appear to be a plausible crux of aesthetic determination, where (as in Goodman and Adorno) we look toward aesthetic determination for a mode of subjective reflection that augments its own determinative scope without lapsing into eccentric or ideological subjectivism. Perhaps it is fair to say that aesthetic experience, inflected by Sartrean choice, echoes Adorno's "movement against the subject for the sake of the subject." It overcomes the polarizing opposition of self and other, which, by its weakness for preemptive negations, inhibits a second reflection. Moreover, we cannot overlook the fact that the transformational imperative of choice that facilitates this "overcoming" may now be perceived to be the place where the aesthetic and the narrative converge upon the locus of subjective action and its motivations.

Thus, the aesthetic agent is charged with a wider exploitation of contextual experience than would be mandated under the terms of a more sensationalistic orientation to the aesthetic object and the more complacent role of the artist that goes with such an orientation. We must now examine the consequences of that charge.

Three Poems: A Case of Lateral Development

The recognition that *Three Poems* is a work deeply embedded in the problematic of human motive and act is most indisputable in the fact that it is a work of prose. To characterize *Three Poems* as prose is to acknowledge that syntactical order—rather than any of the relatively more external elements of prosody, rhyme, metrics, stanzaic arrangement—gives the work its structural integrity. More important, we must observe that the conspicuous number 3 in the title bears on syntactical lucidity in a way that strikingly contrasts with the monological intelligibility of lyric expression. The tripartite structure of Ashbery's narrative ("The New Spirit," "The System," "The Recital") further supports a hypothesis that syntactical order projects us into the temporal realm of act, despite the fact that, by its paradoxical evocation of a multiplicity *and* a unity, Ashbery's title seems to solicit one intuition that would subsume their differences.[10]

Nevertheless, Ashbery's syntax in *Three Poems* is, by its remarkably active complexity, resistant to the integration solicited in its title. The critic's first temptation is in turn to allegorize the multitude of transformations within the text to a general concept of transformative process in order to reconcile the otherwise incommensurable dimensions of form and content. I want to show how we would be, in that way, tempted to read the "style" of the text too reductively as a mimesis of ephemeral mental states. Such a reading would achieve only a valorization of cognitive activity without any cognitive effectivity of its own. We would lose any purchase on the possibility of augmenting reflective capacity, which was what led us to link the aesthetic to the phenomenon of cognition in the first place. After all, a thought about thought that demurs the exigencies and consequences of its own thinking would be the perfect antithesis of the aesthetic project that prompts my reading of Ashbery's prose. For my purposes, and above all else, Ashbery's prose style constitutes a rich source of information about the nature of narrative desire, especially as it bears on the intersecting axes of motive and act.

Moreover, any reading that purports to do justice to the formal complications of this text must treat the cognitive constraints of formal invention as continuous with the cognitive efficacy of that form. It must resist any separation of the question of formal identity from the phenomenon of cognitive activity. My purpose here will be to show that the aesthetic value of this work inheres precisely in its facilitating the workings of such an understanding. Not coincidentally, I will do this in a way that glosses Sartre's "lateral and retrospective consciousness of what consciousness is without having to be it."

If *Three Poems* is nothing else, then, it is a meditation upon the tensions that play between conceptual and empirical life. In an early moment of the narrative, when the typography of the prose almost pedantically mimes its conceptual movements, Ashbery links the formal shape of this work with the conceptual framework of choosing *any particular* formal stance toward the world of one's desires:

> Even as I say this
> I seem to hear you and see you wishing me well, your eyes
> taking in some rapid lateral development
>
> reading without comprehension
>
> and always taken up on the reel of what is happening in
> the wings. (12–13)

Though the pronoun markers are in process of transformation throughout this text, it is important to note that the distance that conditions any distinction between them becomes a veritable fixed point of reference. Here, in particular, pronomial instability gives the venerable I-thou dyad a more malleable scope of reference than it might otherwise embrace. Furthermore, the "lateral development" that our comprehension of the phrase "reading without comprehension" entails—our eyes moving on the prose page—specifically evokes the philosophical context within which we have been thinking. It is the denial of a simple teleology and a de facto acceptance of the consequent vacillation between mutually unacceptable choices of pure subjectivity and pure objectivity. In this passage our effective comprehension of incomprehension in the act of reading qua comprehending reenacts that oscillation.

In fact, the choices have already been posed in mock-philosophical jargon in the very first sentences of this text:

> I thought that if I could put it all down that would be one way. And next the thought came to me that to leave all out would be another and truer way. (3)

Here are the founding platitudes of two strong philosophical traditions, each of which aspires to the totalizing ideal of system: one by dint of exercising the will, the other by disciplined, albeit bad faith, abstinence from the same. In both cases "truth" is the counter of subjective experience, but by virtue of its undecidability. The incommensurability of the two choices is thus revealed to be only the mask of an ever more demonic contingency. And yet the subsequent turn toward a lateral development (which is in effect the turning of the narrative into a process of turning into something else) presents an occasion for reflecting upon the preemptiveness of such conclusions.

In fact, the torsions of lateral movement prompt an intuition that Ashbery's initial posing of the choice—between putting down and leaving out—constituted a false dichotomy. As such, Ashbery's technique must be seen as a rejection of any notion of choosing that could accommodate a truth bound so self-deludedly to the logic of dichotomy. Or, rather, it is the intimation of a truth that is more plausibly "yourself," which, as Ashbery's persona alleges, comes inevitably to stand in the "place" of truth; Ashbery's persona concludes the passage just quoted: "It is you who made this, therefore you are true" (3). The self conceived here is meticulously responsive to the constituting exigencies of its being in relation to others, rather than being merely a malignant symptom of that opposition.

In turn, the falsity of the dichotomy of putting down and leaving out is most glaringly exposed in our simple recognition that there is no way of putting everything down (the dream of semantic fullness) except by presupposing what is left out, an "outside," which cannot be inclusive of itself. If we consider semantics to be a counter for representing presence (*vorstellung*) and syntax to be a counter for the relationality that instantiates presence (*darstellung*), it follows that syntactical fullness (rather than semantic fullness) indicates a solution of the paradox confronted here merely by revealing it, or by accepting it as the case. After all, syntax constitutes an effective leaving out precisely by virtue of its cumulative efficacy. Syntactical order is selective, and thereby exclusive—i.e., syntax gives us a paradigm for leaving out *by putting down,* whereas semantics, by privileging the putting down, can only leave itself out as a plausible agency. Perhaps one could thus conclude that leaving out is the only way of putting down, and this is why reflection (hence personal identity) is more effectively compassed in terms of syntactic rather than semantic knowledge. This leaving out is the effective continuity of transformation and totality.

Aptly, the culminating moment of "The New Spirit," and perforce a transition to "The System," turns upon this theme of eliding totality with transformation. And it does so by a brilliantly complex animation of the figure of turning. In fact, by its turning from the nominal to the verbal modalities of the concept of the turn, the effective "focal point" of "The New Spirit" both compasses the circuit of human reflection (the subject turning into the object, the face in the mirror) and the irresistible turning of visual reflection into cognitive reflection. In this passage the Tower of Babel is the allusive armature of the turning motion. If we note how the act of building the tower (echoes of *bildüng* battle the babble) elicits an image of multiplicity striving for unity, then we may appreciate how this matrix of allusion elucidates the interchange between sense and rationality that we have so problematically anticipated in contemplating the elision of transformation with totality.

As if recapitulating the choice between putting down and leaving out, Ashbery's allusion to the Tower of Babel follows a view of the progression of life in "stages." For Ashbery's persona the confinement of life within strictly teleological terms instantiates human desire so claustrophobically that it impels him toward a paradoxical self-renunciation in his quest for a more adequate self-image. But the antithesis to the tower (i.e., "turning one's back on it") turns out to be both a turning away from and a return to the desires that are reflected in the image of the tower:

> But it dawned on him all of a sudden that there was another way, that this horrible vision of the completed Tower of Babel, flushed in the sunset as the last ceramic brick was triumphantly fitted into place, perfect in its vulgarity, an eternal reminder of the advantages of

industry and cleverness—that the terror could be shut out—and really shut out—simply by turning one's back on it. As soon as it was not looked at it ceased to exist. In the other direction one saw the desert and drooping above it the constellations that had presided impassively over the building of the metaphor that seemed about to erase them from the skies. Yet they were in no way implicated in the success or the failure, depending on your viewpoint, of the project, as became clear the minute you caught sight of the Archer, languidly stretching his bow, aiming at a still higher and smaller portion of the heavens, no longer a figure of speech but an act, even if all the life had been temporarily drained out of it. (50–51)

Though the image of the Tower of Babel annunciates a meditation on the limits of human self-reflection, the efficacy of the reflected image only too graphically does *not* come clear in the spatial terms that promulgated it. What follows the image of the tower, as the passage devolves to more and more speculative abstraction (the progressive dissolution of the image), seems to entail a palpable loss of that perspective upon which our subjective grasp of things as things naturally subsists. I want to assert that, if the image of the tower functions here in a visual register at all, it is only by analogy, or, to use Goodman's terms, by an invidious appeal to strictly functional rather than sense-qualitative criteria.

In a curious way we might say that in this passage the image of the tower functions like an anamorphic cylinder, proffering a reflective unity from diversity/disorder (the stages of life's progression) that cannot be grasped within the immediacy of the very visual register it prevails upon for its self-presentation. The anamorphic cylinder *does* reflect, but not by re-producing a planar perspective. To the contrary, it actively produces that perspective as if from a welter of confused perceptions. Thus, it reveals the necessity for a productive (rather than re-productive) agency to consummate the reflective act.[11] It is worth noting that the anamorphic image was a popular allegorical emblem of the more adventurous forays of eighteenth-century philosophy into the relatively uncharted reaches of the aesthetic. The postulate of a standard for artistic perfection was an effort to move rationality across the threshold of formal logic into the realm of dynamic experience, a so-called creative perception. It intimated the necessity of a reason whose law-giving powers would arise from the activity of making real discriminations rather than from the subsumption of real differences to a prior unitary principle. The integrity of rational law would thus be discoverable in the activity of mind reflecting upon its own powers of lawful discrimination.[12]

That this interaction between the rational and the sensible (visual) is likewise a fulcrum of the meaning of reflection in Ashbery's text becomes acutely apparent in our realization that the persona's "turning one's back" on the tower involuntarily mimes and thus mirrors again the convex curve of the edifice that originally bore, however distortedly, his reflection. Furthermore, the turning away prevails upon precisely that malleability of the spatial dimension that perspective painting presumes upon in its freedom to depart from, rather than to coincide with, the object it professes to reflect. Here is the revelation of the illusory distinction between the visual and the cognitive. In perspective painting the visual is cognitive by virtue of the mathematical calculus through which the image is *made* to appear. The "illusory" perspectival image sought in the spatial register (whether on the retina or on the canvas) is, of course, synonymous with the self-transformative dream of subjective autonomy that is nonetheless at odds with the medium of its self-recognition. This dream springs eternal from a terror of incompleteness otherwise thrust upon us by the illimitable abstraction of independent cognition.

In the Tower of Babel passage that terror is quite deliberately reflected in the ambiguity of the pronoun references that ensue upon the appearance of the tower: "the terror could be shut out . . . simply by turning one's back on *it*. As soon as *it* was not looked at *it* ceased to exist" (my emphasis). The *it* turns between the terror and the tower for its proper antecedent, making a mockery both of the linearity of perspective and the presumption to a secure intentionality of will within which perspective may be presupposed. In this context we cannot forget that the tower, like any rounded object that appears to us in space, ceases to exist at the vanishing point of the curvilinear illusion, which, in the painter's craft especially, would be intended to evoke its invisible *other* side and thus complete its argument of solidity. Correspondingly, the one who turns her back on the tower, who demurs the depravity of illusion, employs the inverse measure of such depravity in the artifice of that renunciative will. It is a hermetic retreat into subjectivity, a flight from the objectivity of "real" space.

The conspicuously spatial cue that punctuates this knowledge, "In the other direction one saw the desert . . . ," recapitulates the previous perspectival confusions and gives us our best initiative for clarifying them.

The turning in the "other direction" is effectively rendered directionless in this context. It constitutes a disorientation that is no less sharply mirrored in the knowledge that the "constellations drooping above it" reflect a desire for self-reflection (the repertoire of astrological signs, a pervasive context of Ashbery's narrative) that is ultimately refractory in its inevitable recourse to signs that must distort what they profess to reflect.

What the whole passage does, therefore, is to intimate a method that might dispel the false dichotomy that inaugurated Ashbery's narrative. I adduced the analogue of the anamorph because, in its "miraculous" unification, it makes eloquent testimony about the intrinsicality of transformation to totality. The optical trick of the anamorph, like the syncretistic continuity between antithetical realms imaged in the Tower of Babel, is an allegory of the striving after divine essence. This struggle ironically expresses the essence of the secular (a rich contradiction in terms in itself) as precisely the act of *making essential*—i.e., it expresses the essentiality of making qua *making* to the enterprise of totalization. Hence, there is no turning away from the tower because there is only turning. By virtue of this knowledge we are made adept in the ways of a lateral (narrative) rather than a vertical (transcendental) development. In other words what "rounds out" our existence in the world of this text is tantamount to the confusion of Nature and artifice epitomized by the convex glass, which magically conjures depth out of relief.[13]

It is no accident that this epistemological project is acknowledged in a subsequent episode of Ashbery's text (no less accidentally entitled "The System") in the mock-worshipful name of "the convex one" (57). In this epithet Ashbery deftly kaleidoscopes diverse planes of thought, once more mirroring the collapsing of divergent spatial planes in the optical mechanics of the convex surface. Indeed, the self-mockery of the epithet speaks eloquently to the narcissistic gaze that otherwise manifests the agency of an overwhelming self-deception.

The "confusion" of diverse planes evokes an expressly (though unexpectedly) rational goal in this context. This is even more dramatically the case if we recall once more how the etymology of the term *confusion,* in eighteenth-century aesthetics, denoted a perceptual corollary to the unity of the manifold endowed by rational concept. Con-fusion, the bringing together of disparate particulars into a perceptual gestalt, offered, as we have noted specifically with respect to A. G. Baumgarten's aesthetic, a possibility of making the sensible world conformable with the rational world.[14] Or at least such would be the case insofar as the sensate manifold was marked as an intersection of the axes of universality and particularity: one that could only be represented through their mutual transformation. Such is indeed the case as I have explained it, in Baumgarten's *Reflections on Poetry* and his *Aesthetica,* where the orderliness of the aesthetic object obtains in the self-differentiating ordination of its sensate particulars, i.e., in its productive agency.

What Ashbery gives us in *Three Poems* is, correlatively, a way of employing confusion for a unitarian end that is not abstractable in either a thematic generality or a sensate immediacy: he makes self-reflection integral to its self-production. This point is usefully contextualized by recalling how Western aesthetic theory has historically vacillated between privileging the subsumptive, legislative aspect of mind (Kames, Hutcheson) or its discriminatory, productive aspect (Hume, Coleridge). Traditionally, confusion, the "productive" extensional sensory gestalt, had been invidiously contrasted with "the legislative" ideal of distinct clarity: the intensive, rational, concept. It was specifically in response to this tradition that Baumgarten, formulated the category of aesthetic in the virtually oxymoronic terms of a "confused or indistinct clarity," proposing implicitly that a principle of coherence rather than a principle of disjuncture mediated the registers of confusion and clarity.

According to this innovation of thinking, Baumgarten had alleged that there could be degrees of confusion insofar as clarity was understood to obtain on a sliding scale of intensive and extensive determinations. Above all other artistic media, the visual image in poetry was for Baumgarten the exemplum of the extensively clear but indistinct or confused representation because it starkly manifested a con-fusion of aspects. Its confusedness was nonetheless orderly—not in its reduction to a logical essence but, rather, in its paradoxical essentializing of a logical activity. The visual image was hereby characterized as both an *assemblage of parts* as well as an intuitively totalizable whole. Contrary to Baumgarten's explicit aim, however, I believe that this account of aesthesis as an assemblage needs to transcend its own exemplification in the visual image in order to engage more directly the temporality of the syntactic order that it adumbrates.[15]

Ironically, yet true to the productivist bias of Baumgarten's aesthetic, I want to show how Ashbery's prose technique gives us a motive for modifying Baumgarten's criteria of "confused clarity," which I am otherwise suggesting *Three Poems* exemplifies so well. Specifically, the passage from "The System" which we have been examinig so closely does approximate a corollary to the painterly visual perspective that Baumgarten appears to privilege in his emphasis on the image. But, particularly in its transitional placement between "The New Spirit" and "The Recital," and in its ever more obtrusive syntactical twisting, "The System" evokes the painter's magical turning of the spectatorial I/eye, so as to reveal the emergent roundness of things that *time,* not space, produces in the tradition of perspective painting. Contrary to all conspicuous appearances, the tricks of single point perspective are in fact temporally, not spatially, inspired. They are predicated explicitly, according to Alberti (*On Painting*), on a ratio of differential subject positions.[16] Time inheres in space where differential perspectives obtain.

Just so, I believe that, in Baumgarten's making the image a touchstone of poetic perfection, there is an implicitly unaccounted for temporal dimension that the phenomenon of syntax in Ashberyan prose expresses. Furthermore, I believe that the continuity of Ashberyan syntax with the precept of confused clarity, by which Baumgarten conferred value upon the image, has explicitly to do with its way of augmenting the determinateness of attentional consciousness. This is its cognitive dimension.

Such speculation is fueled by Baumgarten himself in section #38 of *Reflections on Poetry,* in which he clarifies the mimetic power of the visual image, not in terms of its "picturing" the forms of Nature (as unified in sense experience) but, rather, in *producing* the *effects* of sense experience: "Now to represent images as clearly as possible is poetic. Therefore it is poetic to make them very similar to sensations" (52). The clarity of the image is thus understood as a function of the number of distinctions or divisions within a continuum that it occasions (see sec. #17). I believe that Ashbery compellingly dramatizes the temporality of this logic: he "clarifies" his images by turning the image into syntax. This syntax entails a transformation of contextual boundaries that will not brook semantic plenitude but, rather, proliferates schema within which semantic meanings might be intelligibly configured.

It is no small coincidence that Herder,[17] who was the most decisive and influential disseminator of Baumgarten's aesthetics, strongly condemned the visual register as the touchstone of aesthetic perfection owing to its displacement of time and cognition. In *Plastik* (1778), Herder challenged the notion of the aesthetic as a visual discrimination that sorts particulars according to spatial criteria. Alternatively, Herder pegged the aesthetic to the *activity* of a child who[18] grasps, grips, takes, risks, probes, measuring with feet and hands, creating around itself with certainty and security the first most difficult but necessary concepts of body, form, magnitude, space, distance and suchlike. . . . Here where vision and feeling are ceaselessly bound, and each through the other is investigated, extended, raised, strengthened, is formed here the first judgement. (7–8)[19]

As we observed it to be the case in Ashbery's syntax, so Herder marks a transformative impetus in the most inertly nominalistic terms of cognition. Accordingly, Herder asserts the necessity of acknowledging that what something is depends on what one does with it.

Specifically, in the transitional moment of Ashbery's "The System" such transformability has its animus in the annunciation of a breakdown. The second section of *Three Poems* begins with the declaration: "The system is breaking down." Breakdown, as we have already noted, is the logical prerequisite of transition, so long as we understand that this moment of consciousness has the status of an explicitly temporal illusion. In the transition from one aspect or perspectival line of sight to another there is a moment whose rationality is subject to the belatedness (reflection) of its own experience. One can only see oneself seeing (present tense) by seeing what one saw (past tense): by breaking out of the perceptual mold. In this sense, of course, every moment is a transition, and we risk indulging a fatuous truism about the infinite breakdown of mortal existence. In *Three Poems,* however, Ashbery skirts this banality by seizing upon that image of images that both accepts the passage of time and defies any generalization beyond the particularity that articulates its passage: the motion picture montage.[20]

Where Herder renounced the visual paradigm of aesthetic perfection, he might nonetheless have embraced visual montage (the *techne* of motion picture art) as a vital exemplification of his claim that aesthetic perfection is most fully attainable in activity. After all, his own counterexample to the visual art of painting was sculpture. Our viewing of the work of sculpture, like the anamorphosis evoked by the Tower of Babel, imposes a requirement upon the viewer to move in space. This is a corollary to the child's self-discovery in the handling of the object. The implicit wisdom that plasticity entails a reflective imperative is grasped no less astutely by Ashbery in his invocation of the motion picture. And, not surprisingly, Ashbery invokes the movie *as* a mirror—a mirror of the most flattering and therefore vexing convexity:

We are both alive and free.

If you could see a movie of yourself you would realize that this is true. Movies show us ourselves as we had not yet learned to recognize us—(102)

More important, as we learn in a subsequent passage, the movie is a mirror in which the self's "movements alone define it" (103).

The form of the cinematic image, like the sculptural form, imposes a unique perceptual protocol. It converges on the threshold of cognitive experience without vanishing into the horizon of its enabling perspective—as would be more immediately the case in the picture plane of painting. Consequently, the self made available in the mirror of the movie (like the selves reflected by the tower and the convex glass) is both a product of succession (montage) and an agent of succession. Hence, its mirror efficacy. Hence, its "convex" knowledge of the self as a product of what it cannot see—the individual frame on the celluloid continuum. Motion picture technology marks the necessity that the self see itself by the default of an image qua *spatial image,* as the producer of its own agency of knowing. If the image *is* only in the virtual modality of montage, wherein resemblances are produced by the proliferation of differences, then the narrative integrity of such successiveness inheres in its more and more highly resolving powers of discrimination. Hence, transition governs in the place of any conceivably subsumptive integration as the guarantor of narrative intelligibility.

Re-Citation: Developing the Case

In "The Recital," the final "episode" of *Three Poems,* the movie logic of Ashbery's prose purveys what is perhaps our richest gloss on what was meant by the news that the system was "breaking down." "The Recital" commences with a quintessential and telltale moment of transition: "All right. The problem is that there is no new problem." The locutionary loop of this sentence, whereby the problem recurs as a repetition and a difference, constitutes a breakdown of sequence in the form of a reconfiguration of the terms of sequentiality. It is significantly marked as a shift, or transition, from a semantic to a syntactic threshold of meaning: the "problem" is empty semantically but full syntactically, and vice versa, since the old problem becomes new again by reason of the succession of the "new problem."

This conspicuous foregrounding of meaning, as an eliciting of grounds for further discriminations of contextual sense at the start of the third and final episode of this narrative, contrasts all the more emphatically with that other cathartic model of sequence, or successiveness, that still haunts the text as the ghost of linear, teleological subjectivity. If the narrative of *Three Poems* followed the nominally Aristotelian logic of its tripartite structure, we would expect to be led climactically out of the pattern of problematic successiveness without closure (transition qua transition, the metier of the first two episodes) into some specular integration with all that has come before. We might thereby come to some threshold of allegorical lucidity whereby the proliferating imagistic or semantic particulars of the first two episodes finally sorted themselves out into stable perspectival schemata: the way that the objects in a painted scene ironically begin to cohere as they disappear into the vanishing point. But this mode of totality has been rejected. According to this model of appearance, succession would be supplanted by a purgative disappearance of what is extraneous. We would thus be encumbered with the paradoxical insight that disappearance is the unacknowledged essence of appearance. This would be tantamount to the liquidation of particularity, which Ashbery's practice and Goodman's and Adorno's theories have so energetically fended off.

This is not to say that the rules of linear perspective are simply negated by Ashbery's movie narrative. He does not reject teleological order absolutely. Rather, the rules of perspective are made to function differently. Or we might say of Ashbery's narrative that, in the place of that cathartic episode of recognition wherein constative knowledge supplants performative knowledge, Ashbery gives us an episode in which performative and constative modalities cannot be decoupled. This does not amount to their mutual indeterminacy but, rather, to an acknowledgment that there is a determinate constraint on the phenomenon of determination itself.

For example, in "The Recital," where there are no typographical breaks in the prose to tease out the illusion of a quasi-stanzaic closure (not to mention the multiply framed frame of the motion picture image), we see very clearly how the locutionary inertia of Ashbery's prose is accelerated into more complex relations rather than arrested in schemas of cathartic revelation. Previously, the segmenting typographical breaks allegorized the contextual fissures, or discontinuities, within the overelaborated periodicity of the prose. They gave the idea of disjuncture a quasi-abstract, regulatory status in the text, adducing the effects of spontaneous consciousness as a totalizing conceit. Contrastingly, in "The Recital" contextual disjunctures (typographically *un*marked) appear to be consigned to the metonymic drift of their more prosaic contiguity. Thus do they deny a reader access to any metalevel of intelligibility, rendering the "internal" differences in the prose superficially more numerous but more superficially difficult to discern.

There is, however, and contrary to superficial appearances, a deeper level of coherence based on the solicitation of discernible differences. This becomes ever more apparent in a passage that announces its relevance to my argument by eliding the purview of the visual image (the constative register) with the purview of syntactical transformation (the performative register).

We are like sparrows fluttering and jabbering around a seemingly indifferent prowling cat; we know that the cat is stronger and therefore we forget that we have wings, and too often we fall in with the cat's plans for us, afraid and therefore unable to use the wings that could save us by bearing us aloft if only for a little distance, not the boundless leagues we had been hoping for and insisting on, but enough to make a crucial difference, the difference between life and death. (111)

In isolation the image of the fluttering sparrow eloquently figures the "montage" temporality that has kept the text epistemologically aloft from the opening conundrum announcing the paradoxical ways of totality. And at first glance this sentence, however cumulative in its length, does not proliferate those abrupt transformations of scene and action that Ashbery's syntax seems to induce everywhere else in the text. It is worth noting Ashbery's laudatory characterization of such stylistic effects in Giorgio de Chirico's distinctly nonvisual novel, *Hebdomeros,* as "the cinematic freedom of narration" ("The Decline of the Verbs," 3). In the present passage, however, the montage effect appears to be superseded by the leap to a thematic gloss. The sparrow "sees" itself in the reflective image of the cat. This is roughly an allegory of the constitutive misrecognition scene of Hegelian/Lacanian identity. Such easy thematic lucidity would seem to dispel the otherwise daunting locutionary complexity of the prose that "frames" our recognition of it. That is, the lucidity of the thematic gloss here is purchased at the cost of ignoring its "cinematic" entailment in the syntactical *verstehen* that elides image and act.

If we remember that the sparrow, in its purely visual dimension, is a vantage point of anthropomorphic perspective and, in that way, a narcissistic mirror for any metaphorically minded reader, we will possess our best clue for how to proceed with the successive conceptual/contextual twists and turns of the passage, which dissolve or blur such visual clarity. The appealing simplicity of the allegory of the bird and the cat is shattered like the paradigm of mirror reflection that is the medium of its optical lucidity. It is precisely the one-to-one ratio of reflective knowledge "mirrored" in the allegorical proposition here that is specifically challenged by the ensuing paragraph.

> "It almost seems—" How often this locution has been forced on us when we were merely trying to find words for a more human expression of our difficulty, something closer to home. And with this formula our effort flies off again, having found no place to land. As though there were something criminal in trying to understand a little this uneasiness that is undermining our health, causing us to think crazy thoughts and behave erratically. We can no longer live our lives properly. (111)

The inaugural phrase of that paragraph, "It almost seems"—the tain of that mirror held up to *we* by the image of the sparrow—becomes the lever of a cognition that is markedly cumulative rather than integrative. For, while it reflects back, especially in the deliberately enigmatic antecedence of the pronoun *it,* the locution is simultaneously a transition to a disjunctive context of concerns.

Nowhere is the force of transition, or change (as opposed to identity), so clear, in fact, as in a memorial evocation of the fluttering sparrow in the phrase following "It almost seems": "our effort flies off again having found no place to land." Here the image verges upon the status of act not only by its transformation into a bearer of speculative knowledge about the nature of thinking (ultimately "causing us to think crazy thoughts") but also by the revelation that the image in that capacity is already an act of reflection, a fulcrum for specifically transformative perspectives.

As we anticipated in our reading of Sartrean desire, here we can see, with perhaps greater clarity than before, that what is most vital in the phenomenon of reflection is the imperative of choice. This is because we can see reflection here, in the mirror of the sparrow, as *a solicitation of particularity*. It is a solicitation of particularity that, by its syntactical/ contextual multiplicity, grants a warrant for greater powers of discrimination. Here our effort at interpretation "flies off again" on the wings of the recognition that where we contemplate the difference between figure and what it expresses, between image and analogy, we will produce an augmented expressive capacity. Such expressive capacity will be increasingly determinate as a motive for making transitions from one threshold of intelligibility, one context, to another.

Significantly, the locution "It almost seems" serves as an exemplary transition because it articulates neither a continuous nor a disjunctive contextualization of meaning. In the deployment of the concept of "likeness" (picked up later and ironically in the truism that "every good impulse is distorted into something *like* its opposite") there is something distinctly like a "confused clarity," a Baumgartenian totality whose extensive ordination of meaning is intrinsically transformative. The "effort" that flies off like the sparrow both instantiates the standard of likeness adduced in the phrase "It almost seems" and elicits a new construal of the category of likeness, such that it can accommodate the transformability of the terms it solicits. This is, in effect, its own comprehension of the terms. Here we can see that the locution "It almost seems" is "forced on us," as the speaker attests, because it captures the effective force of any expressive agency that exists in light of the knowledge that no value, subjective or otherwise, can ever be represented except as the result of a transformation. Such expressiveness in turn depends upon a recontextualization, the terms of which are the imperative of new criteria of valuation.

The locution "It almost seems" is therefore the locution par excellence. Locution is etymologically the "act of speech,"[21] an interface of acting and thinking. In this context the stark singularity of the word *locution* is ironically inextricable from the syntactical successiveness it engenders. Furthermore, the locution "It almost seems" induces exactly the act of reflection that would be required to unravel the otherwise vexing entanglement of thought and action originally propounded in the etymology of the word *locution*. In other words, the compounding of constative and performative modalities in the word *locution* is immediately elucidated in a locutionary matrix that devolves from "It almost seems" to an intercalation and imbrication of constative and performative registers of value.

Indeed, the eliciting of differential schema for instantiating the sparrow—such that the imperatives of conceptual construal eclipse the content of those construals—infers the futility of any further attempts to sift out the performative dimensions of "It almost seems" from the constative states it reiterates. Thus, the force of the locution "It almost seems" in its immediate relation to the similitude of "the effort" (of thought) that "flies off" with "no place to land" epitomizes that cognitive activity wherein the solicitation of particulars always entails their transformability. This is a phenomenon we have variously called confused clarity, the prereflective body, cumulation, and cognitive efficacy. Such recognition in turn impels our comprehension of expressive capacity as a variable of changes of state rather than as a status quo. As Ashbery's persona subsequently asseverates: "There is only the urge to get on with it all. . . . There is no vital remnant which would transform one's entire effort into an image somewhat resembling oneself" (111).

Under the constraint of this knowledge we will not easily forget how the title of this final episode, "The Recital," rehearses the ambiguous relationship between the performative and the constative modalities of knowing and acting. Reciting both recognizes and situates one's knowledge, binding both moments in a reciprocal logic. In this way does the title recite the quandary that opened the text upon the sinuous syntactical pathways of Ashbery's prose: How does one go forward without a knowledge of ends? Or, more specifically, how does one posit ends with any expectation of arriving at them, without acknowledging the transformation of the desire for ends that originally determined one's sense of purpose?

These questions, the universally recognized impetus of narrative desire, are banal in themselves. But, if we construe the urge to "get on with it" as neither a teleological self-realization nor a nonnarrative immediacy, then the choice between those "ends" ceases to be a strictly legislative decision, and the text sustains a contrastingly productive protocol of understanding. If the syntax of this text can be accurately described as "extended" because it complicates the end-determinative proposition of syntactical order, we may also remember that the extensive register of determination in philosophical aesthetics (Baumgarten) demands that production be understood not merely as an addition to but also as a reciprocity with what it differentiates itself from.

I believe that this self-differentiation, posited as an answer to the question of how one proceeds without ends, is what Ashbery means to evoke in the "conjugating" procedure that terminates the narrative. The final paragraph of *Three Poems*, driven as it is by the closural imperatives of every literary performance toward the exemplifying status of the constative and acknowledging that performance itself depends upon the recognition of an audience, mock-climactically conjures that audience. Yet Ashbery does so in a way that makes his authorial performance more than a conventional bid for recognition and, so, more than a performative gesture. In the nominally punctual moment of the performance of *Three Poems*,

> there were new people watching and waiting, *conjugating* in this way the distance and emptiness, transforming the scarcely noticeable bleakness into something both intimate and noble. The performance had ended, the audience streamed out; the applause still echoed in the hall. But the idea of the spectacle as something to be acted out and absorbed still hung in the air long after the last spectator had gone home to sleep. (118; emphasis added)

I take the deployment of the word *conjugating* to be the conceptual armature of the passage. The term is explicated through its own etymological recital of the locutionary structure previously annunciated in the etymology of the word *locution*. *Conjugation* comprehends a determinateness that is extensive, which is to say, lacking the intensive distinctness of teleological emplotment. It is epitomized by an alternation or transition between reciprocating modalities of value. *Conjugation* refers to the taxonomic lucidity of that structural whole that denotes the schema of inflexional verb forms in the grammatical system of the language. But it is nonetheless a schema that accommodates a division within itself. It thus juxtaposes a unity and a schedule of differences within a decidedly temporal grid of relations (the system of verb tenses).

What makes the con-fusion of such disparate ends in the etymology of *conjugation* yield such a lucid retrospect on Ashbery's aesthetic practice in *Three Poems* is a rationality grounded in the inherent narrativity of the contingent—what from this point on I will call *narrative reason*. In the persona's account of the emptying of the hall the self-differentiating enterprise of the people "conjugating" the distance (objectivity) and the emptiness (perspective) adduces the realm of contingency without being swallowed up by it. Here people watch and transform only to be transformed through the seeming instability of the temporal relations (futurity and pastness) that coordinate them. So the watching comes after the spectacle.

The applause is dissociated from the audience. The idea follows the act. The consciousness of the act exhausts the active contemplation of it. Most paradoxically, we must accept the proposition that what will be precedes what was: for the "idea . . . to be acted out still hung in the air after the last spectator had gone home." In each strictly provisional event of this final episode of *Three Poems* there is a temporal marker that intimates an integrative succession of moments that should resolve the contingency of futurity into some positive fact/fate. But in its passing, each successive integer of narrative time is effectively reshuffled to make the fact of contingent experience adumbrate a pattern, the coherent terms of which cannot be extrapolated beyond the problematic of choosing between them.

To better understand the motives of the passage we must remember that the ineluctable error of contingency, the fallibility of choice, was the driving anxiety of *Three Poems*, beginning with the inaugural moment of the persona's trying to decide to proceed by putting down or leaving out. This may now be specifically rationalized as a narrative drive. For Ashbery's text, in its conjugating drift, comprehends precisely what was revealed to us on the bodily threshold of Sartrean desire: the impossibility, rather than the inevitability, of our most feared nemesis—a "pure" contingency that would negate narrative will and that narrative must therefore struggle to defeat. After all, the etymological ground of the conjugating will supports the idea that connection and distinction are *not* mutually exclusive but, rather, necessary aspects of totality. This is especially the case as long as we are presuming to treat the aesthetic as an increasingly complex protocol of choices respecting the shifts of contextual horizon entailed by our choosing.

For a richer appreciation of what is cognitively entailed by this relatively "impure" contingency, we might refer ourselves again to Nelson Goodman's term *repleteness*, designating the number of terms or respects within which the variability of any formal composition might be discerned as significant. It is important to remember that variation, in itself, does not satisfy a standard of aesthetic density that Goodman would countenance as contributing to the cognitive efficacy of the artwork. The performance that is declared to be "ended" in the last paragraph of "The Recital" evokes just this impure contingency of Goodman's repleteness in the guise of a proliferation of choices rather than a punctual truth. Such self-deluding truth otherwise lurks in our most impotent fantasies of vanquishing pure contingency. In other words, at the end of "The Recital" (and in the manifest absence of the threat of absolute contingency) the constative ends of performance seem to be articulable only insofar as they are revealed to be inseparable (which is not to say indistinguishable) from new performative imperatives. These always arise out of the split between intentions and consequences prompted by any such postulate of ends in the first place. Indeed, in the conjugating effect of Ashbery's prose I believe he offers a method for rationalizing narrative will that solves the problem of how to begin (whether to put down or leave out): we recognize how the inhibition about beginning at all (which, as we have already noted, is really an anxiety about beginning in error) is a variable of the problem of acting in the knowledge that the act will always surpass the intentions that originally made it desirable. It is in these terms that the final passage of *Three Poems* reveals contingency to be a hinge, not an impasse, between constative and performative modes.

Furthermore, the project of beginning is thus unburdened of the masochistic longing for a reconciliation with unintended (contingent) consequences. Such a reconciliation would itself founder on the inevitably temporal contradiction (between constative and performative thresholds of experience) that was originally posed for the persona in the choice of putting down or leaving out. In order to elude such contradictions we are prompted here to put what is a fundamentally sociological problematic—the conflict between intentional ends (the individual) and the unintended consequences they precipitate (the group)—into the framework of an aesthetic analysis that requires a comparable adequation of particular to general. The notion of the aesthetic I have deployed in this chapter eludes the trap of self-contradiction because its solicitation of particulars is signally an expression of the temporal excess that turns all narrative form into narrative praxis. Here we must accept the presupposition that praxis already inheres in form as a necessary condition for valorizing narrative knowledge in the first place.

We may now imagine that narrative and aesthetic values converge where the horizon of expectations for any intentional project becomes a new criterion for subjective expression. This transformation occurs on the threshold of every expectation's inadequacy to the perspective for self-reflection that emerges in the moment of its being surpassed. In Goodman's terms the horizon of expectations becomes a threshold of plausible repleteness, subject in its turn to normative judgments. It is therefore eminently determinate without being dogmatically deterministic.

The content of such determinateness may in fact be characterized as a prospectively richer ground of motivation for self-reflective subjects. If, as I have alleged, there is a conventional solicitation of the audience in Ashbery's "recital," that audience's "performance" of the duties of reading would require a grounding in reason that does not release the thinking self from the contingencies of meaning by the ruse of any blindly deterministic intentionality. The audience does not strive toward subsuming performative energies to a constative, mimetic standard of lucidity. Rather, the solicitation of the audience ought to be understood, as corollary of an aesthetic solicitation of particularity. Thus, the manifest insufficiency of readerly intention with respect to the text is registered not in the nullification of its meaning but, rather, in the *realization* of the text's *surplus value,* so to speak. As Adorno says, "The surplus of intentions [in the artwork] then proclaims the irreducibility of the work to mimesis alone" (*Aesthetic Theory,* 217).

The advantage gained in this argument may be seen best by comparison with the stock-in-trade poststructuralist antidote to the oppressive determinacy of teleological intentions: the recourse to a dogmatic indeterminacy of meaning. In this radical recourse the interrogation of meaning is rendered an eminently subversive, but ultimately inconsequential, enterprise. By contrast, Adorno's critique of intention does not depend upon making intention external (hence indeterminate, as in Derrida's *hors texte*) to the text. Therefore, in the context of *Three Poems* we may read the particular consequence of Ashbery's recital as making the concept of intention more weightily consequential. We may read it as literalizing the consequentialism of Adorno's "second reflection," which we can perhaps now see more precisely as a refusal to separate intention from its dialectical bond with materiality (see *Aesthetic Theory,* 217). Here we must construe the consequence of action as that which renders the actor a recitor: it renders intention continuous with the changes it precipitates and hence answerable to them as narrative development.

Once again the principle of nonidentity promises a shrewd critical utility. And it does so with an even clearer view of what Adorno might have meant both in his assertion that nonidentitarian thinking is ("in some other way") identitarian and in his assertion that the secret telos of identity is nonidentity. What is at stake in nonidentity is a specifically cognitive efficacy, as was the case when we first took up the issue of aesthetic determination. In his exposition of the dialectics of identity and cognitive self-reflection in *Negative Dialectics* Adorno points out that the mistake of traditional (nondialectical) thinking is that it takes identity for a goal. It seeks to tell us what something "comes under" (what it exemplifies or represents) rather than what it "is." Adorno is emphatic on the point that cognition, as opposed to traditional thinking, is a syntactical relation, not a nominative function:

> The force that shatters the appearance of identity is the force of thinking: the use of "it is" undermines the form of that appearance which remains inalienable just the same. . . . Under its critique [the critique of identitarian thinking], identity does not vanish but undergoes a qualitative change. Elements of affinity—of the object itself to the thought of it—come to live in identity. (*Negative Dialectics,* 149)

To strive to say what something "is" rather than "what it comes under" is thus to acknowledge how syntactical order in general, like the specific compositional strategy of *Three Poems,* accepts the contradiction of preserving the concept of identity ("The concept of identity must not be discarded" [*Negative Dialectics,* 149]) within its critique, which is thereby rendered inconclusive. Yet what is inconclusive in this case is once again *not* aporetic, because identity is reconstituted in contradiction as the vantage point of some predicative agency for which contradiction is the determinant contingency. Adorno concludes that identity is its own contradiction insofar as "[i]dentity is the primal form of ideology. We relish it as adequacy to the thing it suppresses; adequacy has always been subject to dominant purposes and, in that sense, its own contradiction" (148). If standards of adequacy are only expressible in this context as self-suppression, then identity is effectively self-transformative. Thus, Adorno can conclude that the critique of ideology here is constitutive as well as destructive of consciousness.

All of this helps to buttress my assertion that the closural moment of *Three Poems* is recursive for the intentions that give the work narrative coherence. I have already suggested that "The Recital," by strictly elaborating rather than encapsulating what is conceptually staked in the compositional strategy of the text throughout, serves chiefly to reveal how the consequences of such a strategy constitute a deepening of the ground of motivation upon which self-knowledge arises. "The Recital" demurs to be a vehicle for the dissemination of that identity. The mere dissemination of identity would be insupportably subjective, in the worst sense—unresponsive to the intersubjective requirements for recontextualization or reciprocal recognition that attend upon ideological identity. Hence, "consequence" is once again a crux of Ashbery's method. But we are led to resist the linear telos of unreflective (noncontradictory) temporality that obtrudes in the conceptual proximity of consequence to the problematic of causality. In fact, one might now say that the conceptual burden of Ashbery's style here is specifiable as its power to disarticulate those terms.

Closing the Case: The Cognitive Burden of Narrative Aesthetics

The causality of meanings in *Three Poems* is sacrificed to a concern for their consequences. This is the case where the supervening transformability of context reflects an emergent narrative subjectivity that is augmented, not merely revealed, in its unfolding. Ultimately, Ashbery's practice of perpetually shifting contextual boundaries, without substituting a strict protocol of syntactical boundaries, has an effect akin to sustaining the interdependence of identity and nonidentity. Within Ashbery's work we are thus positioned to see how self-knowledge (in general) might be profitably characterized as an aesthetic enterprise. By the means just alluded to it makes the terms of the self more coherent with the unintended consequences (internal contradictions) of the subjective will. This self is thus made more coherent with the ground of productive subjectivity that, according to Adorno's definition of *ideology,* necessarily transcends subjective value in the course of every willful self-expression. In the process Ashbery produces a witty gloss on the venerable apothegm that beauty is in the eye of the beholder. In this work beauty beholds the I to the extent that the reflective capacity of the aesthetic subject is, strictly speaking, its constitutive agency. Here the tyranny of the visual paradigm of aesthetic value is most decisively overthrown.

   This account of self-knowledge as reflection and reconstitution is tellingly conversant with two exotic and complex verse forms employed by Ashbery with notable frequency and commitment in his more generically framed books of poetry: the Italianate sestina and the Indonesian *pantoum.*[22] Both forms deploy a narrative intelligence that, like the compositional strategy of *Three Poems,* recites itself in order to make a progression. Recitation is its cumulative modality. In the sestina there is a shifting pattern of semantic markers that substitute for the unity of rhyme, in turn shifting the principle of coherence from a sensuous to a quasiconceptual ground. But, because the conceptual register is always in transition contextually, it makes sense to see this as a principally syntactical rather than a principally semantic phenomenon.

Even more to this point is the exemplum of the *pantoum*, a form of unlimited length exhibiting an alternation of lines such that the second and fourth lines of one stanza become the first and third of the next. The *pantoum* achieves a nominal closure in a terminal repetition of the first line. But the unspecified length and the thickening weave of intertextualization attenuate that closure to a recognition of its own temporal fragility.

I have already noted that what is most striking about both of these verse forms is their fundamentally syntactical principles of order. In each case the linkage of particulars that obtains in the patterns of repetition (of word and line) instantiates a threshold of intelligibility in inverse proportion to the transformability of context that the repetitions so assiduously articulate. Furthermore, the repetitions are remarkably articulate for the terms of narrative desire that have figured so powerfully in our attempt to read out of Ashbery's *Three Poems* a narrative aesthetic that does not disjoin transformation from totality as incommensurable and, hence, mutually fetishistic terms of experience. In the case of these formal structures, as in the form of *Three Poems,* we are compelled to speculate that the transformability of context is not antithetical to the teleology of the whole. This is true as long as transformability is understood to be the condition of its (the whole's) representability and as long as the whole of representation is given priority over the represented whole.

This reconceptualization of the whole links the act of representation with the cognitive determination of the aesthetic that I have been endorsing throughout this chapter. Such linkage would be impossible were agency to be precipitously swallowed up into telos by its assimilation to the concept of intention. Inasmuch as Goodman and Adorno make the cognitive burden of the aesthetic depend upon a transformative function, we might then see *Three Poems* as an exemplar of the way in which the cognitive determination of the aesthetic produces new situations, not as objects of contemplation (either intentionalist or fatalist) but, rather, as vehicles for mediating the differences between intentions and consequences. In such cases transformability of context redounds to the intentional will of the one who acts in recognition of it *as a transitional impetus*. This gives us a motive for a non-intentional-teleological narration that nonetheless does not renounce ends. Rather, because this narrational paradigm treats ends as products of transformation, it reads out of them the pretext for other transformations. It is on this basis that we may assert a quasi-ethical agenda of narrative aesthetics: the augmenting of a capacity to promulgate distinctions. This augmentation would necessitate a reciprocal transformation of the criteria of assessment by which we discern the significance of such distinctions in the first place.

The cognitive burden of such a narrative aesthetic would be twofold. It would preempt the ideological (in Adorno's terms) dead end of Aristotelian catharsis, in which transformation is doomed to become a trope of resemblance. In Aristotelian catharsis transformation succumbs to the reifying, conceptual, thematic momentum of a recognition that naturalizes difference at the expense of the reversibility of perspectives implicit in difference. Just as important, however, narrative aesthetics would preclude the infinity of transformations that might ensue from a *peripeteia* unchecked by *anagnorisis*. It would force us to accept the proposition that, because transformative subjectivity is intelligible always as an intersubjective recognition of difference—not a subjective proliferation of difference—our assessments of its validity will require a protocol of ever more apt criteria of recognition.

In this way we bring out the cognition of Aristotelian recognition. Thus, recognition is revealed to be the true complement to reversal of perspective. It registers the effect of reversal not as a false culmination of experience, a succinct totalization of meaning (a subsuming truth), but, rather, as a logical principle that remains an active part of the whole it would reveal. Such recognition proposes a more fitting "conjugation" of the distance and the emptiness than we have mastered in our more thematically minded (oddly noncognitive) traditions of cathartic narrative knowing. It marks the necessity of fitting our knowledge to experience without abstractly presupposing the standard of fitness by which we judge. If this looks like a Kantian reflective judgment, it is so in a way that does not relegate judgment itself to a noncognitive margin of human experience. Nor does it release us from the obligation of judging. Rather it makes us more mindful of the procedural complexity of judgment as an indissolubly material part of all substantive acts of mind. To look beyond it would be to dissolve the narrative of the self into that treacherous medium of reflection that swallowed Narcissus up into the most deceptively formless idea of himself.

8

Thinking *Peripeteia* / Peripetic Thinking

In the eyes of the existing rationality, aesthetic behavior is irrational because it castigates the particularity of this rationality in its pursuit not of ends, but of means. Art keeps alive the memory of ends-oriented reason. It also keeps alive the memory of a kind of objectivity which lies beyond conceptual frameworks. That is why art is rational, cognitive. Aesthetic behavior is the ability to see more in things than they are. It is the gaze that transforms empirical being into imagery. The empirical world has no trouble exposing the inadequacy of aesthetic behaviour, and yet it is aesthetic behaviour alone which is able to experience that world.
　　　　　　　　　　　　—Theodor W. Adorno, *Aesthetic Theory*

Beyond Closure and Openness

We may now judge that the historical significance of narrative form does *not* inhere in any representation of holistic reality that the novel divines from the weltering contradictions of temporal successiveness. By far its greater significance inheres in the insuperable and more durably human contradiction between universals and particulars, a contradiction that, however falsely, has long been assumed to be already resolved in the omniscient wholeness of the most canonical novelistic representations.

We are therefore bound to accept the ever more deeply underlying contradiction that what makes the ideal of narrative totality alluring to human imagination is what makes its realization as narrative practice unthinkable: the inexhaustible particularity of experience that it purports to integrate into a noncontingent realm of knowledge. Yet, in this regard, the unthinkable need not preclude laborious thought.

This is seminally the case in the most self-problematizing progenitor of the English novel, *Tristram Shandy* (1761). Laurence Sterne's novel exemplifies the generative power of narration most decisively where it harbors, within its labyrinthine formal complication, the minotaur of an antinarrative intelligibility. Yet the antinarrative mode here is not tantamount to a monstrous irrationality bred out of the conceptual failures of narrative reason. Rather, it is an attempt to seek a more existentially grounded rationality that, because it arises from the most timely and therefore time-conscious vicissitudes of narrative totalizing, reflects the distinctly human proportions of narrative desire that animates, as Aristotle avers in *Poetics,* our most naively mimetic nature.

Sterne's novel is, of course, justly famous for the way particulars obtrude so as to protract the temporal frame of reference intended to contain them within its mock-Lockean hermeticism. Under this circumstance, however, containment is epistemologically conceivable only in virtue of the reversibility of the perspectival lines that connect subject and object, agency of consciousness and the horizon of meaning, character and action. Furthermore, in *Tristram Shandy* this reversibility is reciprocal with respect to the contextual transformations it promulgates, beyond the limit term of *anagnorisis.* Hence the vigorous speculation that the novel was never completed.[1] What goes beyond *anagnorisis* goes beyond any apparent self-reifying imperatives of containment because it subordinates justificatory criteria of value to transformative values.

As we have seen by negative example in the literary readings through which my argument has progressed this far, it is precisely such a necessity of self-understanding that the novel of F. R. Leavis's "Great Tradition" prolifically represses in its expansive access to thematic truths wherein recognition need not yield any reciprocity with action. Nonetheless, the fateful irony of this repression is itself irrepressible: over the course of the novel's history the desire for self-containment has become the ever more problematic nemesis of philosophical protocols of formal perfection in the novel.

We see this irony in the way that the rhetoric of fiction has "naturalized" the internal contradictions of novel form by promulgating a self-conscious criticohistorical master plot. Accordingly, the "history" of the novel exhibits a shrewdly conflictual "progress" from prevailing strategies of containment under the theoretical sanction of categories such as omniscient narration, realism, etc., to a moment of cathartic reversal where consciousness of the futility of containment becomes its own oppressively open-ended gambit of containment. On these epistemic coordinates we could handily plot the progress of the novel from the allegorical unity of medieval romance to postmodern fragment.[2]

Yet I believe that the formalistically self-conscious internalization of this conflict between totality and particularity, especially as promoted by

postmodern novelists, has substantially impoverished the theoretical resources of the novel rather than enriched them. It evades the cognitive
burden of assimilating the historically particular consequences of such
conflict. It thus evades the need to think beyond the terms of closure and
openness as mutually exclusive, and hence strictly heuristic possibilities.
This is a circumstance only too starkly apparent in the increasingly fetishistic alternation of realist and antirealist hegemonies of style promoted in
the historical manifestos of the genre. The intensifying viciousness of this
hermeneutic circle in the late-nineteenth- and early-twentieth-century
novel—the "progression" from romanticism to naturalism to symbolism,
and, finally, modernism—presages the radical millenarianisms with which
the most self-annihilating polemics of postmodernist culture are so self-
righteously infatuated: urgent pronouncements of the end of literature,
the end of history, the end of philosophy. Here is the skeptic's last resort:
to outwit his or her own limits through the trope of an inexhaustible wit.

The insufficiency of novel theory, so end bound in its renunciation
of ends, is, I believe, clearest in its perpetuation of a singularly unproduc-
tive dualism of thought about how the genre, having given up its naive
claims of totality, might nonetheless still be reconciled with competing
realms of skeptical knowledge in the late twentieth century. The pendu-
lum of current debates still swings between narrative-ethical and antinar-
rative-aesthetical dicta. Whereas narrative telos has always purported to
give the genre a trajectory of social purpose, the antinarrative demons of
narration—irony, parody, pastiche, which always haunted its more sobering teleologies—are now seen to annunciate a *purely aesthetic* register of
values. This aesthetic purity purports to resolve the conflicts between
moral telos and aesthetic freedom by ignoring them. Here is the cultural
ennui that Fredric Jameson has perhaps too famously characterized as the
postmodern "waning of affect."[3]

Predictably, the category of the aesthetic has in turn become the
pretext for a righteously political critique of artistic narrative (of the novel
particularly) as a socially derelict form, a judgment that the self-aggrandizing "playfulness" of the postmodern novel in particular has almost
fatally attracted. In any case we cannot ignore the fact that the discourse
of the novel, conceived so reductively in terms of the easy reversibility of
starkly oppositional stances, succumbs to an increasingly formal abstraction. This further undermines the genre's aptitude for the cognitive
efficacy that I have been claiming for it on the basis of its unique comprehension of, rather than its sterile fetishization of, contradiction.

In the course of taking this admittedly schematic historical view of the fate of the novel, however, we might profitably seize an opportunity to redraw the schema. Despite the empty circularity of academic debates about the reality of the novel, the epistemological stakes that are at issue between narrative and antinarrative, political and aesthetic rationalizations of the novel, nevertheless do offer an opportunity to transcend the narrowly dualistic frame of reference within which discussions of genre might otherwise be stranded. If nothing else, the conflict between narrative and antinarrative, or political and aesthetical rationalizations of the novel, suggests the need for a broadening of the methodological repertoire of critical analysis. If we confront the novel genre in terms of the problematic commensurability of aesthetic and political scruples, it becomes possible to construe this genre's historical striving for totality as epiphenomenal of the larger social project of ideology-critique. This striving for totality is clearly borne of the kindred vicissitudes of post-Enlightenment political life. Under the perhaps too brilliant aura of Enlightenment reason the ideal of totality is immediately compromised by the increasingly self-conscious temporality of the act of contemplating it. Especially under the rigors of the current critique of modernity executed by philosophers and political theorists, as well as novelists, the social purposiveness of totalizing narrative may be justifiably seen to be complicit with the totalizing object of instrumental reason, the object of ideology-critique par exellence. In a complementary way, then, the narrative aesthetic I have adduced in these pages, subsisting as it does on its antagonism with the drive for totality, would seem to proffer fresh motivation for the critique of ideology. Indeed, the allegedly problematic aesthetic dimension of the novel might facilitate a methodological recouping of the genre's prodigal capacity for socially responsible action.

Even more important, reciprocal benefits might accrue to the realm of the social from the application of the terms of the literary debate sketched in the previous paragraph. Because the novel is socially and historically such a pervasive paradigm of self-production (*bildung*) in Western culture (however much it is still shrouded in the conceptually dense shadow of Platonist idealism), the recontextualizing of ideology-critique within the formal problematic of literary narration may transform it into a more pragmatic exposition of human creativity. In that way ideology-critique might be helped to transcend the barren ground of invidious comparisons between false consciousness and science, art and truth—the conceptual topoi to which it is frequently consigned by the social and political sciences. And, because the novel instances self-produc-tion as both transformation *and* totality, at least in the device of *peripeteia,* ideology-critique (transformation) and ideology (totality) may be con-strued as ultimately complementary and coherent aspects of a normative, if not holistic, experience. Thus, a conceptually rigorous contem-plation of form in the novel particularly and narration generally might facilitate a more productive theorizing of the phenomenon of ideology as continu-ous with ideology-critique. Such an analysis might make ideology amena-ble to a more dialectical rather than dualistic mode of judgment. By pointing up a furtive continuity between ideology and ideology-critique, we might thereby relieve the so-called science of ideology of the otherwise indisposable burden of truth.[4]

It should be clear by now that in the issues raised around this view of the novel as a weapon against ideology, I am reprising the critique of the narrative-aesthetics opposition that I prosecuted in the previous two chapters, where my chief aim was to free the narrative subject from a self-preempting narrative rationality on the one hand and a self-pulveriz-ing aesthetic sensationalism on the other. In each of the previous chapters this task was taken up in the service of the explication of a specific literary work. In this chapter I take up the case against the dualism of narrative and aesthetics again, and even more pointedly with the purpose of en-abling an expressly social criticism that may enlarge the context in which literature can be seen to verge pragmatically on the life-world. But the strength of such claims must now depend on a more explicit forging of the links between the project of ideology-critique and narrative aesthetics.

For this reason I want to take the work of two contemporary thinkers, Jean-François Lyotard and Jürgen Habermas, for whom the opposition between narrative and aesthetics specifically provides a springboard for ethical claims intended to promote ideology-critique. The respective cri-tiques of Lyotard and Habermas make available a context for seeing yet another way out of the narrative-aesthetic opposition and thus justifying the more widely applicable ethical conclusions I have just proposed. In fact, what we will see as the inability of Lyotard and Habermas to realize ethical ends by specifically anti-aesthetic or antinarrative means will more decisively reveal how the means of ethical judgment inheres as a pragmatic bond *between* narrative and aesthetic practices.

Both Lyotard and Habermas embrace ideals that respect the comple-mentary purposiveness of communitarian freedom on the one hand and ideology-critique on the other. For Lyotard, of course, community (*sensus communis*) is always a deferred moment, while for Habermas it is an imperative of every human *inter*action. But for both Lyotard and Habermas the relevance of the narrative-aesthetic opposition to ethical ideals is relatively straightforward. Communitarianism may be roughly correlated with narrative as a teleological enterprise. Critique may be just as roughly correlated with aesthetics in its detotalizing susceptibility to conceptually indeterminate intensities of feeling. So, in this regard Habermas and Lyotard present oddly complementary and antithetical perspectives. Lyotard wants an antinarrative aesthetics, because he is wary of the instrumentalism of all rationalistic narrative drive. Habermas wants an anti-aesthetic narrative of emancipation because he is wary of the atomization of subjective experience, the subject's inexorable displacement from the "routines . . . and the conventions of everyday action" prompted by yielding the field of discourse to the sensuous play of the aesthetic ("Discourse Ethics: Notes on a Program of Philosophical Justification," *The Communicative Ethics Controversy*, 104).

What Lyotard and Habermas have most in common here, however, is what they both lack. What is most provocatively absent from both accounts is an appreciation of how self-conscious subjective agency (subject as act) is in any way a condition of either aesthetic freedom (Lyotard's goal) or communicative normativity (Habermas's goal). This lack is precisely what Max Horkheimer and Theodor Adorno so vociferously decried in *Dialectic of Enlightenment:* the drift toward a dissolution of the difference between part and whole such as to deny any discrepancy between actor and action. Within such ethical universes there would be no scope for agency as anything but the most abstract presupposition of human history.[5]

My thesis in this concluding chapter, then, will be that it is precisely the maintenance of a split between narrative and aesthetic valuation, as exampled by Lyotard and Habermas, that inhibits the convergence of public and private selves in programs of ethical solidarity. In the reciprocal partiality of their views Lyotard and Habermas both proffer and preclude the goal they share as critics of ideology. Furthermore, by seeing how the narrative and aesthetic axes of human experience might intersect in the postulate of narrative reason and the practices of a narrative aesthetic, I want to suggest a means to restore subjective agency to the project of ethical idealism. Through a rehabilitation of the ethical stances of Lyotard and Habermas, wherein the aesthetic is taken to be a strict corollary of narration, I may in turn suggest a strategy for rehabilitating the artwork as a more effectual political link between individuals and group experience.

Striving toward *Sensus Communis:* From Kant to Fichte

In the preceding chapters I argued—out of the tradition of Aristotle, Baumgarten, and Fichte—that the phenomenon of aesthetic determination exhibits a structural affinity with the dynamism of narrative form. This affinity obtains as the presupposition of a self-determining agency that accommodates both the de-reifying effect of transformation and the reflective normativity of totality. In this presupposition, I have argued, we may find a potent analogue to the structure of *peripeteia,* provided that we stress the irreducibility of recognition and reversal as the condition of any self-determining agency. In earlier chapters I conceded that this treatment of *peripeteia* goes against the traditional reading of Aristotelian emplotment as sublating reversal to recognition.

Correlatively, I pursued J. G. Fichte's inference that a dynamic of reversal and recognition is a structural crux of human subjectivity. I have not, of course, argued that Fichte is following the dicta of Aristotle's *Poetics.* But there is an Aristotelian aspect to the Fichtean philosophy of the subject. Fichte adduces a principle of "self-activity" (*tathandlung*) whereby self-determination is *conditioned upon* self-reflection rather than *deduced from* self-reflection. Indeed, Fichtean self-positing occurs conspicuously in relation to a not-I, as is the case in Kantian epistemology. But, unlike the Kantian intuition of self-determination instantiated through an immediate constraint, or limit, imposed upon its activity, the Fichtean subject sees itself more mediately as *choosing* to see its own constraint. This means that the context of choice, within which recognition of choice is originally possible, is what is most importantly posited in the Fichtean project of self-activity. This, in turn, suggests that the self is contingent upon the transformability of context, i.e., the reversibility of perspective. After all, recognition of a context of choice is contingent upon what is not recognized. What is not recognized therefore remains the ultimate condition of activity itself.[6]

Reflection, in this respect, constitutes a genuinely successive temporal moment, one that articulates identity as a protractive distance from itself. Self-activity thus offers a ground of human self-determination that maximizes free creativity without drawing the self-determined subject into a cul-du-sac of solipsistic consciousness and without sacrificing the practical subject to the noumenal subject. Ultimately, it offers a ground of human subjectivity without decoupling the phenomenon of reflection from the phenomenon of determination. As I have intimated, that decoupling would incur the abstraction of rational subjectivity, which Horkheimer and Adorno diagnosed as the fatal symptom of the Culture Industry.

For this reason my inquiry into the narrative dimensions of subjective act has depended upon a methodological shift from narrative totality to narrative reason. I believe that, like Fichtean self-activity, narrative reason might reveal the necessary continuity of reflection and determination. By closing the gap between aesthetics and narrative, this "faculty" of narrative reason might show forth a way in which the self-determining subject is nothing but the project of its own creativity, while maintaining that such creativity is in no way bound within the precincts of an autonomous and asocial self. The reasons for promoting narrative reason, then, are akin to the reasons that we have so closely attended to the agenda of ideology-critique (key to the ethical stances of both Lyotard and Habermas): to emancipate subjective reflective consciousness from the heteronomous determinations of society (alienating history). This is an incentive to unfetter the creative forces of human culture at large from the narcissistic traps of ideological self-reproduction. Ideology-critique has also always promulgated an ideal of subjectivity that purports to be both free and universal. In other words ideology-critique proposes a means for human agents to inhabit both the subject and object positions of experience. It would free the subject without conceding the incoherence of the will and the world in which the subject recognizes its actions as self-determinative.

Historically, of course, this has always been easier said than done. Since Kant the problem with such ideals has been that subjective universalism preempts the world of objective determinations upon which the subject's conscious bearings are predicated as freedom. What Fichte proposes by his theory of self-activity, and explicitly as a remedy for the Kantian antinomy, is the possibility of making the subject and object coherent according to a principle of self-production. In the Fichtean ethic of activity, contrary to the Kantian categorical imperative, the maxims by which one reflect's one's freedom as a productive agent are emergent in the act of reflection itself. Thus, as we shall see more fully later, is the subject effectively rendered agent and product both.

I have already argued that this is explicitly the state of affairs conjured by Aristotelian poetics (in *peripeteia* and *anagnorisis*). What is not so obvious perhaps is that *peripeteia,* rationalized as self-activity, in effect unites

Aristotle's *poetics* with *phronesis,* a term that otherwise seems to offer the basis of an unsurpassable distinction between the aesthetic and the practical. By viewing *phronesis,* or practical wisdom, through a Fichtean prism, however, we see that it is conceivably the term of Aristotelian ethical knowledge that most persuasively entails the dialectic of recognition and reversal. For, as the deployment of theoretical knowledge in an ineluctably temporal realm, *phronesis* turns toward a self-modifying (hence transforming, or peripetic) register of determinateness.

In contrast with Aristotle, Lyotard's and Habermas's perpetuation of the aesthetic and narrative split specifically violates the spirit of *peripeteia* by stubbornly maintaining subjectivity and objectivity, reflection (theory) and determination (practice), as incommensurable places of knowledge. Lyotard's antinarrative aesthetic can be construed as emphasizing reversal at the expense of recognition, and Habermas's anti-aesthetic narrative can be construed as emphasizing recognition at the expense of reversal. Nevertheless, insofar as the Fichtean premise of narrative reason follows Aristotelian *phronesis* in requiring both reversal and recognition, we may see how both Lyotard and Habermas are themselves, albeit unacknowledgedly, working very much in the framework of poetics (and *phronesis*), very much in the framework of the dynamics of emplotment. This recognition might then be construed as an imperative to link what I would characterize as their otherwise "demotivated" communitarianism with particularly Aristotelian agents.

What is required for my purposes, then, is an analysis of the degree to which their mutual blindness to the usefulness of affirming the continuity of aesthetics and narrative entailed in *peripeteia* makes Lyotard and Habermas into advocates of mutually relevant but mutually exclusive arguments. By this analysis I seek to show how, through exposing each other's weaknesses, Lyotard and Habermas might indicate the need for thinking in terms of narrative reason. In narrative reason they might preserve the higher goal they share as a common strength. This, of course, is the proverbial "higher goal" of all speculative philosophy: a duly ethical reckoning of theoretical with practical experience.

As we have seen in the discussion of self-activity, the motive of Fichte's theory of the subject was precisely to unite theoretical and practical subjectivity. Fichte kept faith with the Kantian claim that this was possible according to a scrupulous discipline of reflective judgment. Nevertheless, Kantian reflective judgment appeals to a common sense, a *sensus communis,* for proof of its universality. For Fichte this seemed to imply a principle of subjective identity that was structurally identical in theory and practice.

But Fichte shrewdly observed the impossibility of inducing such a *sensus communis* because it requires (at least in Kantian terms) uniting a single intuition (reflective judgment) with the idea of totality (determination) in a brute subsumption of particulars to universals. Fichte's recourse, in the name of "creative imagination," was that "Neither of these courses is the one to follow: we should reflect neither on the one aspect alone, nor the other alone, but on both together, oscillating inwardly between the two opposing determinations of this idea" (250). As we know, Fichte finessed the impossibility of a structural identity between theoretical and practical subjectivity by making the criteria of identity (totality) *emergent in,* rather than *a priori to,* the act of choosing between the objects by which one expresses one's standards of judgment.

It is important to see that Fichte is trying to find a way of doing justice to what, in Kant, is an oddly anthropological solution to an epistemological question. In "Analytic of the Sublime" (136) Kant insists upon the need to reconcile the freedom from conceptual determination achieved in reflective judgment (judgment of taste) with the situation of all other people, thus obtaining a ground of universality that is at least presumptively social. I have been suggesting that such a reconciliation is most realistically conceived along the lines of peripetic reversal, because peripetic reversal conditions a reciprocity of divergent perspectives. It is no small point to note that Kant explicitly admonishes us to put "ourselves in the place of" other men.

The Fichtean notion of self-activity, whereby the self solicits its terms of self-understanding from interaction with a nonsubjective world, effectively connects reversal and recognition by its intrinsic contextuality.[7] But, as I have already alleged, and as Frederick Neuhouser, one of Fichte's most sympathetic contemporary exponents explains more fully in *Fichte's Theory of Subjectivity,* self-understanding for Fichte is not simply a matter of distinguishing who I am as an existent being in contrast with the not-I of the world (169). Rather, it is a case of choosing how I will recognize myself as such (170). What affects the distinction between these two selves, then, in Neuhouser's analysis is (even more suggestively than has been previously made out) a reversal of fate construed as a change of the contextual terms of self-understanding. As Neuhouser says, I only ask myself who I am when my contextual coordinates are inadequate to the desire for self-recognition (160). The intuition of new contextual particulars in effect solicits, from outside itself, new terms of recognition in much the way I have been alleging that the aesthetic procedurally entails a solicitation of particulars as its expressive register.

In this respect we might characterize the "Fichtean" solution as one that effectively elides Aristotelian recognition (change of context) with a Hegelian recognition (*aufhebung*). Or it might be more to the point to invoke Hegel's disciple in the dialectic of recognition, Alexandre Kojeve. Kojeve unapologetically suspends the metaphysical trajectory of *geist*, thus making Hegel's "advance" from a Kantian position more polemically stark. In Kojeve the dialectical transformability of context induced by action contexts, or what Fichte calls self-activity, is construed as or entails a choice, a choice to be recognized in one's choice of value, by a particular other.[8] In other words, by this strictly circuitous route, Kantian reflection may be seen to yield to or to become continuous with determination in the phenomenon of reciprocal recognition.

As we have seen, both Habermas (in his construal of communicative action) and Lyotard (in his avowal of a *sensus communis*) are implicated in this problematic of choosing without a coercive or prejudicial, i.e., ideological (or, in Kant's case, conceptual), principle. Both want to construe a subjectivity that does not preempt its free creativity (Fichte's creative imagination) with the very instrumental reason that originally seemed to endow its self-expressive will. Habermas and Lyotard are in this respect, like Fichte and Aristotle, both involved in balancing the demands of reflection and determination. Yet Lyotard's aesthetic of indeterminacy puts the subject on a course of reflexivity (Kantian reflective judgment) that devolves to endless transformation. Habermas seeks to determine the subject within a procedural enclosure of rationalistic discourse that can only reflect itself as a communal "we," mutually exclusive of a pragmatic "I." So, once again, we must observe that both Habermas and Lyotard achieve this balance only through mutual exclusions. In effect, Habermas preempts reflection with determination, and Lyotard preempts determination with reflection.

For these reasons we must now consider the separate paths by which Habermas and Lyotard came to such self-inhibiting reckonings with the realm of contingency, i.e., that which is excluded in the mutually exclusive choice between transformation (narrative) *or* totality (the aesthetic). Only in this way can we begin to specify the means by which narrative reason might effectively mitigate the mutuality of such exclusions.

Lyotard's Antinarrative Aesthetic

Lyotard's aesthetic defies narrative precisely on the model of the Kantian judgment of taste. This defiance is occasioned by what Lyotard calls a moment of "euphony," or relationality between the representative powers of Kantian understanding and imagination "so far as they are determined by a representation" (*Critique of Judgment*, 56). The moment is determined but in a way that is not representable, except through the protocol of a formalism for which no concept of form can be deemed adequate. The phenomenon of determination is thereby disjoined from any reflection of determining agency by the strict inadmissability of any relation/ality of the subject to subjectivity that is not always already and thus only representative. Following the Kantian paralogism that the "I think" (*Ich denken*) cannot think itself, Lyotard insists that "the cognitive I misses itself in its effort to determine itself" (*"Sensus communis,"* 233). The self to be realized in the judgment of taste is therefore necessarily an index of its indeterminacy. Lyotard stipulates that in aesthetic pleasure:

> There is too much for the understanding to think in the forms, especially the very free ones, that imagination delivers to it; and the imagination remains threatened by that regulation that the faculty of concepts could impose on forms, by the intellectual "recuperation" of forms. It is according to this competition of the two powers that, on occasion, sometimes, their possible concert can be heard. (232–33)

The abstract, indeterminate temporality ("sometimes," "on occasion"), to which the judgment of taste is a formal concession here, is the best indication of the degree to which reflection precludes narrative determinateness. Lyotard makes the case here explicitly as a retort to Hegelian synthesis: "Being the opposite of the Hegelian notion that time is a concept, time for Kant is the challenge that thinking has to take up; it is its self-differing, its 'differer'" (*Peregrinations*, 7). The very fact that the excess of form for the faculty of understanding to think, or to "take up," is construed as a temporal excess implies that, for Lyotard, contingency becomes in itself a register of freedom. In the flow of narrative time, by contrast, it is the tension between understanding and contingency that actualizes reflective consciousness as determinate and, hence, plausibly self-determining. The freedom of mind endowed in narrative circumstances is decidedly provisional and contextual. Lyotard would appear to make the threshold of freedom more tacitly absolute.

This absolutism is a pretext of the jargon that links the differer of the self to the ideal of ethical community: the *differend*. For in the differend it is precisely the contextuality of freedom that would render its intelligibility mutually exclusive of its authenticity. As we will see more thoroughly later, the Lyotardian ethical ideal is at the mercy of a derationated will without which it paradoxically makes no claim on existential being. But, of course, paradox is the point. Doxa is that heteronomously determined selfhood wherein self-realization is indistinguishable from an extinguishing violence perpetrated against the self.

Specifically, the differend is a threshold of incommensurability across which we may not pass except under the dispensation of an aesthetic "will" that mitigates all instrumentally willful action. Instrumental will is that epistemological parasite upon subjectivity that Lyotard would dispel by liquidating the host consciousness. Narrative epitomizes that consciousness by its "logical" (instrumental) commensuration of phenomenologically discrepant moments of experience. The differend will vitiate the force of instrumental will, and hence of narrative, by acknowledging what Lyotard calls the "seriality of totality" (*The Differend*, 7), the persistence of contingent experience beyond rational order. The seriality of totality drives the wedge of an infinite irony between human intentions and human actions.

The theme of this contingency is justice, but a justice that submits to the letter of no law. True to the "aesthetic" form of this philosophy, Lyotard's best exposition of the differend proceeds by exemplification rather than generalizable definition. Thus, he "explains" the differend as a wrong sustained in circumstances such as the following: Eualthus, a student of the rhetorician Protagoras brings a suit against his mentor before a tribunal of the law. The student believes himself to have been wronged by the teacher. Subsequent to training, the student has failed to win a single contest of rhetorical skill. But the student underestimates his own victimization. By merely accepting the terms of the litigation against him, Protagoras now has his student in a double bind. If the tribunal rules in Protagoras' favor, Eualthus loses. But should Eualthus persuade the tribunal of the injustice he has suffered, he loses just as decisively, though by new criteria, since he will have thereby succeeded in proving his rhetorical skill. In the spirit of all sophistical taunting we would say he loses because he wins (*The Differend*, 6–8).

Above all, what Lyotard wants to exemplify here is the gist of tort (wrong)—"a damage accompanied by the loss of the means to prove the damage" (*The Differend,* 5). Lyotard's emphasis on means is meant to dramatize a painful aporia of knowledge, the inherent injustice of conjugating means with ends at all. The aporia here is inexorably the "victim's" lack of choice of ends or criteria by which he would seek recognition of his reality and thus be done the justice of being seen *in his own terms.* Reality, Lyotard insists, is "a state of the referent," not a prerogative of the subject. It is a product of what he calls "establishment procedures," the rules by which one is instantiated as an intelligible object. His point is that, where rational objectivity rules, one "inhabits" the judgment of others. This is the case in every solicitation of redress for the grievance of being one's self and, in that capacity, being alone in the world. Within the language game of recognition, Lyotard assures us, one submits self-sacrificingly to rules of truth.

The crux of Lyotard's critique respecting this unjust state of affairs is that the truths of individuals, contrary to the teleological purport of logical reasoning, are in fact incommensurable with the means by which individuals are bound to express those truths. So, for example, the worker who would appeal for an ameliorization of his or her working conditions must officially appeal in the language and logic of capitalism, thereby granting the validity of the terms (and institutional forces) within which he is already victimized. The dilemma is even more starkly revealed for Lyotard in the example of the Martinican French citizen who can plead for his or her rights under the law that makes him or her a citizen but must remain silent about the crimes done him or her by being forced to *be* a French citizen in order to claim rights under that status (*The Differend,* 27).

If one seeks a reprieve from this dilemma, one might well imagine an alternate situation in which one could choose the establishment procedures by which he or she would be known. But once again paradox rears its hydra heads: the logic of rational truth precludes the possibility that the authority by which one grounds one's identity in articulcable rules could be subsumed within those rules. Under this well-known Russellian dictum, Lyotard tells us, the rules will always perpetrate an injustice merely by their application to a necessarily incommensurable circumstance of need (*The Differend,* 8). Hence, Lyotard asserts the urgency of the differend and the corollary project of aesthetizing the realms of logic and politics, over which the logician's will otherwise prevails as bleak oppression.

At this point, however, it will be useful to ask whether Lyotard has not overstated his case and in doing so overlooked the terms for a more just adjudication of human differences. The very impossibility for any free choice of the terms of recognition, which Lyotard laments is the effective premise or the threshold of the differend, is even more nihilistically dictated by the differend itself. Attempting to give a greater affective scope to his indictment of reason, Lyotard sharply opposes narrative determination to the aesthetic freedom proffered in the differend as, above all else, the nemesis of choice. I have myself acknowledged many times that narration falsifies the multiplicity of moments by which self-recognition may be solicited as choice. Within Lyotard's view of narrative we always play the game of recognition according to rules that denature our identity. For the nature we appeal to is abstractly proleptic, the end already present in the beginning. Ironically appropriating the jargon of the most influential of narrative theorists, Gerard Gennette, Lyotard would displace narrative prolepsis with *metalepsis:* a "shifting but sacred frontier between . . . the world in which one tells and the world of which one tells" (cited in *The Differend,* 25). Metalepsis would mire the otherwise pristine formality of past and future in a relentlessly *becoming present.*

Nevertheless, as I have been arguing in these pages, the concept of narrative that Lyotard attacks here is a substantially more narrow one than we need to be satisfied with. I have showed that narrative, considered more in light of the structure of peripetic reversal than totalizing truth, plausibly reconstitutes the game of recognition as a game of re-cognition. In this case, where the cognitive boundaries of narrative do not remain static, where prolepsis thus verges upon metalepsis, narrativity offers the desirable basis for a recognition of what one is that would be fully responsive to the perspectival discrepancies between addressees and addressors. Such discrepancies between addressees and addressors constitute, Lyotard maintains, the structure of their reality. Alternatively, Lyotard's radically antinarrative aesthetic, couched in the incommensurability factor of the differend and demurring every cognitive determination, would render the discrete moments of time it purports to "liberate" a feckless sensationalism. Under such conditions the category of choice, and any substantive dimension of freedom that would depend upon choice, appear perfectly irrelevant. The formal integrity of the discrete moments that constitute a self is preserved by Lyotard at the cost of any intelligibility that would admit grounds for knowing what one wants *for oneself*.

So, Lyotard's aesthetic register purveys freedom from external determination. But it also denies the self all but the most external, which is to say the most patently selfless, possibility of knowledge. On the contrary, it would seem that knowing who one is for oneself ought to be the most elemental precondition for the ideal of self-determination abiding in the differend. This would seem to be all the more compelling given Lyotard's unabashed enthusiasm for the Kantian principle of autonomy according to which the judgment of taste is so scrupulously conditioned. In Lyotard's undisguised recapitulation of Kant we can hear the purport to bridge the ethical and the aesthetic: "the beautiful does not develop. The feeling that it is does not belong to process" (*"Sensus communis,"* 223). But an autonomy without boundaries abstracts the will to know oneself as a willing agent beyond any ethical usefulness. It thereby weakens the motivation for theorizing the aesthetic at all.

Furthermore, by severing the aesthetic from narrative, Lyotard has, in effect, collapsed the Kantian autonomous *Wille* (free will) into the more practical *Willkür* (free choice), a distinction that Kant himself was at great pains to maintain. As Frederick Neuhouser explains in a further treatment of Fichte's attempt to salvage self-determination of the subject as a nonnoumenal subjectivity, the Kantian insistence on equating moral freedom and autonomy threatens to subvert itself. If only autonomous moral acts are free (as Kant stipulates), then immoral acts are unfree and thus *not* susceptible to moral judgment. This leaves no basis for charging individuals with moral responsibility. *Willkür* is therefore the necessary supplement to transcendental autonomy that would preclude precisely the dilemma Lyotard reproduces by his coupling of the differend to a will that eludes cognizable determinates. According to Neuhouser, what is made possible by Kant's maintaining the distinction between *Wille* and *Willkür* is a reflective consciousness compatible with the exercise of will such that it expresses a situational, not a dispositional, nature. Otherwise, the disposition to obey a universal maxim intrinsic to *Wille* consigns us to a realm of experience that remains a priori to the temporality within which the claim that such autonomy is freely chosen is fundamentally imaginable.[9]

But even the Kantian account of *Willkür*, as Fichte sees it, does not go far enough. Though it does effectively supplement a theoretical/ noumenal choice with a practical/phenomenal choice, Kant's *Willkür* remains deeply tautological: *Willkür* chooses in practical experience the maxims by which one's choosing nature is already determined in the form of reason. As Kant stipulates in an important footnote to *Religion within the Limits of Reason Alone* (1793): "The concept of the freedom of the will [*Willkür*] does not precede the consciousness of the moral law in us but is deduced from the determinability of our will [*Willkür*] by this law as an unconditional command" (45). For this reason Fichte adapted his understanding of *Willkür* from Kant. Fichte wanted to justify a threshold of self-determination that would neither be indeterminate (hence, anathema to conceiving form as activity) nor be subject to external norms (hence, a prisoner of what we would now call ideology).

These are two extremes that, as we have seen elsewhere, the dynamics of Fichtean self-activity cannot compass. In my previous treatment of self-activity as a rough analogue to Aristotelian *peripeteia*, I have tried to anticipate how *Willkür* might be seen, in this Fichtean regard, as a mode of selfhood that *gives itself norms in the act of self-reflection*. Fichtean *Willkür* exercises a choice that is indistinguishable from the context of its desire for choosing. As such, it would be self-determining in a way that is not vulnerable to the charge of empty formalism that I have leveled against the Lyotardian aesthetic. On the contrary, the form of experience comprehended in *Willkür* would be more strictly productive of experience. As if in retort to Lyotardian inhibitions, such a construal of will would effectively reconcile us with narrative as a social form that need *not* be repressed as heteronomous coercion, precisely because its maxims are generated *in* its activities. Hence, they possess their own temporal trajectory.

This construal of will would furthermore obviate Lyotard's distinction between what he calls pragmatic master narratives and "little," or "performative," narratives. By this distinction Lyotard hedges against the specter of apolitical idealism that he has otherwise conjured in the differend's inducement to a piously antinarrative aesthetic discourse. As we might expect, Lyotard condemns pragmatic master narratives because they are externally determined. By contrast, he praises little narratives for their aesthetic subversion of the pragmatism of reason. Their epistemological advantage would appear to be that they are local to situations and so resistant to metalevels of systematizing will. But a more important implication, which Lyotard demurs, is that, because such situations constitute conditions of the differend in themselves, they offer no reflective grasp of what distinguishes one situational locality from another. The vulnerability of the theory of little narratives is more fully exposed in considering that Lyotard adduces a self-righteously "pagan" paradigm for little narratives: the oral storytelling tradition of the Cashinahua Indians of Peru and Brazil. By transmitting stories without ever situating them within the context of faithfulness to the teller, or addressor, the Cashinahua license what I believe Lyotard too facilely calls an "artistic" level of independence from an inherited and coercive culture (*Just Gaming*, 33).

Ultimately, Lyotard trivializes his own example by valorizing the freedom of this pagan practice largely in terms of the teller's dubious license to "ham it up": "one invents, because one inserts novel episodes that stand out as a motif against the narrative plot line" (*Just Gaming*, 33). Here Lyotard gives us a characterization of narrative freedom intended as an invidious contrast with traditional Western narrative practices. Yet the form of this freedom is indistinguishable from that most venerable subgenre of the European novel, the picaresque, and from the epistemological free play of canonical "postmodern" metafiction. Both, in this respect, cast a fatally rationalizing light back upon the formal history of the novel genre.

In fact, the profoundly orthodox Western narrative practices of the picaro and the postmodernist in the increasingly local and atomized episodic structure of their plotting lend themselves more readily to the Culture Industry's standard of "entertainment value" than to any putative task of social liberation. The stubbornly episodic moment of such narrative knowledge is inaccessible to any larger framework of reflection, which, like peripetic reversibility, would *relate* episodes through change. Such narrative knowledge therefore fails to muster any critical leverage against its own complicity with the very fetishized forms of dominant and dominating culture that the picaresque was born to deride.

In an Adornian vein we would criticize both picaresque and metafiction as precipitous flights from identity that all too glibly evade the identitarian logic of nonidentity. And I would argue that it is this critique that elicits the strongest basis for identification of the Cashinahuan narratives with their Western antitypes. Such susceptibility to untoward identification might be the fate of all little narratives that ignore the matrix of identity out of which they realize their negative potencies.

An even more devastating liability of Lyotard's argument is that his favoritism toward little narratives hinges, in a most un-Cashinahuan way, on his deployment of the highly technical jargon of "the phrase." Scaled to the practice of little narratives, the phrase is taken to be the minimal unit of ethical discourse. As a self-presupposing entity, the phrase would seem to elude the conceptual instrumentalism of the logical proposition. In fact, Lyotard deems the phrase to be strictly precategorical, however deterministic, of all categorical knowledge. In this capacity the phrase essays to *institute new relations between addressors and addressees*.[10] Such new relations would guarantee that the incommensurability of the states of being of addressors and addressees is not preempted by a universalizing rule applicable exclusively to the circumstance of one of them. In this way the phrase explicitly negotiates the logical detour of the differend.

Deployed as a counter of aesthetic activity, however, "phrase power" quickly reveals its most problematic aspect: since the phrase cannot be understood as the implementation of a rule, it must be treated as the instantiation of a circumstance that would only warrant the formulation of a rule. This is bound to be a rule that experience will necessarily falsify, since what Lyotard calls the "future anterior" status of such a rule exempts any protocol of applicability. That is to say, the phrase adduces a rule that is forever deferred in our consciousness of its necessity. The gross inconsequence of whatever aesthetic activity might be conceivable according to this protocol of phrasing is further indicated in Lyotard's paradoxical assigning of it the quasi-intentional status of the "faculty of narratives."[11] The narrative faculty purveys a combinative and transformative aptitude claimed to be articulate in the phrase itself. But the lack of any sense of the transformation as mediated by a choice that is not pregiven renders all particular combinations virtually identical, precisely insofar as they are free. This moots the value of taking combination-transformation as a fulcrum of critical energy. It even more seriously vitiates the distinction between big and little narratives that it was meant to buttress.

This is not to say that Lyotard naively liquidates the very capacity to make distinctions upon which his claims to political "activism" would seem to stand. The phrase, by its very refusal to submit to definition, gives distinction the rather redundant status of a given. But distinction takes on a perversely nominalistic character in the context of this givenness. This is especially clear by contrast with the more highly individuated distinctions entailed in any protocol of practical choice, where one is always elucidating grounds of distinction in the course of their proliferation. The differend notwithstanding, it would seem that any protocol of choice instantiates an aesthetic practice as a philosophy of making. Ironically, only an aesthetics of production offers the purview for moral improvement that indisputably drives Kantian and Lyotardian ethics and that Lyotard, even more conspicuously than Kant, fails to delineate.[12] Or, to repeat an earlier critique of Lyotard's reasoning here, we might simply say that, inasmuch as Lyotard's construal of the narrative is incomplete—he gives us reversal without recognition in the exposition of little narratives—it seems reasonable to allege that his construal of the aesthetic is similarly incomplete. It instantiates a virtually mindless solidarity that thereby claims credit for brooking no material differences between minds.

By contrast, my previously stated willingness to see the logic of *Willkür* as a necessary supplement to the noumenal will stands for nothing but the integrity of individual minds. It furthermore constitutes a threshold for meeting the kind of ethical challenge of choice presented in the differend, i.e., two situations that demand to be reconciled under one rule. Because *Willkür* has its provenance in temporality, it meets the challenge not by the provision of a new criterion of choice, a new establishment procedure that is uniquely and therefore justly chosen for a particular subjective circumstance. Rather, *Willkür* promotes a consciousness of the fact that the subjective choosing of a criterion *changes* subjective circumstances in such a way as to require a more elaborate criterion of choice. We must see that this is both pragmatically narrative in its positing of ends and performatively narrative in its positing of ends within a shifting horizon of means.

Though, for Lyotard, big (pragmatic) narratives and little (performative) narratives are antithetical, his subsequent evocation of the differend as a topos of human suffering nonetheless teases the thought of a proto-utopian agency that would "unite" them. Or, at least, Lyotard intimates a reconciliation of big and little narratives in a trajectory of moral self-improvement that likewise obtains in Kantian ethics between the poles of the pragmatic and the performative. Lyotard even intimates this link between pragmatic and performative narratives in the parlance of a moral *ought*. The differend, he explains, is "that which must be able to be put into phrases [but] cannot yet be" (*Differend*, 29–30). What ought to be phrased is preempted by the necessarily prescriptive rhetoric that would be its medium. For prescription, as Lyotard says, effectively confuses "the referent" (the establishment procedure) with "reality." By this preemption of descriptive differentia, prescription infinitely perpetuates the incommensurability of perspectives that issue as the differend. Nevertheless, the moral force of the indeterminate ought, which we are left with in the absence of prescription, is hard to appreciate with any degree of moral urgency.

I would suggest, therefore, that, out of a Fichtean concern to preserve the practical scope of *Willkür* as a feature of self-determination, we might try to treat Lyotard's ought with a bit more practical purpose by proposing its inseparability from an *is* that is determinately knowable because it requires recognition. Recognition in this context entails the construal of a relation of one to an other as a successive moment of cognition. Both *ought* and *is* are thereby susceptible to a logic of choice and are thereby integrable to a project of rationality. If, as Lyotard avers, "to give the differend its due is to institute new addressors, new addressees" (*Differend*, 13), the novelty he solicits in that project is not so clearly incompatible with the normativity that narrative recognition promotes through reversal.

Lyotard, of course, would prefer to see the differences between the *ought* and the *is* as epitomizing the differend's "duty" to an antinomical representation of the unrepresentable. But I would argue that, by this deferment of knowledge beyond the temporality of recognition, Lyotard misses an important ethical possibility: that the capacity for choice that the differend proposes to do justice to might be conceived of as the *production* (not merely the acknowledgment) of a material difference. In that way it might be seen as a counter of recognition. In other words difference need not be conceived of according to Lyotardian dicta as merely the sublime transcendence of choice. Especially if we accept Neuhouser's proposition that self-determination is only ever an issue in the absence of a context of value, in the immediate dissolution of context, we can think how the occasion of choice is always the revealed illusoriness of a perceived equivalence: the absence of any criteria of recognition. Out of the misrecognition of the different-as-same there arises a subtler rationality of difference than Lyotard can discern.

In this circumstance the criterion by which one recognizes one's need for a criterion of distinction is itself indistinguishable from the transformation of the self. This transformation proceeds through a proliferation of perspectival markers that mime the conceptual slippage between contextual grounds and the contexts they instantiate. This is, of course, the pattern of determination that has appeared through all of the example literary texts, adduced in the foregoing chapters of this work as a principle of syntactical transformation. I have been trying to show that the realization of such transformations, at least in narrative aesthetics, is not a concession to the radical heterogeneity for which the differend purports to be the only just testimonial. The realization of such transformation is, instead, a necessary rearticulation of subject-object relations. Further-more, this rearticulation may justifiably be deemed productive (that is to say, duly aesthetic) insofar as it is sustained in an activity for which some future moment will suffice as recognition of its *insufficiency*. It denotes a necessary becoming.

In this regard we have resumed thinking of the aesthetic in narrative terms, as a solicitation of particulars and implicitly as a reversibility of perspectives. Where there is a desire for subjective recognition, the consti-tution of a contextual domain that further determines the context of desire, subject and object are rendered reciprocal. We might now see more starkly how the differend, proffered as the condition of the aesthetic, is proffered—as Adorno might have put it—much too naively. For, just like the highly calculated attitude of "naïveté," which, according to Horkheimer and Adorno, abets the deceptions of the Culture Industry, the differend induces us to treat the subject and object as virtually indis-tinguishable, even if, according to Lyotard's account, their indifference to each other is predicated on the insuperability of their differences. We have seen that Adorno's aesthetic theory preserves a strict "internal" connection between subject and object as a check against any presumptu-ous naïveté that would configure them as radically opposed. That would be to court an overly facile conceptual resolution. The concept per se is officially anathema to Lyotardian aesthetics. But conceptual resolution in the guise of the irresolvable conflicts of the differend remains the obstacle to any Lyotardian ethical pragmatism that could be said to share the stakes of a narrative aesthetic.

Habermas's Anti-Aesthetic Narrative of Enlightenment

It is precisely a vital "internal" connection between subject and object that Jürgen Habermas claims the aesthetic has vitiated in the service of Enlightenment rationality. In fact, Habermas links the demon of rational instrumentalism that conflates subject and object with the "idle" pleasure of the aesthetic. He construes them both as fatally symptomatic of what he calls the *production paradigm* of knowledge.

Habermas's anatomy of the production paradigm, in *The Philosophical Discourse of Modernity* (1987), offers a useful context for seeing how his attack on the aesthetic is anchored in an ideal of communication, for which subject and object both remain vital coordinates of knowledge. The production paradigm for Habermas stands for the Enlightenment ego even more ruthlessly bent upon the domination of Nature. The production paradigm follows a trajectory of human will that constitutes a flight from the social, a leap into the transcendental ether, and, only too fatefully, an ironic "return" to the ruthlessness of pre-Enlightenment dogmatism. Communication stands in an antithetical relation to the production paradigm because it is means oriented rather than ends determined. Or, to put it in strictly Habermasian jargon, communication orients action to the goal of *understanding* rather than the goal of *success*. In this way the communicative paradigm subordinates brute forms of self-justification to the normativity of social cohesion, a standard of justice that is socially productive.

By critiquing the aesthetic in the guise of the production paradigm, Habermas says he wants to "transfer the concept of praxis from labor to communication" (*Philosophical Discourse,* 321). He would thereby realize the potential of Enlightenment by freeing it from its successes, from its self-alienating products. We can never forget that labor here is Habermas's codeword for Hegel and for what he considers to be the burdensome ethical legacy of praxis philosophy. The identification of Hegel as the culprit of the production paradigm points to its betrayal of community-building creativity to solipsistic, instrumental, hence conflict-mongering, criteria of value. According to Habermas, this inevitability follows from Hegel's grounding of the dialectic in the laboring subject's struggle against lifeless materials and the projection of this conflict onto the social relations of domination and victimization that describe the master-slave agon.

But Habermas does not simplistically or even globally reject the Hegelian tradition. Rather, he sees the Hegelian account of self-realization as a project derailed by its own excesses of speculative abstraction. For Habermas the history of production paradigm begins propitiously—as it does for the young Hegel, whom Habermas praises—by discovering new criteria of self-justification in recognition by an other. But the production paradigm ends by tragically precluding the very contexts of justification within which discovery is originally possible, when recognition is sublated into a codex of regulatory rules—as it is for the old Hegel, whom Habermas repudiates. In other words, what begins beneficently in the Hegelian project of self overcoming ends, in Habermas's appraisal with a grotesque transfiguration of the human ego. It is a distortion perpetrated by that sublimely superhuman theoretical monstrosity known only too familiarly to the culture of modernity as Romantic genius.

Genius grandiosely frees the subject from contexts of justification altogether. This results in the unharnessed theorizing and moralizing of the life-world, a process of historical "aestheticization," remanding us to a circumstance in which we are hopelessly cut off from "the routines of *everyday perception* and the conventions of everyday action" (Habermas, "Discourse Ethics," 104). For Habermas the aesthetic epitomized in genius unites the ideals of autonomy and self-realization "in such a way that the objectification of human essential powers loses the character of violence in relation to both external and internal nature" (*Philosophical Discourse,* 77). Such objectification syphons off from the objectifying subject the "violent" self-consciousness of its contingency vis-à-vis other minds and other acts. For Habermas justification would be the antidote to production insofar as it induces consensus. Thus, justification would redeem the creativity of the Enlightenment by putting the good of social formations before the good of individual desires. So, the cultural task of communicative ethics is effectively to separate justification from production.

But the weakness of this schematization of the fate of reason is conceded by Habermas himself when he admits that "the internal connection between contexts of justification [reception] and contexts of discovery [production], between validity and genesis, is never utterly severed" (*Philosophical Discourse,* 323). That would be to ignore the dialectic of knowing and not knowing, which Habermas holds to be the core of communicative action. Even he must grant that communicative action would be inconceivable without some account of its own genesis: "The task of justification or, in other words, the critique of validity claims carried out from the perspective of a participant, cannot ultimately be severed from a genetic consideration that issues in an ideology critique" (323–24).

Nevertheless, if we examine the theory of communicative action, as he elaborates the terms of its consensus, we will see that a gap remains between the justificatory imperative, presupposing community, and the generative imperative (of discovery), presupposing agency. Though he imputes its existence, Habermas himself lacks terms for specifying any "connection" between justification and discovery, even one that would sustain the energy of his critique of production. I will suggest that the gap between justification and discovery is analogous to the gap between narrative and aesthetic determination. Therefore, it may be bridged by a theory of recognition expressed as contextualization. In fact, only in this way does the Habermasian ethic escape the charge of circularity, which is so often leveled at it.

Hedging against this charge of circularity, Habermas himself insists that communicative ethics is a procedure for testing moral maxims, not for generating them ("Discourse Ethics," 100). But we will see that the lack of scope in communicative ethics for generating maxims renders its moral claims upon practical life relatively moot. If we furthermore see that what Habermas condemns in the aesthetic similarly elides any generative agency, then we might have a basis for rethinking his position. We might conclude that only a notion of the aesthetic that possesses a generative as well as a regulative capacity will show us how Habermas's ethical theory can be made to keep faith with the life-world of modernity from which it purports to derive.

One of Habermas's most telling accounts of the inadequacy of the aesthetic to the epistemic dilemmas of cultural modernity presumes upon the reciprocal causality that he posits between meaning and validity. The special challenge of modernity is characterized by Habermas as a crisis of "time-consciousness," wherein the intelligibility of the present moment requires its redemption to a previous historical order instantiated as a ground of identity. The reciprocal causality of meaning and validity is symptomatic of this time-consciousness because it presupposes that the horizon of meaning in any linguistic utterance is indexical for a prior moment. But Habermas makes an even stronger claim here, to the effect that the *connection* between meaning and validity must not eliminate the *difference* between them. What guarantees that difference is the principle that meaning can never exhaust validity.

Habermas believes that in contradiction of these premises the production paradigm, and implicitly the aesthetic, depend upon the assertion of meaning as exclusively a subsumption of experience to criteria of validity: a fatal identification of "meaning-horizons with the truth of meaningful utterances" (*Philosophical Discourse*, 320). When Habermas insists that meaning does not exhaust validity I believe that he wants to dispute the mistaken impression, fostered by the production paradigm, that meanings prompted in validity claims and the justificatory frameworks that endow those meanings are identical. On the contrary, meaning for Habermas does not arise in the satisfaction of criteria of validity per se. In such cases meaning and validity would be falsely conflated with each other and thereby placed in the service of a hypostatized truth. The horizon of ethical meaning does not change through social practice to coincide with validity claims. Rather, Habermas explains, it is only the "conditions of validity" (justificatory frameworks) that change with the horizon of meaning. And because "it is only the *conditions* for the validity of utterances that change with the horizon of meaning—the changed understanding of meaning [still] has to prove itself in experience and in dealing with what can come up within its horizon" (320).

Here we might infer that validity reflects the degree to which the horizon of meaning and its validity claim are *not* conformable and in that way constitute an exigency of change, or what Habermas refers to earlier on the same page as "the transformation of world-view structures" through which all self-comprehending subjects discover their motivation. Habermas's scrupulous distinction between validity claims and "conditions of validity claims" permits us to imagine something like the generation of validity from horizons of meaning. This amounts to assigning a generative capacity at the heart of the reciprocity of meaning and validity. This is precisely what Habermas seemed to disallow in his critique of production. Yet it is precisely the principle I have wanted to adduce by stressing the interdependence of justification and contextualization as a corollary of aesthetic agency.

Nevertheless, this is where the explicit direction of Habermas's argument seems to yield inferences that drift in the opposite direction. Indeed, Habermas gives due credit to Hegelian praxis philosophy for producing a subjectivity that is emergent through what he designates as the "learning process." The learning process seems to obtain in the contextual slippage between the background of social practices that instantiate identity/lifeworld and the "transformation of world-view structures" that any reflective purchase on those practices occasions. But praxis philosophy is judged by Habermas to have suffered gross distortions in the hands of the propagators of the production paradigm. This distortion is correlated with the production paradigm's failure to "exploit" its own best resources for expanding the horizon of meaning by screening out "of the validity spectrum of reason every dimension except those of truth and efficiency" (*Philosophical Discourse,* 320). As far as Habermas is concerned, meaning and validity, in the purview of the production paradigm, are bound to converge in the dogmatism of propositional discourse.

The irony here is that this repudiation of the production paradigm parallels my own account of how pure *aesthesis* perpetrates the very epistemological errors of unreflective immediacy that I am suggesting narrative-aesthetic determination might serve to ameliorate. Furthermore, if we look at what Habermas says we have to gain by "dropping the production paradigm" altogether, we will see that he entertains the very interdependency of transformation and normativity that my account of narrative aesthetics proffers as an inherently moral edification. Despite Habermas's explicit words to the contrary (but as Habermas himself implied in the axiom that meaning does not exhaust validity), I believe that the dropping of the production paradigm would let us see how justification effectively *becomes* contextualization under the pressure of reciprocal recognition. Thus, it is transmuted into a renewed warrant for production.

To give the force of this "becoming" more argumentative ballast it is necessary to traverse more slowly the ground I have so quickly mapped out as a plausible pathway from Habermasian communication to narrative aesthetics. In his most unequivocal formulation Habermas asserts that, by dropping the production paradigm, we could "free" ourselves to "affirm the internal connection between meaning and validity for the whole reservoir of meaning—not just for the segment of meaning of linguistic expressions that play a role in assertoric and intentional sentences" (*Philosophical Discourse*, 321). Though this is most explicitly a diagnosis of the ills of the production paradigm, it is no less perspicuously a formulation of the stakes of communicative action. It reiterates how the possibility of communicative action hinges on the preclusion of production. But in this context we can see that communicative action aspires to an expansion of the horizon of meaning tantamount to the productive trajectory of narrative aesthetics as I have formulated it in these pages.

Communicative action purports to expand the horizon of meaning specifically by making validity a variable of the greatest mutual understanding of participants in a discourse. And, as would be is the case in narrative aesthetics, this communication is strictly predicated upon recognition: "I call interactions 'communicative' when the participants coordinate their plans of action consensually, with the agreement reached at any point being evaluated in terms of the intersubjective *recognition* of validity claims" (Habermas, "Discourse Ethics," 63; emphasis added). Accordingly, the expansion of the horizon of meaning, with respect to a credible standard of communication, entails the inducement to the greatest number of participants, or what, for Habermas, is the underwriting claim of "universalization." This is his so-called bridging principle between reason and the potentially "irrational" diversity of all possible value commitments: "I have introduced 'U' [universalization] as a rule of argumentation which makes agreement in practical discourses possible whenever matters of concern to all are open to regulation in the equal interest of everyone" ("Discourse Ethics," 71).

As a corollary to this stance, we can profitably observe that, in a chapter of *Philosophical Discourse of Modernity* specifically entitled "The Obsolescence of the Production Paradigm," communicative action, evoked in exactly the terms of mutual understanding through recognition that have just been stipulated, is furthermore seen as a specifically "emancipating perspective" (82). If we correlate this with the narrative drive of emancipation projects in general, we might see more forthrightly what Habermas acknowledges to be the "transcendental pragmatic" basis of communicative action. Transcendental pragmatism is a procedure for locating the necessity rather than the truth of a proposition. It shows how the way questions get posed and dealt with indicates the commitments without which discourse would be impossible. Transcendental pragmatism shows us that it is in the conditioning imperatives of such commitments alone that we can secure the most potent force of discursive rationality. The truths of a transcendentally-pragmatically grounded discourse are a function of its reference to presuppositional realms within which the discourse is minimally conceivable. Communicative action thus seeks to justify acts by reconciling them with the most universalizable pragmatic presuppositions. This effectively puts emphasis on the *processural* imperative of the principle of universalization.[13] In this way justification proceeds necessarily through a juxtaposition of contexts.

So here, as I have anticipated (and notwithstanding Habermas's claim that context is irrelevant ["Discourse Ethics," 79]), justification tends to blur into contextualization insofar as its narrative transformations are the index of its rationality. We might sharpen this point by suggesting how communicative action here exhibits a rule governedness that is also rule generative. In fact, rules function through their transformations. Habermas himself observes, in an endorsement of K. O. Apel's pragmatic ethics, that, where transcendental pragmatics is concerned, rules are said to be "proved," not "justified." The force of such rules is indicated as an inevitability determined by the constitutive recognition that no alternative construal of rule would be possible.

The impossibility of alternative construals, and hence the crux of universality here, is guaranteed by the predication of rules, not on a metaphysical a priori or even a logical premise but, rather, on the condition of a "performative contradiction."[14] A performative contradiction is the assertion of a proposition in a discursive situation that specifically contradicts the content of the assertion, e.g., "I do not exist here and now." The so-called inescapable rules that can be imputed as the conditioning presuppositions of discourse in such cases are justificatory of the recognition of contradictions they occasion. This instantiates an intersubjective, which is to say emphatically temporal, frame of reference. In other words, the condition under which "proof" displaces "justification," to take Apel's view, seems to presuppose contexts of expectation and dialogue as the crucial coordinates of knowledge. It is, in effect, an inducement to a reciprocity of perspectives rather than a deductive or teleological argument.

I would like to suggest that the thinking here follows the precedent Habermas has already defended of "justifying" meaning by reference to changing conditions of validity rather than by reference to the changed horizon of meaning itself. Though we might not have seen it as clearly before, in that case, too, justification was subtly elided with contextualization where Habermas went on to claim that validity would henceforth inhere in "the potency to create new meaning which . . . retains the contingency of genuine innovative forces" (*Philosophical Discourse*, 321). Contingency in this case is a counter for the kind of determination exhibited in performative contradiction, whereby the recognition of contradiction mandates a reconstruction of the enabling grounds of discourse or a reconfiguration of new contextual boundaries. Furthermore, in both cases in which justification elicits contextualization ("Discourse Ethics," 93), contextualization takes on the dimensions of an aesthetic project: it verges upon a logic of production, even if it is only the production of new contextual contingencies that must be taken account of.

Habermas's unwillingness to grant this perspective might be explained as a perversely complementary willingness to indulge what Seyla Benhabib has shrewdly diagnosed as a confusion between ethical cognitivism and ethical rationalism in his work. By proposing this distinction, Benhabib means to emphasize the fact that Habermas, however unconsciously, sleights the knowledge that "we are not born rational but we acquire rationality through contingent processes of socialization and identity formation" (Benhabib, "Afterword: Communicative Ethics and Current Crises in Practical Philosophy," in *The Communicative Ethics Controversy*, 365). Contingency again emerges as an index of contextual transformation. The distinction that Benhabib insists upon is designed to establish the scope of this transformability as crucial to any final assessment of communicative action.

Ethical cognitivism in this context thus refers to "the view that ethical judgments and principles have a cognitively articulable kernel, that they are neither mere statements of preference nor mere statements of taste, but that they imply validity claims" (Benhabib, "Afterword," 356). By contrast, ethical rationalism "views *moral judgments* as the core of moral theory" (354), presuming the moral self to be a moral geometer. The social consensus toward which Habermas strives in communicative action is unequivocally a discipline of validity claims and in that regard cognitivist. But here Benhabib is pointing up the danger that Habermas's reliance upon a procedural standard such as performative contradiction will preempt the very narrative (which is to say contextual) dimension of discourse that Habermas himself assumes in crediting the emancipatory power of communicative ideals.

In other words, by imputing to Habermas a confusion between ethical cognitivism and ethical rationalism, Benhabib seeks to relax the universalist rigidity of Habermas's thought, which impels him to make communicative action exclusively a procedure for testing validity claims instead of a procedure for generating them, in which case context is rendered increasingly apodictic. For Benhabib, Habermas's de facto "screening out" of the phenomena of generation, or production, is linked to the mistake of treating consensus secured on a procedural basis, like consensus secured in performative contradiction, *as a goal in itself*. For the reasons already given—that we acquire rationality through contingent processes of socialization—Benhabib prefers to see consensus as a process (Benhabib, "Afterword," 345) wherein the validity of a claim would be less one-sidedly presuppositional. In other words validity would be less a question of what constraints make moral conversation amenable to all participants (and, so, originally possible) and more a question of how that conversation might *continue* in some realistic temporal purview. This temporal purview would mandate some transformational capacity as intrinsic to the community of consensus.

For example, Benhabib can easily appreciate the procedural lucidity that dictates our promulgating a principle that individuals ought not to inflict unnecessary suffering on one another. Thus, we avoid a devastating performative contradiction. For the act of inflicting unnecessary suffering would seem to preclude the possibility of a discursive community that could, let alone would, espouse it. But, by the same token, adherence to a strictly presuppositional ground in this case would preclude the otherwise realistic possibility of a community of masochists and sadists. The life-world would, in effect, be preempted by the consensus in which any such ethical principle was originally presumed to matter. Rationalism masquerades as cognitivism here. The only remedy would be a recognition that has temporal vectors, whereby the transformation of a community into sadomasochists would not preclude the possibility of its perpetuity: where value judgments would not be judged as constitutive of community and in that way render community an inert content, the mere contingency of a formal rigor mortis.

This is exactly what Habermas himself seems to preclude when he insists (though he almost immediately qualifies the insistence) upon what he calls "a moment of *unconditionality*" as "built into *factual* processes of mutual understanding . . . " (*Philosophical Discourse*, 322). This is a phrase that wants mightily to elude the temporal perspective within which communication ensues from communicability. This would effectively mitigate contextualization as a determinant of value by making all contexts equal: they would be equally contexts for consensus and thereby lose all but the most formalistic bearing on the validity claims they embody. According to this protocol, the theory of communicative action would become more strictly a narrative enterprise but more and more deliberately evade the consequences of invoking any particular narrative contexts.

In the context of the kinds of arguments I have been pursuing in these pages, we might appropriately say that the narrative form posited here needs an aesthetic complement, much as recognition needs reversal in order to bear its Aristotelian burden of productive insight. As I have already alleged, Habermas's theory is effectively all recognition and no reversal as long as it remains insulated, within his unconditional moment, from the existential circumstances of its dissemination.

I believe that it is out of a comparable understanding that Benhabib counters Habermas's position with the strong assertion that "communicative actions are actions through which . . . we *practice* the reversibility of perspectives implicit in adult human relationships (Benhabib, "Afterword," 359; emphasis added). Though she does not posit it as such, I believe that, for Benhabib, this reversibility of perspectives is construable as a principle of choice, a virtual solicitation of contextual particulars, and hence an aesthetic imperative consistent with the terms of the narrative aesthetic I have been pursuing in the chapters of this book. Otherwise, the sense of volitional practice conjured in Benhabib's critique of Habermas is diluted to the point of banality.

Or I should say that Benhabib's critique issues a warrant for my own "strong assertion": that the reversibility of perspectives constitutes choice because, as in Fichtean self-determination, whatever presuppositional grounds are necessary to instantiate self-consciousness entail the need to consider the alternative selves that might be knowable as the contingencies of such a recognition. Because this aesthetic imperative would be sufficiently distinct from the sensuous or practical determinism that Habermas decries in the production paradigm, it might thus be fairly construed as a necessary correlative to the demand for recognition that he has built into the definition of communicative action. This demand for recognition threatens to dissolve into pure counterfactuality as long as it remains cut off from production.

The advantage of this supplemental view of Habermas's communicative ethics is that the normative value of communicative action as a testing or justificatory procedure would be sustained. But it would not be sustained at the expense of the contextual transformability that its premise of recognition seems to depend upon. Habermas seems to presuppose this premise of recognition by making his own refutation of the production paradigm hinge upon an "internal relation" between horizons of meaning and validity claims (*Philosophical Discourse*, 321) and between "contexts of justification and discovery" (323). The very contextuality of knowledge that obtains in either case necessitates the transformability of the judging subject's self-reflection.

Benhabib's elaboration of the premise of reversibility, to the effect that it requires both narrative and interpretive skills, strengthens the admittedly inferential thrust of my thinking here. Particularly if we remember Habermas's invidious comparison of the internal relation between meaning and validity with the more "external," and therefore reified relations that are allegedly valorized by the production paradigm, we see why Benhabib goes on to stipulate that the narrative and interpretive skills implicit in reversibility enjoin three distinct domains of moral action that do not succumb to a teleological judgment or to an epistemological synthesis.

According to Benhabib, the domains of moral action are: "the assessment of one's duties; the assessment of one's specific course of action as fulfilling these duties; and the assessment of one's maxims as embodied expressly or revealed in actions" (Benhabib, "Afterword," 361). The assessment of actions with respect to duties projects the narrative scope of moral acts. The further "interpretive" entailment, by which maxims are deemed to be expressively determined, is significantly explicated by

Benhabib as "a willingness to see oneself under various act descriptions." I would argue that Benhabib's characterization of the interpretive aspect of moral action as a mandate to solicit different descriptions, especially in the context of narrative normativity, presents a stance that is coherent with my own claim for the interdependence of the narrative and the aesthetic. And this stance is put forth to the same argumentative end: to promote the idea that what is really at stake in the prospect of ethical community (community has always been proffered, albeit along asymmetrical lines, by both narrative and aesthetic theorists) is not the possibility of its mere perpetuation of social forms but, rather, of their transformation.

Especially in the context of Benhabib's reversibility principle, we might more readily accept the proposition that *only* where one sees one's duties as changing can one trust the possibility of a community wherein self-interest might be transcended and promote a compelling interest in the question: "How does the self co-exist with other selves?" Thus, under the terms of this analysis the otherwise vaguely delineated internal relationality of meaning and validity—so crucial to Habermas's notion of ethical life—might be said to denote an openness approximating what I have elsewhere called an agency without a telos. Benhabib's claim about the meaning of reversibility helps us to see more clearly that such a proposition might now be persuasively construed as an assimilation of objective telos to that process of change. It would be an assimilation whereby the individual's relation to society obtains as a demand that society, in a sense, grow bigger. It is a demand for a greater number of discursive places of recognition from which the subject may gain some reflective purchase.

In fact, Benhabib cites both Kant and Hannah Arendt as locating the motivation for ethical judgments in the prospect of "an enlarged mentality," in which one's own sense of motive requires being able to tell a story of motivation that will be accepted by others. Habermas's internal relationality of meaning and validity gains a cognitivist warrant here that eludes subjectivism (even in the name of the subject). This cognitivist warrant, we will remember, was the sine qua non of Adornian subjectivity. For now the choice to act requires a transition to another choice: the choice of which recognition of one's actions might be self-consciously sustained as reciprocal with the context out of which it arises.

I would want to take this line of thought one step further by backtracking through the lessons of the Frankfurt School to show that the ethical trajectory of this enlarged mentality is already articulated in Adornian second reflection, as I have previously characterized it. The cognitive protocol of second reflection eloquently captures the idealism of Benhabib's admonition to deploy narrative and interpretive skills in the service of the reversibility of perspectives. By always presupposing the mediatedness, which is to say the shifting temporality of aesthetic judgment, second reflection also produces a kind of "reconciliation" between narrative and interpretive modes, such that the transformability of the world of the artwork always takes precedence over the autonomy of the work itself. Hence, Adorno's famous caveat that art does not follow historical changes. Rather, "history is intrinsic to the truth content of aesthetics" (*Aesthetic Theory*, 489). We must, of course, be careful to see that for Adorno reconciliation, though it certainly denotes a relation of the subject and the world through the work of art, is nonetheless a critically inflected term. It denotes not an identification between subject and world but, rather, the very self-alienating dimension of all identificatory desire that sustains the desire as a processual, not an intuitive or instrumental, order of subjectivity. Precisely because the aesthetic is ordained as second reflection, the reflective consciousness that obtains here already entails the reversibility upon which the continuity between narration and interpretation, between contexts of justification and contexts of production, equally depend.

It therefore becomes possible to assert that Adorno's second reflection is perhaps the strongest premise upon which to establish a narrative aesthetics, chiefly because it does, in that respect, precisely what Habermas and his disciples claim it cannot do: it shows that reconciliation and communication are not contradictory. Albrecht Wellmer has carried forward the communicative ethics attack on Frankfurt School aesthetics by asserting that the artwork, set up as a model of reconciliation, de-reifies the objectality of the instrumentalized world in such a way that it metaphysically insulates itself within the philosophy of consciousness.[15] If, however, we grant that Adorno's reconciliation is nonidentical, then it is potentially communicative by dint of its own internal connection with those conditions under which its negations are elementally possible. These conditions, because they cannot be absorbed, hence must be reengaged. It is in this respect that Adorno can assert, almost in anticipation of Wellmer, that "the process enacted by every art work—[is] a model for a kind of praxis wherein a collective subject is being constituted" (*Aesthetic Theory*, 343). Any confusion that the "we" subject annunciated here is merely subjectified into its own reifying will is dispelled by Adorno's stipulation that, "if works of art have any social influence at all, it is not by haranguing, but by changing consciousness. . . . The only subjective orientation that corresponds to the cognitive quality of art works is a cognitive one" (344–45). Reconciliation and communication are thus more fairly judged to be enabling conditions for each other because the cognitive basis of subjective agency is not distinct from that of any putative social agency.

Finally, the ultimate justification for this cognitivist perspective is that narrative aesthetics, couched in such terms, definitively becomes what narrative by itself has failed to become, especially in the most unselfconsciously thematizing gestures of the novel: a transformational act qua transformative agency. That is, the truth of narrative must reconcile form with act in such a way that form constitutes the recognition of a motivational stance inherent to its form of presentation. Only in its aesthetic capacity is narrative a vital reservoir of motivation rather than a preemptive moral codex. We have seen that this is so inasmuch as it is the contextuality of transformation that adduces the need for justification and the corollary appeal to motive. Conversely, motivation is exactly what would be most egregiously lacking from a realm of abstract contextuality such as that entertained in the exclusively justificatory precincts of Habermasian consensus. Even more important for our purposes, without a context of motive any schematization of the aesthetic as a proliferation of particulars, as durable in time, would be impossible. In the end it is perhaps fitting to say that the aesthetic is nothing but motive made ethically vital through submission to the narrative tempers of time.

Notes

1. For a full discussion, see Foucault's *Archaeology of Knowledge,* 67. See also the commentary by Dreyfus and Rabinow in *Michel Foucault: Beyond Structuralism and Hermeneutics.*

2. Much of what I have to say about contradiction and totalization here, and in subsequent chapters, arises from my reading of Althusser, who pursues the problem on many fronts. Though in the course of my argument Althusser's presuppositions are substantively modified, his stance in "Contradiction and Overdetermination," in *For Marx,* remains an important reference point. The notion of "interpellation" gets its fullest exposition in the important essay "Ideology and Ideological State Apparatuses," in *Lenin and Philosophy.*

3. Here I ought to forestall a possible confusion. In all of this discussion I mean to eschew the so-called vulgar Marxist notion of ideology as a veil of false consciousness. Rather, as I have already indicated, my frame of reference is Althusser's provocative reformulation of ideology as "a representation of the imaginary relationship of individuals to the real conditions of their existence." Since "real conditions" are knowable for Althusser (as in the Freudian unconscious) only through the textual play of condensation and displacement, he is bound to assert that ideology is omnipresent. This is a claim that becomes increasingly consequential for my own efforts to link narrative and act. Precisely insofar as the form of the mimetic novel solicits the most naive reifications of closure—e.g., sense and nonsense, fact and fantasy--it is complicit in the vulgar concept of ideology. It is on this basis that we *can* meaningfully contrast our relation to ideology with our relation to the novel. Again, see Althusser's influential exposition in "Ideology and Ideological State Apparatuses" with my further discussion in chapter 2 of this work.

4. Here it is worth considering Ricoeur's treatment of the highly conventionalized nature of realist "style," such that we must recognize a point of no return wherein the ultimate codification of realist form is indistinguishable from the essence of literary artifice. See *Time and Narrative,* vol. 1, and a more extended treatment of the relation between reality and identity in *Lectures on Ideology and Utopia,* 136–39.

5. See Bürger's *Decline of Modernism* for an insight into the paradoxical reciprocity between naturalism and aestheticism. For Bürger the paradox is precipitated by the inadequate theorizing of the subject that underlies the distinction between naturalism and aestheticism (94–126).

6. The by now canonical figures here include John Barth, Robert Coover, Thomas Pynchon, Raymond Roussel, Alain Robbe-Grillet, Francis Ponge, and Philippe Sollers.

7. For a fuller discussion of the Hegelian-materialist controversy, see Coward and Ellis, *Language and Materialism*, 84–87.

8. In such texts as *Criticism and Ideology* and the more recent *Ideology of the Aesthetic* Eagleton's thematizing profoundly inhibits the very dialectical procedures he valorizes within the historical horizon of his arguments. See also Tony Bennett's recent *Outside Literature* for evidence that the persistent thematizing practices of Marxist literary critics lead paradoxically to a renunciation of the aesthetic as a counter for judging works of art.

Chapter 2

1. Derrida's "White Mythology," de Man's "Form and Intent in the American New Criticism," and Hillis Miller's "The Critic as Host" offer useful coordinates upon which this polemic is frequently mapped. For a critique of this "school" of thought, which usefully contextualizes my own discussion of the liabilities of de Manian reading in this chapter, see Cole's "The Dead-End of Deconstruction."

2. See Ragland-Sullivan's helpful gloss on the epistemological trajectory of Freud's *Ich*, in *Jacques Lacan and the Philosophy of Psychoanalysis*, 51–59.

3. In *The Ethics of Criticism* Siebers indicates the scope of internal contradiction that so vexes Aristotle's attempt to reconcile poetics and ethics:

> Moral philosophy in Aristotle tries not to expel its own theories in the form of literary judgments but to retain its literary formulations in their most antithetical and threatening forms within the scope of moral philosophy. Literature for Aristotle reveals the instability of human existence and the difficulty of living morally in such a world. Aristotle's approach was decidedly anti-Platonic but his goals were not. (22)

4. For a fuller discussion of the pragmatics of metaphor as it bears on the relation of trope to act and identity, see the introductory chapters of my book *A Metaphorics of Fiction*. Here, with deference to the magisterial work of Paul Ricoeur on this subject, I try to clarify the trajectory of thinking that is conditioned by epistemological constraints of metaphor.

5. The relevant text here is, of course, "Two Aspects of Language and Two Types of Linguistic Disturbance."

6. See Jameson's *Political Unconscious*, 27–58. Althusser's original discussion of structural causality is found in Althusser's and Balibar's *Reading Capital*, 186–90.

7. See Holquist's penetrating introduction to *The Dialogic Imagination* for a fuller context (esp. p. xx).

8. I am thinking here of Kristeva's early collection of essays, *Desire in Language,* and Foucault's later works, *Discipline and Punish* and *The History of Sexuality.*

Chapter 3

1. It must be remembered that de Tracy asserted a continuity between physiologically determinate experience and ideas. In fact, he considered ideology to be a branch of zoology. It is the positivistic fulcrum of ideological theory that gave critical leverage against the dogmatic practices of traditional culture.

2. See Fekete's fuller account of how "Richards' methodology also happens to eliminate questions relating to the social ontology of labor" (*The Critical Twilight,* 35–36), resulting in the obfuscation of his stated ends.

3. See Ricoeur's meticulous excavation of the notion of mimesis from the corpus of Aristotle: in particular, *The Rule of Metaphor,* 43–70, and *Time and Narrative,* 1:54–64.

4. Lentricchia has the fullest exposition I know of the idealizing momentum of New Critical aesthetics, in *After the New Criticism,* 7–26.

5. I am mapping Bersani's argument across the boundaries of three distinct but related texts: *Baudelaire and Freud,* "The Other Freud," and, with Ulysse Dutoit, "Merde Alors."

6. In "On Narcissism" Freud argues that secondary narcissism is a specular desire arising from the perceived autonomy of another. In the context of the present discussion the self-shattering of the "victim" serves to conjure a fantasy of autonomy vis-à-vis the inertia of the torturer.

7. Jameson derives his understanding of the expressive model, specifically, from Althusser's critique of Hegel. The clearest account of this genesis and its fullest exposition as an aspect of Jameson's own project appears in the long theoretical chapter that opens *The Political Unconscious.*

8. The best account of *heteroglossia* must rely upon the full complement of cross-fertilizing texts and notes in Bakhtin's/Volosinov's bibliography. It is a mistake to attempt to isolate a single definition when in the course of its evolution the concept undergoes the very dialogism it purports to explain.

9. In *Mikhail Bakhtin: The Dialogical Principle,* Todorov explains that Bakhtin pairs the term *exotopy* with *transgradience* "to designate elements of consciousness that are external to it but nonetheless absolutely necessary for its completion, for its achievement of totalization." Todorov observes the implicit contradiction between the openness of exotopy and the formal closure of transgradience with its privileging of the authorial role. Todorov finds a resolution of this contradiction in Bakhtin's revision of *Problems of Dostoevsky's Poetics.* Here Todorov pinpoints "a radical transformation" of Bakhtin's thought: "now the best exotopy is precisely the one Dostoevsky practices, insofar as it does not confine the character in the consciousness of

the author and puts into question the very notion of the privileging of one consciousness over another" (103). Much of what follows in my treatment of Bakhtin is implicitly in agreement with Todorov's findings.

10. It is important to remember in this context that Bakhtin's notes toward a reworking of the Dostoevsky book indicate a relegating of the concept of monologue to the status of an abstract ideal (*Problems*, 315).

11. Bernstein's superb *Philosophy of the Novel* gives perhaps the most complete and sympathetic account of Lukácsian irony, tracing the "performative contradiction" at issue here to Kant's two worlds theory and thereby arguing the continuity of the Lukácsian problematic with the mainstream of Western idealism.

12. Jay's *Marxism and Totality* provides a clear and comprehensive view of the liabilities of Lukács's argument with a view to the entirety of his career (21–127).

13. See Jay's discussion of the consequences of this appropriation (ibid., 112–13).

Chapter 4

1. The influential texts in this regard are Derrida's, who has so notoriously problematized speech as a locus of meaning. I take the key disseminators of a narratology focused on the problematic of voice—Jonathan Culler, Seymour Chatman, Gérard Gennette, A. J. Greimas—to be working directly out of or at least presuming upon fundamentally Derridean assumptions.

2. Here it is worth consulting Cascardi's unambiguously Lukácsian account of McKeon's argument in *The Origins of the English Novel:*

> McKeon's work . . . has sought to explain how the relationship between genre as a "conceptual" category and a series of quasi-objective social facts can "dialectically" explain the origins of the novel as a category that both pre-exists and is precipitated by its own conceptual formation. (*The Subject of Modernity*, 78)

3. The Bakhtin revival can be credited in large measure to Holquist's volume, *The Dialogic Imagination*, which led to the reissue of a broad range of Bakhtinian texts dealing directly with the question of the subject: *The Formal Method in Literary Scholarship, Marxism and the Philosophy of Language* (Volosinov), *Problems of Dostoevsky's Poetics*, and, most recently, *Speech Genres and Other Late Essays*. The recent publication of Clark and Holquist's *Mikhail Bakhtin* and Todorov's *Mikhail Bakhtin: The Dialogic Principle* have brought this question even more starkly into the foreground of Bakhtinian theory.

4. This group includes theorists of the novel such as Lukács and Macherey, neo-Marxists such as Althusser and Jameson, and narratologists working within the poststructuralist paradigm such as Culler and Gennette.

5. Bakhtin's discussion of parody in *Problems of Dostoevsky's Poetics* is particularly noteworthy insofar as it abandons the structural crux of mimicry

and broadens the scope of the term to include the reciprocity of all social significations. It thus precludes any idealizing "fusion of voices": "In carnival, parodying was employed very widely in diverse forms and degrees: various images . . . parodied one another variously and from various points of view; it was like an entire system of crooked mirrors, elongating, diminishing, distorting in various directions to various degrees" (127).

6. See especially the discussions of utterance in *The Formal Method*, for their bearing on the analysis of ideological representations (120–21).

7. This title is given by Clark and Holquist to a set of fragments (written between 1918 and 1924) in which Bakhtin initially posed the problem of the relations between self and other. Clark and Holquist characterize it as: "a treatise on ethics in the world of everyday experience, a kind of pragmatic axiology. Ethical activity is conceived as a deed" (*Mikhail Bakhtin*, 62).

8. See *Problems of Dostoevsky's Poetics*, 30.

9. See Taylor's further development of this argument in the full text of his essay "Language and Human Nature," in *Human Agency and Language*, 215–47.

10. In *Hegel's Dialectic and Its Criticism* Rosen gives an excellent account of the conceptual grounds upon which I base my claim that we might connect Adorno's critique of Hegel with the problem of mediation in Bakhtin (158–64).

11. See *Problems of Dostoevsky's Poetics*, 36.

12. See Benjamin's account of "discontinuous finitude" in *The Origin of the German Tragic Theater* in tandem with Buck-Morss's account of Adorno's reading of the term.

13. See how Bakhtin intimates this definition as a corrective for what he judges to be Engelhardt's more naive account of the so-called ideological novel. In the novel of ideas Bakhtin believes ideation is inherently monological in the manner of a Hegelian synthesis. *Problems of Dostoevsky's Poetics*, 22.

14. In *Late Marxism* Jameson gives some indication of the necessity to privilege Adorno's assessment of Benjamin's coinage here. For Adorno the "juxtaposition of extremes" that instantiates "constellation" possesses a rational lucidity chiefly because it does not sacrifice "knowledge" to "truth" (see esp. p. 54 of Jameson's excursus).

Chapter 5

1. Within the category of thematic criticism I embrace the broadest tradition out of Plato, which predicates the meaning of the literary text upon the possibility of its conceptual abstraction. As I argue in the following pages, such abstractions would tend to unify an array of syntactical particulars under the aegis of a fundamental semantic principle.

2. The attachment of ethical value to the project of thematization reflects the terms of Kantian morality set forth in *Groundwork for a Metaphysic of Morals*. The split between desire and duty warrants the transition from particular to universal value.

3. In this context it is important to note the close relationship between work and form annunciated on pp. 236–38 of *Phenomenology of Mind*.

4. See Benhabib's *Critique, Norm, and Utopia* for a compelling generalization of the "work model" of expressive action (139–40).

5. For a convincing contextualization of the following argument, see the full text of "Lordship and Bondage," in Hegel's *Phenomenology of Mind* (esp. 237–39).

6. See especially Book Zeta of Aristotle's *Metaphysics*. Staten's reading of the priority given by Aristotle to *eidos* is particularly persuasive in *Wittgenstein and Derrida:* "Aristotle uses the word *eidos* to refer to both the form of the individual entity we perceive and the species to which the individual belongs; this means that the *eidos* is prior to the distinction between singular and universal" (6).

7. Here my understanding of Hegel's relation to Marx accords with Ricoeur's account of the function of ideology in terms of *Tätigkeit*. Appropriately enough, this is a term from Fichte's exposition of self-activity in *Science of Knowledge*. Ricoeur credits Roger Garaudy for this insight in *Lectures on Ideology and Utopia* (61).

8. On p. 138 of "Living On," an essay on Blanchot's *récit*, Derrida explains: "(The *non-lieu* is a strange judgement in French law that is worth *more* than an acquittal: it fictively annuls the very proceedings of indictment, arraignment, detention and trial [cause], even though the proceedings have taken place; the transcript of the remains, and the certification of the *non-lieu*.)"

9. See "Différance" (in *Margins of Philosophy*) for Derrida's full discussion of *différance* as "temporization" and *différance* as "spacing" (13).

10. Gasché gives the most precise exposition of grammatological inscription for my purposes in *The Tain of the Mirror* (158).

11. For Giddens the reciprocity of structure and action is conceived in terms of a recursive principle. In his account of human agency this recursivity operates all self-reproducing systems. See pp. 75–77 in *Central Problems in Social Theory*.

12. See p. 92 of Buck-Morss's very important account of Adorno's attempt to distinguish image from figure in *The Origin of Negative Dialectics*.

13. Again Buck-Morss supplies the best context for this hypothesis; see *Origin of Negative Dialectics*, 20.

14. See Blanchot's full exposition of "the neuter" in his essay "The Narrative Voice," reprinted in *The Gaze of Orpheus*, 133–41.

15. See *Reflections on Poetry*, 42–43, for Baumgarten's full treatment of extensive and intensive qualities.

16. Here I am indebted to Gasché's excellent and original commentary on this aspect of Baumgarten in "Of Aesthetic and Historical Determination," in *Post-Structuralism and the Question of History* (147–49).

17. See my discussion of the prolepsis of Aristotelian unity, in *A Metaphorics of Fiction*, 122–23.

18. I am indebted to Bernstein's *The Philosophy of the Novel* for the critical view of Lukács that I am taking here. Bernstein argues that the universalizing thrust of Lukács's argument tends, like the Hegelian state, to mystify difference as an abstract harmony (198).

19. See especially p. 151 of Gasché's essay for the basis of my extrapolation from Baumgarten to Blanchot.

20. See Baumgarten's discussion of the dynamics of the thematizing mind in *Reflections on Poetry* (62). Here Baumgarten renounces the tendency to let individual acts of mind stand "unconnected" in relation to a plausible whole, as "it is interconnection which is poetic." In this passage Baumgarten is at odds with his own need to ground aesthetic determination in the particular, that proverbial nemesis of Enlightenment idealizing. This apparent contradiction is somewhat ameliorated by Aschenbrenner, in his introduction to *Reflections*. Aschenbrenner equates Baumgarten's formulation of theme with Leibniz's principle of sufficient reason. If theme is that which contains the sufficient reason of other representations that do not reflect its own sufficient reason in them, there is effectively only one theme. Thus, the term takes on a more heuristic function and introduces less analytical dissonance into any discussion of how well it may be integrated with the larger context of the rest of the argument.

21. See *Gaze*, 41. Here Blanchot deploys the term *worklessness* to denote the absence of the work as an intentional act. This is *not* to be confused with the expressive capacity of *arbeit*.

22. See the full text of "Literature and the Right to Death," in *Gaze*, for a discussion of the status of the cadaver in Blanchot's thinking, 21–62.

23. See Rockmore's authoritative commentary on the "absolute self," in *Fichte, Marx, and the German Philosophical Tradition*, as well as his contribution to "Fichte and Contemporary Philosophy," a special issue of *Philosophical Forum* (Winter-Spring 1988). My point in this regard is that the absolute self is effectively displaced (except as a heuristic) by the drama of striving, which I want to conflate with the threshold of aesthetic valuation.

24. See *Fichte, Marx, and the German Philosophical Tradition*, 16, for the particulars of the argument behind this assertion.

25. It is important to realize that Fichte begins from a now widely accepted premise of reflection philosophy: where one member of a relation, the "I," is posed as an absolute, its constitutive other is necessarily excluded from that sphere; the totality that it designates is completely undetermined but nonetheless distinctly determinable.

26. See Foucault's influential exposition of this term in "Nietzsche, Genealogy, History," collected in *Language, Counter-Memory, Practice*.

Chapter 6

1. See Rorty's discussion of the hegemony of ironic consciousness in the high modernism of the novel, in *Contingency, Irony, and Solidarity* (100–106).

2. See p. 56 of Ricoeur's *Time and Narrative*, vol. 1 for a discussion of the paradigmatic features of Aristotelian plot as they bear on the phenomenon of action.

3. Ricoeur assimilates Gallie's position to the problematic of poetics most explicitly in *Hermeneutics and the Human Sciences*, 277.

4. It is for this reason that Bernstein and Jameson have argued for the *inevitability* of a Marxist framework of analysis in any theory of the novel that would seek to reconnect this genre with the historical world of its origin. My shifting the emphasis to the dynamics of transformation and totality, action and recognition, is meant to challenge this inevitability.

5. See Benhabib's discussion/formulation of this paradox in *Critique, Norm, Utopia*, 209. I disagree, however, with Benhabib's extrapolation that nonidentity is conceivable for Adorno only aesthetically, "not as a social or interpersonal condition" (212). It is true that Adorno designates "the beautiful in Nature [as] the residue of non-identity in things." But he goes on to stipulate that "nature does not yet exist in the dimension of beauty except in an inchoate and ephemeral kind of way" (*Aesthetic Theory*, 108, 109). As I have implied, and as we will see in more depth, the social imperative of nonidentity is revealed to the degree that when art takes over from the beautiful in nature it is under the constraint of "second reflection."

6. See Buck-Morss's *Origin of Negative Dialectics* for the particulars of Adorno's response to and modification of Benjamin's theory of allegory.

7. This criticism is perhaps most succinctly voiced in Cascardi's recent essay "Narrative and Totality." Also see Dews's *Logics of Disintegration*, 139–43, for a convincing refutation.

8. These issues constitute the substance of chapters 1 and 2 in *Time and Narrative*, vol. 1.

9. I am presuming upon Ricoeur's etymology of this expression in *Time and Narrative*, 1:45–46. Here he stipulates that any simple equating of the meaning of *mimesis* and *muthos*

> does not completely fill up the meaning of the expression *mimesis praxeos*. We may . . . construe the objective genetive as the noematic correlate of imitation or representation and equate this correlate to the whole expression "the organization of the events," which Aristotle makes the "what"—the object—of mimesis. But that the praxis belongs at the same time to the real domain, covered by ethics, and the imaginary one, covered by poetics, suggests that mimesis functions not just as a break but also as a connection.

10. See Buck-Morss's discussion of this term in *Origin of Negative Dialectics*, 235.

11. See Handwerk's *Irony and Ethics in Narrative* for a corroboration of this perspective on Schlegel.

12. See especially de Man's essay "The Epistemology of Metaphor" for a useful elaboration of this distinction.

13. See Taylor's historical sketch of the theories of language acquisition, particularly his commentary on Herder, in *Human Agency and Language*, 1:215–47, for the basis of my speculation in these pages.

14. See "The Agency of the Letter in the Unconscious: Or Reason since Freud," in *Ecrit*, 114–17.

15. See also Caramello's essay, "Portrait Narration: Generals James and Stein," in *Intertextuality and Contemporary American Fiction*, ed. Patrick O'Donnell and Robert Con Davis. Caramello discusses at length Stein's acknowledgment of James as a precursor for her own syntactical innovations, though in her description of them she takes up issues divergent from my own line of argument.

16. See James's references to Trollope throughout *Theory of Fiction*, but especially the excerpt from his 1883 essay "Anthony Trollope":

He took a suicidal satisfaction in reminding the reader that the story he was telling was only, after all, a makebelieve. He habitually referred to the work in hand (and in the course of that work) as a novel, and to himself as a novelist, and was fond of letting the reader know that this novelist could direct the course of events according to his pleasure. (175)

17. As a context for the following, see both Fichte's *Science of Knowledge* (219–21) and Lachs's essay "Is There an Absolute Self?" (in the special Fichte issue of *Philosophical Forum*). Lachs especially features the controversial aspects of this Fichtean concept, which proffers a resolution of the conflict between ideal and real selves. Also see my discussion above in chapter 5, n. 23.

18. See Baumgarten's *Reflections on Poetry*, 62.

19. See *Reading Capital*, 186–88.

20. See *Art of the Novel*, 347, and Sprinker's *Imaginary Relations*, 59.

21. James gets this from Flaubert. See *Art of the Novel*, 347.

22. See Rowe's *Theoretical Dimension of Henry James* (esp. p. 227).

23. See *Henry James and H. G. Wells: A Record of Their Friendship, Their Debate on the Art of Fiction and Their Quarrel*, edited by Leon Edel and Gordon N. Ray.

Chapter 7

1. See Caygill's *Art of Judgement* for a precise and exhaustive discussion of the tensions between productive and legislative theories of mind in the eighteenth century (38–102).

2. See Todorov's influential discussion of the transformative aspects of narrative in *Poetics of Prose*. Here he asserts that there are three levels of analysis: the verbal, syntactical, and semantic. These levels conform to my own account of the syntactical armature of narrative transformation insofar as they are held to be dialectically relational. In fact, Todorov's concluding words on this point specifically endorse my view of narrative activity as a syntactical relationality that plays between resemblance and difference:

"transformation represents precisely a synthesis of difference and resemblance, it links two facts without their being able to be identified. Rather than a 'two-sided unit,' it is an operation in two directions: it asserts both resemblance and difference; it engages and suspends time" (233).

3. See also Danto's embellishment of the notion that the work of art ought not to be subject to a transparency theory, or what he calls an "ephemeralization" process, in *The Philosophical Disenfranchisement of Art*, 9.

4. Again Caygill gives a useful survey of this history, in *Art of Judgement*, 38–98.

5. See Butler's full consideration of Sartre's place vis-à-vis the poststructuralist inheritors of Hegel, in *Subjects of Desire*, 172–76.

6. See Butler's account of the debate (*Subjects of Desire*, 133). She is giving her own translation of the transcript originally published in *Bulletin de la Société Française de Philosophie* 13 (June 1948):49–91.

7. In *Poetics* Aristotle vitiates the determinative vitality of reversal with the identificatory logic that prevails over it in recognition (*anagnorisis*).

8. Sartre specifies what he means by affectivity: it is to be contrasted with an intentionality conditioned by "pure affective qualities" (*Being and Nothingness*, 330):

> Affectivity as introspection reveals it to us is in fact already a constituted affectivity; it is consciousness of the world. All hate is hate of someone. . . . In these various examples a transcendent "intention" is directed toward the world and apprehends it as such. Already therefore there is a surpassing, an internal negation; we are on the level of transcendence and choice.

9. See Butler, *Subjects of Desire*, 134–35. My proposal that prereflective agency might be both mediate and immediate is a retort to Hyppolite's assertion that the prereflective is merely absurd if it is neither mediate nor immediate, as Sartre implies.

10. Ashbery speaks explicitly about his decision to write in prose, stipulating what he has called "the freeing impulse of a prosody of syntax":

> suddenly the idea of it occurred to me as something new in which the arbitrary divisions of poetry into lines would get abolished. One wouldn't have to have these interfering and scanning the processes of one's thought as one was writing; the poetic form would be dissolved, in solution, and therefore create a much more—I hate to say environmental . . . but more of a surrounding thing like the way one's consciousness is surrounded by one's thoughts." (cited in *Poet's Prose*, 130)

11. See Baltrušaitis's *Anamorphic Art*, for a view of the intellectual underpinnings of catoptrics and related scientific enterprises bearing on the illusionistic aspects of reflection.

12. See Baumgarten's *Reflections* (esp. secs. 40–43) in which the distinction between the intuitive register of pictorial art and the cognitive register of verbal art hinge explicitly upon the possibility of *making distinctions*.

13. Ashbery gives his own eloquent gloss on this phenomenon in his poem based upon Parmigianino's experiment with a three-dimensional canvas, "Self-Portrait in a Convex Mirror," in the collection of the same name.

14. See above, p. 223.

15. This is, in fact, a gesture that Baumgarten himself makes in his comparison of visual and verbal representations in *Reflections*. It is, however, abortive to the extent that his emphasis on the necessity of poetry to approximate sense immediacy seems to privilege the image as a static, hence noncognitive, feature of aesthetic form. This false appearance was widely disseminated by Baumgarten's followers and constitutes the urgency of Herder's subsequent "correction" in *Plastik*.

16. See the notes for *On Painting*, 107–13.

17. Caygill gives a helpful summary of Herder's defense of Baumgarten in *Art of Judgement* (174–76).

18. It is worth noting that philosophical anthropology follows this line of thought, especially in the work of George Herbert Mead (*Mind, Self and Society, The Philosophy of Act*) and Arnold Gehlen (*Man in the Age of Technology*).

19. Here I am following Caygill's translation of Herder, in Johann Gottfried Herder's *Sämtliche Werke III*, edited by Bernhard Suphan (Berlin 1878), 7–8. See Caygill, *Art of Judgement*, 180.

20. For a full consideration of the motion picture medium as an art form with profound philosophical ramifications, especially along the lines projected in this discussion, see Deleuze's *Cinema 1: The Movement-Image*. Though Bergson is the informing philosophical mind here, the consequences of thinking about the time-consciousness of the motion picture image in this work bear upon the German tradition that animates my own argument.

21. See the *Oxford English Dictionary* for this definition.

22. I owe this insight to Stewart's splendid anatomy of Ashbery's poetic in *American Poetry Review*, "The Last Man."

Chapter 8

1. See Arthur H. Cash's *Laurence Sterne: The Later Years* (London: Methuen, 1986), 259–61.

2. This progress is emplotted implicitly and explicitly in historical purviews as various as Watt's *Rise of the Novel*, McKeon's *Origins of the English Novel*, Caserio's *Plot, Story, and the Novel*, Bernstein's *Philosophy of the Novel*, and Todorov's *Poetics of Prose*.

3. See Jameson's influential essay "The Crisis of Capitalism in Post-Modern Culture."

4. Thompson credits both Anthony Giddens and Jürgen Habermas with this insight about the continuity between ideology and ideology-critique in his useful survey *Studies in the Theory of Ideology*. See his chapters 7 and 8.

5. See especially "The Culture Industry," in *Dialectic of Enlightenment,* for the consequences of this presumption.

6. This discussion of the recognition as a variable of choice is persuasively traced to Fichte and acknowledged as a significant ground for Hegelian dialectic in Pippin's somewhat controversial rereading of that philosophy, *Hegel's Idealism* (see esp. p. 56). See also Williams's *Recognition,* 49–94.

7. See the logical spectrum of this interaction in Fichte's account of the "I am" in *The Science of Knowledge,* 94–97. Fichte arrives at his most unambiguous characterization of self-activity as *Tathandlung* in the following passage (I, 96): "The self *posits itself,* and by virtue of this mere self-assertion it exists; and conversely, the self *exits* and *posits* its own existence by virtue of merely existing. It is at once the agent and the product of action; the active, and what the activity brings about; action and deed are one and the same" (97).

8. Kojeve's perspicuous disentanglement of Hegelian recognition from the metaphysics of *Geist* is an underpinning of my own claims about how the dialectic bears on narrative time. The corollary entailment of choice in recognition is implicit in Kojeve's assertion that "man can only truly be 'satisfied' . . . in and by the formation of a society . . . in which the strictly particular, personal, individual value of each is recognized as such" (*Introduction to the Reading of Hegel,* 58).

9. See especially the connection between *Wille* and *Willkür* in Neuhouser, *Fichte's Theory of Subjectivity,* 144–51; and Silber's preface to Kant's *Religion,* "The Ethical Significance of Kant's Religion," xcv–xcvi.

10. See Lyotard's own mapping of the "phrase universe" denoted in this goal, in *The Differend,* 12–14.

11. This point is buttressed by Weber's commentary in the postscript to *Just Gaming* to the effect that Lyotard becomes the "great prescriber" himself, who makes us abide by the rules of the game of prescribing.

12. For the fullest and most acute account of this failure on Lyotard's part, see Dunn's excellent article "Radical Resentment: The Ethics of Lyotard's Differend," *Boundary 2* 20, no. 1 (Spring 1993).

13. Here it is worth considering Benhabib's critique of transcendental pragmatics on the basis of its valorization of consensus as an end in itself. See her afterword to the volume (edited with Fred Dallmayr) *The Communicative Ethics Controversy* (see esp. p. 345).

14. See Apel's "The Problem of Philosophical Foundations," in *After Philosophy,* ed. Kenneth Baynes, James Bohman, and Thomas McCarthy, 272–83 for an account of the reflective infrastructure of transcendental pragmatics. My own stance is more sympathetic to the conditions of possibility for intersubjective validity stipulated here than the immediate context of my analysis suggests.

15. For a gloss on this argument, see Wellmer's chapter "Truth, Semblance, Reconciliation" in *The Persistence of Modernity.*

Works Cited

Adorno, Theodor W. *Aesthetic Theory*. Edited by Gretel Adorno and Rolf Tiedemann, translated by C. Lenhardt. London: Routledge and Kegan Paul, 1970.
———. "Die Idee der Naturgeschichte." In *Gesammelte Schriften*, 23 vols. Edited by Rolf Tiedemann. Frankfurt am Main: Suhrkamp Verlag, 1973.
———. *Negative Dialectics*. Translated by E. B. Ashton. New York: Seabury Press, 1973.
Alberti, Leon Battista. *On Painting*. Translated by John R. Spencer. New Haven, Conn.: Yale University Press, 1966.
Althusser, Louis. *For Marx*. Translated by Ben Brewster. London: Verso, 1979.
———. *Lenin and Philosophy*. Translated by Ben Brewster. New York: Monthly Review Press, 1971.
Althusser, Louis, and Etienne Balibar. *Reading Capital*. Translated by Ben Brewster. London: Verso, 1979.
Altieri, Charles. *Act and Quality: A Theory of Literary Meaning*. Amherst: University of Massachusetts Press, 1981.
Apel, Karl-Otto. "The Problem of Philosophical Foundations in Light of a Transcendental Pragmatics of Language." In *After Philosophy*, edited by Kenneth Baynes, James Bohman, and Thomas McCarthy. Cambridge, Mass.: MIT Press, 1987.
Aristotle. *Poetics*. Translated by W. Hamilton Fyfe. Cambridge, Mass.: Harvard University Press, 1962.
———. *Metaphysics*. Translated by Richard Hope. Ann Arbor: University of Michigan Press, 1968.
Ashbery, John. *Three Poems*. New York: Viking, 1978.
———. "The Decline of Verbs." *Book Week* 4, no. 15 (18 December 1966):5.
———. "The Impossible." *Poetry* 90 (July 1957):250–54.
Bakhtin, M. M. *The Dialogic Imagination*. Edited and translated by Caryl Emerson and Michael Holquist. Austin: University of Texas Press, 1984.
———. *The Formal Method in Literary Scholarship*. Translated by Albert J. Wehble. Cambridge, Mass.: Harvard University Press, 1985.

————. *Problems of Dostoevsky's Poetics*. Edited and translated by Caryl Emerson. Introduction by Wayne Booth. Minneapolis: University of Minnesota Press, 1985.

Baltrušaitis, Jurgis. *Anamorphic Art*. Translated by W. J. Strachan. London: Abrams, 1977.

Baumgarten, A. G. *Reflections on Poetry* [1735]. Translated by Karl Aschenbrenner and William Holther. Berkeley: University of California Press, 1954.

Baynes, Kenneth, James Bohman, and Thomas McCarthy. *After Philosophy*. Cambridge, Mass.: MIT Press, 1987.

Benhabib, Seyla. *Critique, Norm, and Utopia: A Study of the Foundations of Critical Theory*. New York: Columbia University Press, 1986.

Benhabib, Seyla, and Fred Dallmayr, eds. *The Communicative Ethics Controversy*. Cambridge, Mass.: MIT Press, 1990.

Benjamin, Walter. *Illuminations*. Translated by Harry Zohn. New York: Schocken, 1969.

————. *The Origin of German Tragic Drama*. Translated by John Osborne. London: Routledge and Kegan Paul, 1977.

Bennett, Tony. *Outside Literature*. London: Routledge and Kegan Paul, 1990.

Bernstein, J. M. *The Fate of Art: Aesthetic Alienation from Kant to Derrida and Adorno*. University Park: Pennsylvania State University Press, 1992.

————. *The Philosophy of the Novel: Lukács, Marxism and the Dialectics of Form*. Minneapolis: University of Minnesota Press, 1984.

Bersani, Leo. *Baudelaire and Freud*. Berkeley: University of California Press, 1977.

————. "The Other Freud." *Humanities in Society* 1 (1978): 35–49.

Bersani, Leo, and Ulysse Dutoit. "Merde Alors." *October* 13 (1980): 23–35.

Blanchot, Maurice. *Death Sentence*. Translated by Lydia Davis. Barrytown, N.Y.: Station Hill Press, 1981.

————. *The Gaze of Orpheus*. Edited with an afterword by P. Adams Sitney, translated by Lydia Davis. Barrytown, N.Y.: Station Hill Press, 1981.

————. *The Madness of the Day*. Translated by Lydia Davis. Barrytown, N.Y.: Station Hill Press, 1981.

Buck-Morss, Susan. *The Origin of Negative Dialectics: Theodor W. Adorno, Walter Benjamin, and the Frankfurt Institute*. New York: Free Press, 1968.

Bürger, Peter. *The Decline of Modernism*. Translated by Nicholas Walker. University Park: Pennsylvania State University Press, 1992.

Butler, Judith P. *Subjects of Desire: Hegelian Reflections in Twentieth-Century France*. New York: Columbia University Press, 1987.

Caramello, Charles. "Portrait Narration: Generals James and Stein." In *Intertextuality*, edited by Patrick O'Donnell and Robert Con Davis. Baltimore, Md.: Johns Hopkins University Press, 1990.

Cascardi, Anthony J. "Narrative and Totality." *Philosophical Forum*, Winter 1991, 1–15.

————. *The Subject of Modernity*. Cambridge: Cambridge University Press, 1992.

Caserio, Robert. *Plot, Story and the Novel: From Dickens and Poe to the Modern Period.* Princeton, N.J.: Princeton University Press, 1979.

Cash, Arthur H. *Laurence Sterne: The Later Years.* London: Methuen, 1986.

Caygill, Howard. *Art of Judgement.* London: Blackwell, 1989.

Clark, Katerina, and Michael Holquist. *Mikhail Bakhtin.* Cambridge, Mass.: Harvard University Press, 1984.

Cole, Steven. "The Dead-End of Deconstruction: Paul de Man and the Fate of Poetic Language." *Criticism* 30, no. 1 (Winter 1988): 91–112.

Coward, Rosalind, and John Ellis. *Language and Materialism.* London: Routledge and Kegan Paul, 1977.

Crewe, Jonathan. *Unredeemed Rhetoric.* Baltimore, Md.: Johns Hopkins University Press, 1983.

Croll, Morris W. *Attic and Baroque Style: Essays by Morris Croll.* Edited by J. Max Patrick and Robert O. Evans. Princeton, N.J.: Princeton University Press, 1966.

Danto, Arthur C. *The Philosophical Disenfranchisement of Art.* New York: Columbia University Press, 1986.

Davidson, Donald. *Essays on Actions and Events.* London: Oxford University Press, 1980.

Deleuze, Gilles. *Cinema 1: The Movement-Image.* Translated by Hugh Tomlinson and Barbara Habberjam. Minneapolis: University of Minnesota Press, 1986.

de Man, Paul. *Allegories of Reading: Figural Language in Rousseau, Nietzsche, Rilke, and Proust.* New Haven, Conn.: Yale University Press, 1979.

———. "The Epistemology of Metaphor." *Critical Inquiry* 5, no. 1 (Autumn 1978): 13–30.

———. *The Resistance to Theory.* Minneapolis: University of Minnesota Press, 1986.

Derrida, Jacques. *Dissemination.* Translated by Barbara Johnson. Chicago: University of Chicago Press, 1981.

———. *Margins of Philosophy.* Translated by Alan Bass. Chicago: University of Chicago Press, 1982.

———. "Living On: Border Lines." In *Deconstruction and Criticism,* edited by Harold Bloom, 75–176. New York: Continuum Books, 1979.

———. "White Mythology: Metaphor in the Text of Philosophy." Translated by F. C. T. Moore. *New Literary History* 6 (1974): 35–75.

Destutt de Tracy, Antoine Louis. *Eléments d'ideologie.* 4 vols. Paris, 1801–15.

Dews, Peter. *Logics of Disintegration: Post-Structuralist Thought and the Claims of Critical Theory.* London: Verso, 1987.

Dunn, Allen. "Radical Resentment: The Ethics of Lyotard's Differend." *Boundary 2* 20, no. 1 (Spring 1993).

Eagleton, Terry. *Criticism and Ideology.* London: Verso, 1978.

———. *The Ideology of the Aesthetic.* Oxford: Blackwell, 1990.

Edel, Leon, and Gordon N. Ray, eds. *Henry James and H. G. Wells: A Record of Their Friendship, Their Debate on the Art of Fiction and Their Quarrel.* Urbana: University of Illinois Press, 1958.

Fekete, John. *The Critical Twilight: Explorations in the Ideology of Anglo-American Literary Theory from Eliot to McLuhan*. London: Routledge and Kegan Paul, 1977.

Fichte, J. G. *The Science of Knowledge (Wissenschaftslehre* [1794]). Edited and translated by Peter Heath and John Lachs. New York: Cambridge University Press, 1988.

Foucault, Michel. *Archaeology of Knowledge*. Translated by Alan Sheridan Smith. London: Tavistock, 1972.

————. *Discipline and Punish*. Translated by Alan Sheridan. New York: Pantheon, 1977.

————. *The History of Sexuality*. Vol. 1. Translated by Robert Hurley. New York: Pantheon Press, 1978.

————. *Language, Counter-Memory, Practice*. Translated by Donald F. Bouchard. Ithaca, N.Y.: Cornell University Press, 1977.

————. *The Order of Things*. Translated by Alan Sheridan. New York: Pantheon, 1973.

Freud, Sigmund. *Standard Edition*. London: Hogarth, 1953–74.

Gaddis, William. *Carpenter's Gothic*. New York: Viking, 1985.

Gasché, Rodolphe. "Of Aesthetic and Historical Determination." In *Post-Structuralism and the Question of History*, edited by Derek Attridge, Geoff Bennington, and Robert Young. Cambridge: Cambridge University Press, 1987.

————. *The Tain of the Mirror: Derrida and the Philosophy of Reflection*. Cambridge, Mass.: Harvard University Press, 1986.

Giddens, Anthony. *Central Problems in Social Theory: Action, Structure, and Contradiction in Social Analysis*. Berkeley: University of California Press, 1983.

————. *The Constitution of Society: Outline of the Theory of Structuration*. Berkeley: University of California Press, 1984.

Goodman, Nelson. *Languages of Art*. Indianapolis, Ind.: Bobbs-Merrill, 1968.

————. *Of Mind and Other Matters*. Cambridge, Mass.: Harvard University Press, 1984.

Habermas, Jürgen. *Moral Consciousness and Communicative Action*. Translated by C. Lenhardt and S. W. Nicholsen. Cambridge, Mass.: MIT Press, 1990.

————. *The Philosophical Discourse of Modernity*. Translated by Frederick Lawrence. Cambridge, Mass.: MIT Press, 1987.

————. *Towards a Rational Society*. Translated by C. Lenhardt. London: Heinemann, 1971.

Hall, Stuart. "The Hinterland of Ideology," *Working Papers in Cultural Studies* 10 (1977): 129–59.

Handwerk, Gary J. *Irony and Ethics in Narrative: From Schlegel to Lacan*. New Haven, Conn.: Yale University Press, 1985.

Hartman, Geoffrey. *Beyond Formalism*. New Haven, Conn.: Yale University Press, 1970.

Hegel, G. W. F. *Hegel's Science of Logic*. Translated by A. V. Miller. Atlantic Highlands, N.J.: Humanities Press International, 1990.

――――. *Phenomenology of Mind*. Translated by J. B. Baillie. New York: Harper and Row, 1967.

Horkheimer, Max, and Theodor W. Adorno. *Dialectic of Enlightenment*. Translated by John Cumming. New York: Continuum Press, 1990.

Jakobson, Roman. "Two Aspects of Language and Two Types of Linguistic Disturbance." In *Fundamentals of Language,* edited by Jakobson and Halle. The Hague: 1956.

James, Henry. *Art of the Novel: Critical Prefaces*. New York: Scribners, 1937.

――――. *Theory of Fiction*. Edited by James E. Miller, Jr. Lincoln: University of Nebraska Press, 1962.

――――. *What Maisie Knew*. London: Penguin, 1971.

Jameson, Fredric. "Imaginary and Symbolic in Lacan: Marxism, Psychoanalytic Criticism, and the Problem of the Subject." *Yale French Studies* 55–56 (1978): 338–95.

――――. *Late Marxism: Adorno, or, The Persistence of the Dialectic*. London: Verso, 1990.

――――. "Marxism and Historicism." *New Literary History,* Winter 1979: 41–73.

――――. *The Political Unconscious: Narrative as a Socially Symbolic Act*. Ithaca, N.Y.: Cornell University Press, 1981.

――――. *Postmodernism, or The Cultural Logic of Late Capitalism*. Durham, N.C.: Duke University Press, 1990.

Jay, Martin. *Marxism and Totality*. Berkeley: University of California Press, 1984.

Kant, Immanuel. *Critique of Judgment*. Translated by J. H. Bernard. New York: Hafner, 1951.

――――. *Groundwork for a Metaphysic of Morals*. Translated by H. J. Paton. New York: Harper and Row, 1956.

――――. *Religion within the Limits of Reason Alone* [1793]. Translated by Theodore M. Greene and Hoyt H. Hudson. New York: Harper and Row, 1960.

Kermode, Frank. *The Sense of an Ending*. London: Oxford University Press, 1986.

Kojeve, Alexandre. *Introduction to the Reading of Hegel: Lectures on the Phenomenology of Spirit*. Translated by James H. Nichols. Ithaca, N.Y.: Cornell University Press, 1969.

Kristeva, Julia. *Desire in Language*. Translated by L. Roudiez. New York: Columbia University Press, 1980.

――――. *La Révolution du langage poétique*. Paris: Seuil, 1974.

Lacan, Jacques. *Écrits: A Selection*. Translated by Alan Sheridan. New York: W. W. Norton, 1977.

――――. *The Four Fundamental Concepts of Psycho-Analysis*. Translated by Alan Sheridan. New York: W. W. Norton, 1978.

Lachs, John. "Is There an Absolute Self?" *Philosophical Forum* 2–3 (Winter-Spring 1988): 169–80.

Lacoue-Labarthe, Philippe, and Jean-Luc Nancy. *The Literary Absolute: The Theory of Literature in German Romanticism*. Translated by Philip Barnard and Cheryl Lester. Albany, N.Y.: SUNY Press, 1988.

Lukács, Georg. *History and Class Consciousness*. Cambridge, Mass.: MIT Press, 1971.

———. *The Theory of the Novel*. Translated by Anna Bostock. Cambridge, Mass.: MIT Press, 1971.

Lentricchia, Frank. *After the New Criticism*. Chicago: University of Chicago Press, 1980.

Lyotard, Jean-François. *The Differend: Phrases in Dispute*. Translated by Georges Van Den Abbeele. Minneapolis: University of Minnesota Press, 1988.

———. *Just Gaming*. Translated by Wlad Godzich. Minneapolis: University of Minnesota Press, 1985.

———. *Peregrinations: Law, Form, Event*. New York: Columbia University Press, 1988.

———. "*Sensus communis:* The Subject in *statu nascendi*." In *Who Comes after the Subject?* edited by Eduardo Cadava, Peter Connor, and Jean-Luc Nancy. Translated by Marion Hobson. London: Routledge, 1991.

Macherey, Pierre, and Etienne Balibar. "Literature as an Ideological Form: Some Marxist Perspectives." *Praxis,* no. 5 (1981): 38–59.

McKeon, Michael. *The Origins of the English Novel 1600–1740*. Baltimore, Md.: Johns Hopkins University Press, 1987.

Nashe, Thomas. *The Unfortunate Traveller and Other Works*. 1594. Reprint. London: Penguin, 1972.

Neuhouser, Frederick. *Fichte's Theory of Subjectivity*. New York: Cambridge University Press, 1990.

Nietzsche, Friedrich. *Philosophy and Truth: Selections from Nietzsche's Notebooks of the Early 1870's*. Translated by Daniel Breazeale. Atlantic Highlands, N. J.: Humanities Press, 1979.

O'Donnell, Patrick, and Robert Con Davis, eds. *Intertextuality and Contemporary American Fiction*. Baltimore, Md.: Johns Hopkins University Press, 1990.

Pippin, Robert. *Hegel's Idealism: The Satisfactions of Self-Consciousness*. Cambridge: Cambridge University Press, 1989.

Richards, I. A. *Principles of Literary Criticism*. London: Oxford University Press, 1924.

Ricoeur, Paul. *Hermeneutics and the Human Sciences*. Edited and translated by John B. Thompson. Cambridge: Cambridge University Press, 1981.

———. *Lectures on Ideology and Utopia*. Edited by George H. Taylor. New York: Columbia University Press, 1986.

———. *The Rule of Metaphor: Multidisciplinary Studies of the Creation of Meaning in Language*. Translated by Robert Czerny with Kathleen McLaughlin and John Costello, S.J. Toronto: University of Toronto Press, 1977.

————. *Time and Narrative*. Vols. 1–3. Translated by Kathleen McLaughlin and David Pellauer. Chicago: University of Chicago Press, 1984–88.

Rockmore, Tom. *Fichte, Marx, and the German Philosophical Tradition*. Carbondale: Southern Illinois University Press, 1980.

Rorty, Richard. *Contingency, Irony, and Solidarity*. Cambridge: Cambridge University Press, 1989.

Rosen, Michael. *Hegel's Dialectic and Its Criticism*. Cambridge: Cambridge University Press, 1984.

Rowe, John Carlos. *The Theoretical Dimension of Henry James*. Madison: University of Wisconsin Press, 1984.

Sartre, Jean-Paul. *Being and Nothingness: An Essay on Phenomenological Ontology*. Translated by Hazel E. Barnes. New York: Philosophical Library, 1956.

————. *What Is Literature?* Cambridge, Mass.: Harvard University Press, 1988.

Siebers, Tobin. *The Ethics of Criticism*. Ithaca, N.Y.: Cornell University Press, 1988.

Simmel, Georg. *The Conflict in Modern Culture and Other Essays*. New York: Teachers College Press, 1968.

Singer, Alan. *A Metaphorics of Fiction: Discontinuity and Discourse in the Modern Novel*. Tallahassee: Florida State University Press, 1984.

Sprinker, Michael. *Imaginary Relations: Aesthetics and Ideology in the Theory of Historical Materialism*. London: Verso, 1987.

Staten, Henry. *Wittgenstein and Derrida*. Lincoln: University of Nebraska, 1984.

Stewart, Susan. "The Last Man." *American Poetry Review* 17, no. 5 (Sept.–Oct. 1988): 9–16.

Taylor, Charles. *Human Agency and Language: Philosophical Papers*. Vol. 1. London: Cambridge University Press, 1985.

Thompson, John B. *Studies in the Theory of Ideology*. Berkeley: University of California Press, 1984.

Todorov, Tzvetan. *Mikhail Bakhtin: The Dialogic Principle*. Translated by Wlad Godzich. Minneapolis: University of Minnesota Press, 1984.

————. *Poetics of Prose*. Translated by Richard Howard. Ithaca, N.Y.: Cornell University Press, 1977.

Tugendthat, Ernst. *Self-Consciousness and Self-Determination*. Translated by Paul Stern. Cambridge, Mass.: MIT Press, 1986.

Volosinov, V. N. *Marxism and the Philosophy of Language*. Translated by Ladislav Matejka and I. R. Titunik. Cambridge, Mass.: Harvard University Press, 1986.

Von Wright, Georg Henrik. *Explanation and Understanding*. Ithaca, N.Y.: Cornell University Press, 1971.

Weber, Samuel. *The Legend of Freud*. Minneapolis: University of Minnesota Press, 1982.

Wellmer, Albrecht. *The Persistence of Modernity: Essays on Aesthetics, Ethics, and*

Postmodernism. Translated by David Midgeley. Cambridge, Mass.: MIT Press, 1991.

Williams, Robert R. *Recognition: Fichte and Hegel on the Other*. Albany, N.Y.: SUNY Press, 1992.

Index

Action, 9, 85
Adlerian psychoanalysis, 61
Adorno, Theodor W., 1, 3, 9, 13, 18, 55, 91–97, 100, 117, 145, 148, 156, 162, 167, 193–98, 202, 222–26, 232, 244, 248, 259–61; *Aesthetic Theory*, 1, 18, 95–97, 148, 152, 162, 193–95, 202, 222, 260, 261; "Die Idee der Naturgeschichte," 94; *Negative Dialectics*, 1, 93, 148, 167, 222–23; on negative dialectic, 81, 118, 124, 154; on nonidentity, 154, 167, 177, 198, 260; on preaesthetic, 193–95, 197; on second reflection, 14, 202–3, 222, 259–60
Aesthesis, aesthetic, 14, 84, 86, 252; and cognition, 188–90; creative, and consumption, 177; and determination, 187, 202; expressive, 140; and history, 147, 260; narrative, 14–15, 36, 185–88, 190, 230, 232, 257, 261; and reason, 182–83, 232; rules of, 95; as structure of action, 176; and subject formation, 182–83; and totality, unity, 10, 106, 130, 151, 157, 170; and the visual, 210–11
Aesthetic Theory (Adorno), 1, 18, 95–97, 148, 152, 162, 193–95, 202, 222, 260–61
Alberti, Leon Battista, 211
Alienated history, 234

Alienation, 108; of labor, 11
Alienation effect, 178
Allegories of Reading (de Man), 8, 38
Allegory. *See* Benjamin, Walter
Alterity, 85, 90
Althusser, Louis, 3, 8, 19, 23, 25, 46–47, 51, 52, 56–57, 81, 178; on the aesthetic, 178; *For Marx*, 52; on interpellation, 18–19; *Lenin and Philosophy*, 25, 178; on structural causality, 46–47, 168
Altieri, Charles, 23–24
Ambassadors, The (James), 166
Anacrisis, 84, 86
Anagnorisis, 5, 109, 123, 185, 201, 226, 228, 234. *See also* Recognition
Anamorphism, 207, 209, 213
Antinarrative, 9, 16, 238
Apel, K. O., 254–55
Arendt, Hannah, 259–60
Aristotle, 2, 8, 24, 37–39, 42, 44, 46, 56–57, 134, 144, 166, 201, 226, 233–35, 237, 242, 257; on ethics related to poetics, 166–67, 179, 188, 198; on identity/*eidos*, 111, 163; *Nichomachean Ethics*, 39, 188; on *phronesis*, 165, 188, 235; and plot, 123, 185; *Poetics*, 12, 109, 153–54, 188, 191, 228, 235
Ashbery, John, 14, 161–62, 188–90, 203–25 passim; "The Decline of Verbs," 215; "The Impos-